about the author

Award-winning* journalist David Bennun began his career at *Melody Maker* and went on to become *Loaded*'s first features editor, a job he has likened to that of zoo-keeper at the chimpanzees' tea party. Since taking up writing full time, he has been a contributor to among others. *The Mail On Sunday*, *The Guardian*, *The Observer* and GQ. He has also co-written three series of the successful BBC TV show, *Clarkson*. A selection of his work can be found at http://bennun.biz.

Millionaire playboy David lives in Brighton, 'because it's handy for my yacht'. His interests include the arts, fine dining and breaking into nearby safari parks to fight lions with his bare hands. 'I fear my exploits may have been a little exaggerated,' he says, with a modest chuckle. 'Thanks, and here's your fifty quid.'

*Best Junior Dog Handler, Nairobi Kennel Club Show, 1981

tick
bite
fever

For my family

tick bite fever

DAVID BENNUN

EBURY
PRESS

First published in Great Britain, 2003

1 3 5 7 9 10 8 6 4 2

First published by Ebury Press
Random House, 20 Vauxhall Bridge Road, London SW1V 2SA

Random House Australia (Pty) Limited
20 Alfred Street, Milsons Point, Sydney, New South Wales 2061, Australia

Random House New Zealand Limited
18 Poland Road, Glenfield, Auckland 10, New Zealand

Random House South Africa (Pty) Limited
Endulini, 5A Jubilee Road, Parktown 2193, South Africa

The Random House Group Limited Reg. No. 954009

www.randomhouse.co.uk

A CIP catalogue record for this book is available from the British Library.

ISBN 0 09 188689 9

Typeset by Textype, Cambridge
Cover design by the Senate

Printed and bound in the UK by Mackays of Chatham plc, Chatham, Kent

Papers used by Ebury Press are natural, recyclable products made from wood grown in sutainable forests.

acknowledgements

This ought to contain a long list of thank-yous. It doesn't.

There's no shortage of people to whom I owe debts of gratitude. But I have to consider the embarrassing possibility that any such list might well outnumber the eventual readership of this book. So I'll keep it brief and hope that nobody takes offence.

I'm deeply appreciative of my many friends and colleagues who over the years have supported me in my work; likewise, those editors who have paid me for it and even, now and then, printed it. Thanks to all of you, I have already got away with calling myself a writer for longer than I ever thought possible.

I must single out Ben Marshall and Jon Wilde, great writers and even better friends. If not for their help and encouragement, I might never have attempted a book. Blame them.

I'm also very grateful to everyone who has assisted me with the book along the way. Needless to say, any errors, flaws and lapses of judgement are entirely their responsibility, while the good bits are mine alone.

Above all, my thanks and my love go to Kavita, without whom nothing would be worth doing in the first place.

Out of Africa, with Some Relief

AFRICA-BOUND from Heathrow Airport, at 30,000 feet over the Mediterranean Sea, I politely announced that this had all been very nice, but I'd like to get out now.

It was 1971. I was three, and already demonstrating the keen pragmatism of a child half my age. Over the next two decades, my understanding of reality failed to improve much.

My parents came to despair of me. 'What world do you live in?' my father would ask, frustrated. It was a good question. We lived in Africa: first, briefly, in Zambia, after that in Kenya. Yet my Africa seemed to be set on an entirely different planet from theirs.

As I grew up, I would come to think of myself as being, by default, African. I didn't look, or sound, or act African, by any stretch of the term. Still, there didn't seem to be an alternative.

I should explain why we were flying to Africa that day in 1971. We were flying to Africa because it was a surefire means to get away from England, where my family had just concluded a spell of nine drab, grey, parochial years. Part way through that spell, I had been born in a place as far from exotic as it is from the equator: Swindon. It wasn't my idea.

To be fair to my parents, it wasn't their idea either. I came as a surprise, and they resolved to make the best of me. I don't doubt that they succeeded, given what they had to work with.

What they had to work with was me, the presumed subject of this book. But the book isn't really about me. It is about Africa, about my family, about the mishaps and calamities and freakish occurrences in which I was so often an unwitting pivot or accidental catalyst. It is about a life – my own – where I have figured largely as a baffled spectator. Others meet danger with cunning and fortitude; I overcame it through a mixture of blind luck and not falling over too often. My childhood passed in a haze of delirium familiar to me from several intriguing diseases, including the one that provides the book's title. Maybe I never fully recovered from it. That would explain a great deal.

I moved back to Britain permanently over ten years ago. Since then, the level of weirdness in my life has dropped to approximately zero. I can tell myself it was all Africa's fault, and none of mine. Occasionally, I even believe it. That's why I've stayed here in Britain. To keep the weirdness at bay.

When you already have enough weirdness to fill a book, there are only two things to do. The first is to sit tight and hope you don't encounter any more of it. The second is to fill a book.

chapter one

Family Snapshots

'WE ARE never the men our fathers were,' my father, Max, once said to me. While I believe he was absolutely right, it would have been easy to take that comment the wrong way. But I know that he was thinking of himself and his own father, Naphtoli, rather than of me.

Naphtoli – 'Toli' for short – was born in 1904, in Lithuania, into a family of tanners by the name of Misnuner. They ran a leather factory in the country town of Wilkomir, 50 miles to the north of the capital, Vilna. Wilkomir is still there, and so is the factory. The Misnuners are gone. They were massacred in the summer of 1941 – along with every other Jew in the vicinity – by the German Einsatzkommando 3 death squad and its enthusiastic local collaborators.

Toli eluded this catastrophe thanks only to the earlier misfortune of his father, Yitzchak. One day in 1926, Yitzchak had climbed into a giant tanning drum to clean it out. An employee, unaware, set the mechanism rolling. Yitzchak, as befitted a man who worked with rawhide, was a tough customer. He braced himself against the sides of the spinning cylinder for a full ten minutes before succumbing to dizzy exhaustion, and was tumbled into oblivion.

This left Toli in the charge of his uncles, of which he had several. They decided he should be sent to South Africa. Yet more uncles had set up another leather business in Port Elizabeth, on the Western Cape, where Toli was seconded in a junior capacity. He arrived that same year, a penniless young man with a letter of introduction, a chemistry degree and not a word of English.

By now, the South African branch of the family had shamefacedly changed its name to Bennun, after a rogue Misnuner went doolally and took a pot shot at a colonial governor. While some might see this, in retrospect, as a laudable act of insurrection, it was a grave embarrassment at the time. Our errant relative had not been engaged in a misguided attempt to better the lot of humanity. He was simply mad as a bucket of eels. His aim proved to be no sounder than his wits, but this only made it worse, and the name change fooled nobody. 'That's one of those Bennuns who used to be a Misnuner,' people would say. 'They're a bunch of lunatics, and they can't even shoot straight.'

* * *

SIMPLY IN marrying my grandmother, Miriam, Toli showed himself as a young man to be reckoned with. Miriam came from the wealthy, long-settled Silberman clan, whose elders considered Toli no more than an upstart hick – a view with which Toli's own uncles less than generously concurred. The only point in Toli's favour was his Lithuanian origin. Had he been a 'Peruvian' – a Pole, acronymically nicknamed for the Polish Emigrants Relief Union, the body which assisted Polish Jews in their removal to South Africa – he would have settled even further down the social scale.

But Toli was deemed sufficiently base as it was. When he began to court Miriam, the uncles were indignant. They forbade the match, and chose for him a bride better suited to his own lowly station. He married the girl under threat of dismissal from the family business. After a month of unconsummated torment, he consigned the family business to perdition, filed for divorce, booked passage on a Cape Town Castle liner, and eloped with Miriam to Lithuania. There they married, in 1934, on the day Toli's decree absolute was granted.

The couple returned to South Africa, where Toli opened an analytical laboratory. His clients were miners wondering if their hunks of rock enclosed precious metals, or just smaller hunks of rock. Toli was the first person in the country to refine platinum; my grandmother always wore on her wrist, with pride, a plain bracelet cast from that pioneer batch. Eventually Toli went prospecting for gold himself in the Northern

Transvaal. To say this venture was a washout would be harsh but accurate. Toli soon thought better of it. With his younger brother Boruch, who arrived from Lithuania just in time to escape the Holocaust, Toli opened a tannery of his own, and prospered.

As a matrimonial deterrent, the stern disapproval of both the Bennuns and the Silbermans scarcely ranked beside Miriam's own forceful personality. On the plus side, she was fiercely intelligent. On the minus, she was, quite simply, fierce. Her opinions were unshakeable, her manner imperious, her temper notorious. She didn't require a husband so much as a wrangler.

My grandmother always loomed large in my own childhood, when she had become, if possible, more belligerent and set in her extraordinary ways. I remember her conviction that my mother was personally at fault for failing to produce any redheaded offspring.

Nobody has ever been able to figure out why my grandmother was so fervent about redheads. All else aside, red hair and the accompanying pale and vulnerable skin were a serious liability on the sun-dazzled African plains. But *her* side of the family had always delivered redheads, and by God, she wanted more of them. By the time I was born, Miriam had made this perfectly clear to my mother. And yet there I was, another baby whose darkly fuzzed scalp, Miriam concluded, could only be the consequence of sheer, wilful gall. This notion is absurd not only for obvious scientific reasons, but also because it suggested my mother might be capable of spite.

* * *

MIRIAM HERSELF had produced two sons – the younger, in 1939, being my father, and neither of them being redheads. She promptly lost the ability to talk about any other subject at all. For a woman who had been a society lioness, this was a disaster. In the salons and drawing rooms where politics, ideas and the world at large were discussed, the latest utterances of her treasured offspring were of limited interest, and the interest was limited to Miriam. Oblivious to this fact, she continued to relay these bon mots as if it were Noel Coward and not little Maxie who had, for instance, made such an endearing and precocious remark about the gardener. Before long, the invitations stopped coming. Miriam never forgave her former friends, and never for a minute stopped to consider her own role in the matter.

She now concentrated her full and formidable attention upon the boys, and did so with the single-mindedness that marked every aspect of her existence and theirs. To this day, my father cannot touch peanut butter – the result of an unwise gesture at the age of seven, which he soon learned not to repeat. Finding a peanut butter sandwich in his school lunchbag one day, he came home and told Miriam how much he'd enjoyed it. For the next five years, his lunches took the form of a peanut butter sandwich.

'Please, Ma,' he would beg, 'no more peanut butter!'

'But you *like* peanut butter,' she replied, indignantly, each time. 'You said so yourself.'

My father can't abide red wine or brandy either, but that aversion came about much later and was entirely self-inflicted, involving as it did all-night poker games and a significant portion of the output from the Cape's KWV vineyards.

When my father was approaching the age of college – and of all-night poker games – he was invited to Toli's study to discuss his future.

'You can be either a doctor or a lawyer,' Toli informed him. 'Your brother is already going to be a lawyer. So you'll be a doctor.'

Off Max went to the University of Cape Town. To hear him tell it, his studies were conducted in the manner of Sigmund Romberg's romantic operetta, *The Student Prince* – all foaming flagons, comradely cheer and hearty drinking songs. Not to forget the poker games, and Oxbridge-style pranks adapted to fit the locale. These entailed citing obsolete by-laws, which permitted vast herds of borrowed livestock to be driven down the main street at six o'clock in the morning. That might well strike you as a good idea after you've been up all night playing cards and drinking KWV brandy.

My father was also a keen competitor at rugby, a fact that has more to do with subsequent events than seems strictly likely. He turned out for his college team with eagerness and a will, until the day they were drawn against a rival side from some Godforsaken corner of the veldt called Nêrensnieburg or Hundwater or similar. These were hulking farmers' boys, with arms like legs and legs like baobab trees. They trained by tossing tractor wheels, sacks of feed, prize bullocks and other everyday items from one end of the *dorp* to the other. Half of them were already lined up for South Africa's then redoubtable national side, the Springboks.

The match could have passed for an historical society's recreation of the sacking of Constantinople. Had you reversed the score after ten minutes, you would have obtained each side's casualty figures. Any attempt on the part of the Cape Town XV to press forward was not so much rebuffed as shrugged off with amusement. When the opposition got the ball, which they invariably did, they surged ahead to the far touchline, handing off tackles as if they were swatting away midges.

Finally, a moment arrived which my father had dreaded. A team-mate caught the ball and, with an agility born of terror, ducked between two converging behemoths, then passed the cursed object on to him. Within milliseconds, the horizon vanished behind a wall of charging manflesh. One of the forwards paused, nonchalantly plucked my father from his boots and the ball from his hands, upended him, dropped him on his head and thundered onwards.

My father was carried from the field, bloody and considerably bowed. For some days after he was crumpled in the middle, and stood a good three inches shorter, when he could stand at all. He was certainly in no fit state for that evening's engagement: the Good Hope College annual ball, a very salubrious dance at a highfalutin girls' school, to which he was to escort a young lady named Sarah. Sarah viewed my father as quite the prospect. She might well have persisted – and succeeded – in her intentions, had her beau not veered and stumbled about the ballroom like a rum-happy matelot, eyes rolling, knees sagging beneath him, giving slurred replies to the last question but two.

Sarah swiftly and tearfully vanished from both the dance and the scene. Shortly afterwards, my father met my mother, Mavis. Luckily for him then and me later, she has displayed a lifelong tolerance towards boys who have been dropped on their heads, or at least behave as if they have been.

* * *

MY MOTHER came from Salisbury, now Harare, in what was then Rhodesia, now Zimbabwe. Her father, Herbert, had been the second of his countrymen to volunteer for the British Army when war broke out in September 1939. Later that month, my mother became the first child born to a Rhodesian on active service. Herbert fought with the Desert Rats in North Africa, and was nearly left for dead on the battlefield. Returning home at the end of the war, he worked as a commercial manager in the coalfields at Wankie, on the Northern border, requiring him to spend long periods away from home.

Mavis's mother, Rene, was a self-absorbed and difficult woman from whom Mavis gradually became estranged as she grew up. Rene's love for her daughter, while genuine, was seldom transformed into care or affection. A fashionable and high-living would-be entrepreneur, she sank money into one feckless scheme after another. She sold the jewellery Mavis had inherited from her paternal grandmother and lost the proceeds investing in an ostrich farm. Mavis was ensconced in a grim boarding school for girls in Bulawayo, and went on to train as a teacher in Cape Town, where she met Max.

In 1960, my parents married. They planned to leave South Africa and move to England for reasons of expediency. My father deemed it expedient not to be locked up by the apartheid government for ferrying explosives around in the boot of his car – this being his contribution to a campaign of resistance by sabotage, conducted by the banned African National Congress, targeting railway lines and power stations.

In addition to smuggling dynamite, my father acted as a chauffeur for such senior ANC officials as Govan Mbeki, father of future president Thabo. On one of these outlawed journeys, through the Transkei in 1961, he was repairing a puncture by the roadside when a Boer policeman pulled up beside them. Max had to pretend that Mbeki, a man he held in absolute reverence, was his lackey. 'The bloody kaffir forgot to pack the spare tyre,' he grumbled, and roundly cursed his idol in Afrikaans, a language that even at its most tender sounds like a series of heartfelt insults.

The government took a very dim view of ANC activity, and my father decided he wasn't going to wait to get caught. In 1963, shortly after the birth of my brother, Leon, my parents upped sticks. At that stage Leon was probably the only male Bennun who wasn't active in the ANC, although I wouldn't put it past him.

My parents lived in Woking, then Swindon, then Bedford. Within a year of arriving in Britain, they had my sister, Lesley, and after a decent interval, me.

* * *

IN MARCH 1968, when a bumpy afternoon car ride successfully bounced my overdue mother into the maternity ward of the Victoria Hospital, Swindon was a small, bland and dispiriting assembly of cookie-cutter housing. It appeared to have been constructed with the principal intention of spoiling some otherwise quite attractive countryside.

The town is very different now. It's bigger. The list of things that originate in Swindon is short and undistinguished, a circumstance my arrival did little to alter. It includes the onetime glamour model Melinda Messenger, and the Honda Civic. I once met Melinda Messenger (which I won't mention again), and have on several occasions driven a Honda Civic, badly, along the world's most hazardous stretches of road (which I will).

To my parents' way of thinking, England was just a stop-off, where my father could pursue his profession and my mother raise a family. As a registrar, my father specialised in gynaecology and obstetrics, because, he claimed, that was the last lecture he had attended before departing Cape Town.

The stop-off lasted almost a decade. That decade happened to be the sixties, but this meant little to my parents. The sixties were something which that happened to other people – people who didn't have three small children and a precarious toehold on solvency.

My parents were waiting for the Apartheid government to fall, as they were sure it must, so that they could return home. By 1971, it was clear that, far from crumbling before the popular will, South Africa's racist regime was becoming ever more entrenched.

For a while, Britain had felt like a safe haven following the chaos and uncertainty of Africa. After a dose of Swindon, chaos and uncertainty may have looked the better option. In 1971, we moved as far south as we safely could: to Zambia, where we would find chaos and uncertainty aplenty, much of it caused by me.

chapter two

The Scapegrace of Lusaka

WE LIVED on the outskirts of Zambia's capital, Lusaka, in an upmarket neighbourhood called Mulungushi Village. Mulungushi had been built, in the loosest sense of the word, to house visiting dignitaries at a political summit conference organised by the United Nations or the Organisation of African Unity or some such pork barrel confederation. It began to fall down before they left.

By the time we arrived, it was crumbling. The dark wood used so prolifically by the Czech construction company made a banquet for termites. During the rainy season, with a dependability seldom encountered in any other aspect of Zambian life, two feet of muddy water sluiced down the hill and washed gently back and forth upon the nearest level ground, which happened to be our living-room floor. On schooldays we paddled out to the car in our bare feet, carrying our socks and shoes.

The Mulungushi houses, each placed in its own broad plot of acreage, were set around a rectangular roadway which in turn enclosed a *vlei*, or open tract of common grassland. Grand and handsome from a distance, close up our own villa had the shabby, uncertain and menacing air of a once-proud heavyweight on his uppers, slouching between punch-drunk and outright plastered. Not that I precociously conceived such an image of it then. As far as I was concerned, cracked cement and shaky masonry presented one more opportunity to imperil myself and keep my parents on their toes, a position to which they must have become better accustomed than the lead couple of the Bolshoi Ballet.

My talent for putting myself in jeopardy may have blossomed in Zambia, but it was budding before we left England. On a caravan trip to the New Forest in 1970, having just learned to walk, I wandered off into the woods. When my father came looking, he found me sat, gurgling contentedly, directly behind the hooves of an irascible wild pony – a mare with a newborn foal.

It was one of those moments when, in the movies, everything slurs into slow motion, as the action hero mouths a drawn-out 'Noooooooooooo!' and lunges towards the camera. My father scooped me up and hurled me aside just in time to receive the full benefit of a two-footed, one-horsepower pounding smack in the ribcage. It would probably have taken my head off.

He flew 20 feet like a stuntman jerked backwards on a rope, and remained flat on his back for several minutes, winded and severely bruised, while I paraded around him, clapping and uttering squeals of delight. If he had guessed what lay ahead, he might have chosen to stay supine on the forest floor indefinitely. He had, it's true, already undergone a strenuous test of his nerve by taking on the quasi-fascist South African regime. But I had not yet begun to vex.

* * *

ALL SMALL children are sociopaths. That said, the thoroughgoing detachment I brought to being the agency of crisis and havoc, following our move to Zambia, must surely have ranked me in the upper and more frightening percentiles. Even my brother, who as a toddler had somehow contrived to burn down the family home, was placed further down the graph. He was a one-trick pony, who never followed up this *coup de theatré*, and what was more, he was sorry. What I lacked in grand set pieces, I made up for in consistency, combined with blithe indifference.

It was lucky for me, if not the rest of my family, that we now lived in a country where crisis and havoc were perfectly normal. I blended in seamlessly with snakes, bushfires, robbers, car crashes, tropical diseases, food shortages, deranged governance and the regular floods. My name became another standard answer, no details required, to the all-too-frequent question, 'What happened?'

My techniques were diverse and unpredictable, but I did favour two particular gambits: disappearing, and falling into things. Strictly speaking, falling into things was just another way of disappearing, which was my true forte. Sometimes I disappeared on purpose, sometimes I just disappeared. This fine distinction meant little to my parents, who, to their credit, always tried to find me. 'He can't have got far,' they would reassure each other, although experience had taught them otherwise. A nipper with the whole of Lusaka at his feet could go a lot further than you'd think. And even when I hadn't got far at all – no further than the *vlei* opposite the house – the elephant grass concealed me so effectively that I might have been on Pluto.

I suppose I did something with my days other than ramble around Mulungushi Village. I have a fuzzy, lingering mental picture of a nursery school on a hill. It had a green lawn, *Janet and John* books in the classrooms, and other children, which was a change. I never thought of my sister and brother as other children. They were simply one of life's painful actualities, like hornets and salad and bedtime. Their major function was to supply at least one of the heads that my infuriated father was forever threatening to knock together.

Of my fellow pupils I recall only one in any detail – a little girl who shared my birthday. When I suggested this meant we must be friends, she stared me down wordlessly, then ran away and hid. Despite this setback, it wasn't long – only another 25 years or so – before I became perfectly at ease in the company of girls.

The *Janet and John* books gave an early indication that my own life was not normal. Set in a 1950s British village Arcadia, they portrayed a pair of siblings whose blond locks and limited range of interests hardly chimed with my own appearance and hobbies. Janet and John spent most of their time watching a little dog run. 'See the little dog run,' the text urged. 'Can you see the little dog run?' I could, but the authors weren't about to take my word for it. 'See the little dog run,' they insisted. I assumed this was what children did back in England. They saw the little dog run. I didn't seem to be missing much.

I had far more exciting things to do than track the progress of little dogs, however athletic they might be. I was a three-foot Magellan and Mulungushi Village was my Pacific. I fared better than Magellan in my dealings with the locals. As a senior teaching physician posted to Zambia by Britain's Overseas Development Agency, my father was apparently quite important. At any rate, our neighbours were diplomats, government bigwigs, corporate Pooh-Bahs and the like. Many of them were no doubt involved in the complicated process of wrecking the country. Still, they were always very nice to me, and made a point of returning me to my parents whenever, having disappeared, I resurfaced in their vicinity.

One chap, who I think was something high up in Zambia's rudimentary health service, and was therefore one of my father's bosses, was always delighted to see my sister and me. He would play patriotic choral songs for us on his record deck. I still find myself humming them today, although most of the words have escaped me, forcing me to improvise: '*Hmm*-hmmm, hmmm-hmmm-hmmm-hm. *Zam*-bia, stro-ong and free. *Dum* dum, deedle dum dum. *Milk*-shake, haddock and peas.' For all the good such sentiments did Zambia, my new lines could be the real ones.

Zambia was already a fair way along the crooked downhill path trodden by so many African nations at the expense of their people. A country of opulent good looks, mineral-rich and fertile, it could have been an Elysium for visitors and the breadbasket of Southern Africa, had it been run on even vaguely pragmatic lines.

This understanding comes with hindsight. My memories of Zambia are made up not of comprehension but of colours, of greens or browns, depending on the season. Images, rather than facts or events, lodged in my four-year-old mind. Tall, yellowed grass stems cracking in the heat on highway verges. Headlamp beams bumping through darkness and dust along endless dirt tracks. A journey to the copper belt, where a road cut into massive, vertical slabs of rock wound its way down to vast excavations, and Zambian children barely my seniors crafted amazingly intricate working models of bicycles and trucks out of leftover wire. Already, I was a permanent tourist, disconnected from everything and everyone I saw and marvelled at through the back-seat window.

* * *

AT THE peak of the dry season, the Lusakans torched the *vlei* that faced on to our house, driving out a host of snakes remarkable for both its number and its variety. Many of these slithered straight onto our property, where some common serpentine instinct guided them to the square, paved courtyard at the centre of the house. It wasn't unusual to hear a rhythmic thump and clang in the rockery as my mother methodically beat to death a writhing puff adder with a garden spade.

My parents were generally delighted to know I was in the courtyard, as this meant I couldn't be anywhere else. All the same, come bushfire time, they tried to discourage me from sharing it with a lively selection of cobras, mambas and boomslangs. Under the circumstances, this was generous of them: there must have been times when it felt more tempting to leave me in harm's way than pluck me out of it. Modern child-rearing orthodoxy frowns on chaining youngsters to radiators and the like, but I wouldn't blame my parents had they taken this measure with me for my own protection. Perhaps the only thing that stopped them was the fact that we had no radiators.

On hot days, which meant all of them, the courtyard was cool and welcoming, snakes permitting. Its regular reptilian population was of a friendlier bent. We kept chameleons there; or rather, they kept themselves there, so we adopted them as pets. They weren't the most affectionate of creatures, but they were great fun, when you could find them. Much more so than my brother's stick insect, which was equally hard to spot, and had little to offer if you succeeded. Its only trick was looking like a twig, so once you'd located it, the sport was as good as over.

A chameleon's mood may be deduced from its colour. If the creature was an affable green, that meant it could be used as a targeted anti-insect device. In the courtyard, all manner of buzzing and humming invertebrates clouded the air, settled on the climbing vines, plummeted into your drink or immolated themselves on the barbecue. There were things with dots and things with stripes. Things with rugby-sweater bands of colour. Things with armour plating, things with stings. Things with wing cases like the treasures of the pharaohs. And flies. Lots and lots of flies.

It was deeply satisfying to coax a chameleon onto your bare arm, where its lizard claws gripped with a sensation exquisitely poised between ticklish and painful, then point it at a giant, droning bluebottle. The chameleon's eyes, which bulged spherically under drooping lids and rotated independently of each other, swivelled balefully forward and zeroed in on the quarry. As if on a trigger, the tongue uncoiled, shot out and withdrew faster than human sight could register. No video game I've played since has been remotely as pleasurable; the fly might as well have vaporised.

All too often the same went for me. One night I pulled off a particularly convincing disappearance, with the help of a playmate called Amanda – a born mischief-maker, and in my eyes an honorary boy – who lived a mile or so away. We had the whole thing planned. She would tell her parents I had gone home, but I would be crouched on a pillow in her bedroom cupboard. What we hoped to achieve is hard to say. It just seemed like a clever thing to do. I, presumed to be in one place, would in fact be in another. No Moriarty nor Lex Luthor nor Ernst Blofeld could have been better pleased with his most fiendish and intricate stratagem than Amanda and I were with this piece of idiocy. At no point did it occur to us that, although we might fool Amanda's parents, there was a fair chance mine might notice my absence.

Our plot worked well enough at first. There was no room in Amanda's big, floor-level cupboard, so I climbed up on the shelves to a tiny cubby hole near the ceiling and Amanda pushed the door shut behind me with a broom handle. It was cramped and lightless, and something with 17 legs was unhurriedly crawling up my ankle, as if it knew it had all night. I heard voices. They were muffled and they echoed, adding to my sense of furtive adventure.

'Why have you got the broom in your bedroom?'

'I was playing Sweep-Up, Mummy.' Through the cupboard door, I could picture Amanda's wide-eyed face and feel the adorable innocence beaming from it like sunlight. With the admiration due to one devious little troll from another, I thought, Well done.

'Give it here. Have you brushed your teeth?'

'Yes, Mummy. Good night, Mummy. I love you, Mummy.' Immediately, I sensed our scheme was in peril. Like many another talented artist in the grip of hubris, Amanda had a tendency to overreach herself.

'What's going on in here?' said Amanda's mother, instantly suspicious. Finally persuaded that all was as it should be – or, more likely, that whatever Amanda was up to, it wasn't going to be a police matter, so it could wait until morning – Amanda's mother switched off the light and closed the door behind her. Almost immediately a creaking and dull thumping rose in my direction. Amanda swung back the cupboard door, while balancing on the shelf below like a miniature steeplejack in floral pattern pyjamas.

'Are you all right?' she whispered. Amanda had that child's stage whisper that can pierce reinforced walls impervious to high-calibre ordnance.

I winced and murmured, 'Yes, I'm fine.' I wasn't fine. I was bored, sleepy, thirsty and uncomfortable, and I couldn't complain to an adult about it. But I wasn't about to back out now.

The choice was taken out of my hands. At the far end of the room, the door clicked open and a block of light from the corridor framed a silhouetted head. If a silhouette could look irritated, this would have been the silhouette to achieve it.

'What *are* you doing?' said Amanda's father. Although nobody could see it but me – and only dimly, at that – Amanda's expression automatically composed itself into her familiar model of cutie-pie purity.

'I'm playing Monkey, Daddy,' she replied, as if through a mouthful of unmelted butter.

I shrank back into the cupboard as Amanda's father lifted her down.

'What have you got in there?' he said.

'*Nuh*thing,' simpered Amanda, and I knew the jig was up. That was the most flagrantly false 'Nothing' a child ever uttered.

Riding home in the back of his car, I saw our garden, the *vlei*, the whole of Mulungushi Village, illuminated as if in an attempt to make itself visible from space. Lantern beams and torch bulbs bobbed across every bit of the surface. The entire neighbourhood was out scouring the area for me. It was, so it turned out, a police matter after all. Every officer in the district and a fair few from outlying areas had been roped into the search by a senior policeman who lived a few doors away. It may well have been the greatest mobilisation of manpower seen in Lusaka since the Second World War.

I thought it was a sensational spectacle, a magical, fairy-lit wonderland of thoroughly disgruntled human fireflies. I was so thrilled by it that, until we pulled up in the driveway, I forgot I was in trouble.

My father was beyond angry. He had been shot through Angry with a cannon and landed on the far side in an unexplored emotional netherworld where he could find no appropriate outlet save for a hissing noise issued through a rigidly locked jaw, punctuated by the occasional convulsion. My mother simply looked stricken.

I don't recall being punished. They couldn't think of anything to do to me that would measure up against the upheaval I had caused. If I'd been older, my father might have enlisted me in the army. Any army. Over the next few weeks I often caught my parents watching me. Their expressions blended nervous relief with outraged incredulity, alongside an intimation that should I suddenly sprout horns and a tail, thus revealing my true form, they would not have been much surprised.

It wasn't long afterwards that my mother compared me to the acknowledged repository of all human evil – supposedly because of my hair, which I had sleeked diagonally across my forehead with a wet comb. But I'm not sure the two events were unconnected.

'Oh my God!' exclaimed my mother, as though struck by a flash of clarity. 'You look like Hitler.'

In photographs from that time, I do indeed bear an eerie resemblance to the Boys from Brazil.

'Who's Hitler?' I said.

My brother eyeballed me, much as a chameleon might, nodded knowingly and replied, 'He was a very bad man.'

'Oh,' I said, unperturbed.

* * *

HAVING ALL but perfected the disappearing manoeuvre, I now shifted my complete lack of attention to the art of falling into things. I was very accomplished. If it was larger than I was and contained any kind of liquid, you could guarantee I would wind up face down in it. Swimming pools were no challenge, but I fell into them anyway, because they were there. To up the ante, I developed the knack of falling into them with the lightest of splashes, so that the first hint of anything amiss was a faint but desperate gurgling from the deep end. And it was always the deep end.

I even managed to fall into our own pool at home, which was quite a feat. The pool was one of those overground build-it-yourself jobs with a four-foot polythene wall. It stood higher than I did. This time, my parents were one step ahead of me, and retrieved me with minimum fuss. It wasn't always so easy. Fully clothed adults leapt into swimming pools the length and breadth of Zambia on my behalf. One sunny Sunday, as oblivion greeted me in a hotel lido, the manager, a family friend, performed a spectacular distance dive and split his trousers all the way up the seat. I was too far gone to recall that specific incident, but I do remember watching my mother iron the banknotes from my father's wallet after a similar stunt. The Zambian kwacha wasn't the most stable of currencies, but it was worth even less wet.

Munda Wanga Gardens, a lush Lusaka park founded by a Belgian emigrée and gifted to the state, was a civic Eden yet to find its serpent, which was probably hanging out with its pals in our courtyard. Here were soft lawns. Rare trees. Flowers. Fern leaves which curled together at the touch of a finger. A zoo with a dam populated by sleek and dainty otters, which swam nimbly up to my outstretched hands and accepted lumps of cheese. And on a mossy lake, giant lily pads, which could sustain the weight of a four-year-old boy. I wasn't that boy. In I went, and had to be fished out by my heels, thrashing about and shedding fat drops of green slime like a large, indignant toad.

A tape-recording survives from those Lusaka days. It serves to show how no opportunity to make a nuisance of myself eluded my grip. My father made it on his reel-to-reel player, the first in a series of such machines. This thing had arrived amid a fanfare worthy of *Aida*. For weeks, my father had been bending my mother's ear over the possibilities.

'We can record hours of music on it. Whole tapes for parties,' he enthused.

'That's good,' said my mother, encouragingly.

'We can buy albums on the reel-to-reel format, too. They won't click off in the middle the way they do on the eight-track.'

'That's good,' said my mother.

'You know the way the eight-track clicks and changes track in the middle of a song? This won't do that,' said my father, who could never explain anything just the once. 'It'll play the song all the way through. For hours. Depending on what speed you use. The quicker the speed, the higher the quality, but the less time you get.'

'That's good,' my mother said. 'Have you seen Davie's shoes anywhere? He's done something with them.'

'We can play entire symphonies without a break to change the record over. We can record ourselves for fun, and to keep the memories. Like photographs, only in sound.'

'Well, if you took them off in the vegetable garden and didn't put them back on, they must still be there,' said my mother. 'Go and get them. Yes, Max, that's good.'

When the machine was at last cleared by customs and had been collected from the airport, my father summoned the entire family to the living room, lined up in honour-guard formation, to witness what he patently considered to be the greatest technological miracle of the age. He plugged it in, rigged up a spool of tape, and set the controls to Record.

MY FATHER: 'Testing, testing. This is the Tandberg 72B tape recorder, combined with a Sony handheld microphone – David, get away from there. . .'

MY MOTHER: 'Come here, darling.'

MY FATHER: '. . . Sony handheld microphone. Present are Max Bennun, Mavis Bennun, son Leon, daughter Lesley, son David – I told you to get away from there.'

MY MOTHER: 'Come *here*, darling. No, over here.'

MY FATHER: 'Wouldn't anybody like to say something?'
[Pause]

MY SISTER: 'Are we finished?'

MY MOTHER: 'Please, Davie, leave that alone.'

MY FATHER: 'Would you hold on to him, Mavis?' [Sound of scuffling]

MY SISTER: 'Are we –'

MY BROTHER: 'No.'

MY SISTER: 'Who asked you?'

MY BROTHER: 'You did.'

MY SISTER: 'I didn't.'

MY BROTHER: 'Yes you –'

MY FATHER: 'Stop it now or I'll knock your heads. *David, will you get away from th–*' [Ominous thunk. The rest, as *Hamlet* has it, is silence.]

These few feet of tape make me wish that I had been the worst problem my family had to contend with. But even the most thoughtless, hapless and intractable child – and while I hesitate to claim that title for myself, others were less reluctant to bestow it on me – is no match for an entire country. I couldn't begin to compete with what Zambia had to throw at us.

hole large enough for me to fall into.

When I came to, I was in an unfamiliar room, and the bottle drip-feeding into my arm was also quite a novelty. My father and brother were sitting by the bed.

'Didn't we like the other hotel?' I said.

If we didn't, we'd have had good reason.

* * *

THE HOTEL in Livingstone was a motel-style arrangement of separate bungalows, with glazed, flat-metal frames for doors. There my mother and sister spent the night and the next day waiting for word of my condition.

A message was delivered, belatedly, by the front desk. It told my mother that I was going to survive, and that my father was already on his way back to Livingstone.

'Go and get your bag from the bedroom,' said my mother to my sister a few hours later, hearing the crunch of footsteps on the gravel path. My mother went to meet my father at the door and instead found herself separated by a thin sheet of glass from a pair of machete-wielding bandits.

My slight, gentle-natured mother grabbed the handle and, summoning the maternal strength of a she-bear, wrestled against the thugs' attempts to wrench it open. All the while she and my sister set up a cacophony of howls and shrieks for help fit to wake the dead. Had the dead been vacationing in an adjacent cabin, help might have come much sooner. As it was, the two of them grappled and screamed for what seemed like half an hour, but was probably a matter of minutes.

The braver and more resourceful of the two attackers had by now procured a giant boulder, which he heaved through the pane directly at my defenceless mother on the other side. Had it hit her, it would probably have killed her. She desperately twisted out of its path amid a blizzard of glass fragments.

'Hoi!' somebody shouted, and the sound of running feet approached. The intruders were gone in a second.

'I told you,' said one of the rescuers, a woman, to her husband, who was heavy set and short of breath. By way of response, he wheezed and flapped a dismissive hand. 'I did tell him,' she added, for my mother's benefit. 'He thought it was just somebody hitting his wife. But I said it didn't sound normal.'

My mother was cut, bruised and too shocked to say very much. My father arrived 15 minutes later to find her shaking in a chair. My sister was hiding in the bedroom and wouldn't come out until she heard his voice.

Later, we all agreed that even by our family's standards, this had been a torrid weekend. It heralded a wretched spell. I began it in hospital, getting stuck with needles on a twice-daily basis. My mother took the afternoons off from her teaching job at a Lusaka kindergarten to visit and bring me Smarties, which in Zambia were as prized, rare and luxurious as nylon stockings in wartime Britain.

Once, my mother and the Smarties failed to show for hours. 'I'm so sorry I'm late,' she said. 'I was tear-gassed by the police.'

The supposed target for this no-nonsense display of law enforcement had been a tumultuous demonstration outside the French embassy, next door to my mother's kindergarten. I don't know what the French had done to annoy the citizenry of Lusaka – blown something up, probably – but the citizenry of Lusaka was exceedingly piqued. They aimed rocks, colourful songs and even more colourful insults at the French compound. For an angry mob, they possessed both a strong sense of entertainment value and, more importantly, direction.

An hour into the rally, the riot squad arrived, and swiftly made plain their intentions, if not their accuracy, by firing off half-a-dozen CS canisters into the neighbouring playground full of kiddiewinks. It was a pre-school Ypres. Only when a small deputation of embassy staff braved the protestors' fury, and pointed out that nobody was demonstrating against the kindergarten, did the police realise their error. Still, these novel policing tactics worked. Protestors, cops and bewildered diplomats all broke off to watch my mother, weeping and choking, attempt to corral and evacuate several dozen hysterical pre-schoolers. Then everybody went home.

My mother, still traumatised by the incident in Livingstone and terrified even of walking into our own house, was obliged to deal with this, and everything else, on her own. In Britain, my grandfather

Toli had succumbed to heart disease. My father flew north on his sad mission, returning a few weeks later with my grandmother.

* * *

I SCARCELY knew Toli, which is now a matter of regret for me. The more I have learned about him, the more remarkable I find both the man and his life.

I recently discovered that early in 1939, he once again visited Wilkomir, in an attempt to persuade our family to leave Lithuania. It was a brave undertaking. The journey obliged him to pass through Austria, by then under German control. He was detained in Vienna by the Gestapo, and released after ten days thanks only to the intervention of the South African consul.

The fate of those who stayed in Lithuania had their fate concealed by the fog of war until 1945. Then a letter arrived for Toli in Port Elizabeth. As my father watched him read it, Toli fell down on the floor in a dead faint. Only weeks later, Toli received another letter, from the Gestapo officer who had arrested him in Vienna. The letter reminded Toli that he had been treated kindly in prison, and begged him to send food parcels. Toli did so – an act of magnanimity and forgiveness both astonishing and humbling.

Toli's death meant little to me at the time. It was something abstract which had happened far away. My understanding of death was as limited as any very young child's, but, for some reason, much gorier. Putting some information I had heard or read through the scrambler of my juvenile brain, I was under the delusion that on one's deathbed, the skin peeled away from the body, depositing one's innards upon the sheets.

'We have some bad news,' my mother and father told me. 'Your Grandpa Toli has died.'

'Didn't it make a big mess?' I said.

They both looked at me in a way that was fast becoming familiar: two parts bafflement to one part awe at my talent for making a bad situation worse.

To cheer everyone up, and because my brother was in the cast, we went to see the International School of Lusaka's student production.

The ISL's name was misleading. Its choice of play gives a hint as to just how international the school really was: *The Wind in the Willows*. The ISL saw no reason not to conduct itself as if it had been transplanted from Berkshire to this tropical Oz by a freak tornado. I would wind up attending a series of schools just like it. At least they never made me dress up as a rat, the way Leon had to. He was still wearing his costume when we went to find him after the show. His face betrayed all the joy you would expect in a schoolboy who, disguised as a rodent and surrounded by his peers, spies three generations of kinsfolk bearing down on him.

'I thought you were very good,' said my mother, who had made the outfit from brown felt.

'I look stupid,' he muttered, elbowing me aside before I could stand on his tail.

'The character is called "Ratty",' said my father. 'You knew the risks.'

Another boy's grandmother was introduced to us. I had never knowingly met someone else's grandmother before. Like my own grandmother, she was small and had white hair. I was amazed. I thought they must be related.

My grandmother went on to survive Toli by 25 years; her lifetime all but spanned the century. She spent much of those 25 years referring to me as 'an id-yot'. I miss her very much, and have yet to prove her wrong.

* * *

ONE WEEKDAY morning in 1973 my father put me in the family car to take me to my own school. My mother had gone on ahead in her tiny red Honda with my brother and sister. As we rounded the *vlei*, I saw a Honda just like my mother's upended in a ditch beside a nearby junction, its indicator lights still blinking. I clearly recall my immediate reaction, which was to hope that this was the identical tiny red Honda driven by another resident of Mulungushi Village.

It wasn't. As we drew closer that became all too clear. What I witnessed next is seared on my memory as if with a branding iron: it is the image of my mother, her limbs utterly slack, being lifted horizontally from the car by my father and two passers-by. Her eyes were lightly closed, her face placid, as if she were dozing, and her head and body were slathered in blood. The men carried her in what I would later recognise as a ghastly, inadvertent parody. To this day, the sight of a cabaret turn hoisted horizontally aloft, Marilyn Monroe-style, by a chorus line of performing drones in dinner jackets, instantly takes me back to that roadside. So, for many years, did the frozen, tragic classical tableaux in the books on Greek mythology given to me by my grandmother.

Lesley, who had broken her arm, was consumed with quiet, racking sobs; Leon, bruised and missing a tooth, was calm – as usual – but pallid and quite silent. I don't remember who went where with whom after that. My recollection loops from the driveway to the ditch and round again.

The fact that all the adults around me kept saying that everything would be all right was of little assurance. I'd heard the same thing from the nurses when I begged to be spared my injections while convalescing from meningitis.

'Just this one,' they would promise cheerfully each time. 'After that, you won't have to have any more.'

That went on for a month. Did the silly sisters think I wouldn't notice when my arm was being skewered every morning and night? So it wasn't until I saw my mother sitting up in bed with her eyes open that I believed she wasn't dead.

Once again, the hospital became the nexus of our family life. Now it was she who lay on the ward, her legs so badly injured that surgeons were obliged to remove portions of her knees, and I who came to visit. I would have brought Smarties, if I'd known where to get them. I'd probably have eaten them in the car. But the thought was there.

Eventually my mother came home with her legs encased in plaster, and got about on crutches. The driver who had swerved across the junction, at speed, with no signal or warning or right of way or third party insurance, who had broadsided and crushed the little red tin can carrying most of my family, walked away with neither a scratch nor an apology. It was an instructive year for me. It taught me that life is unfair, and that for some things, there is no redress.

* * *

THAT WAS also the year we left Zambia. We had undergone two years of turmoil and misfortune, and the way things looked, we were only slightly ahead of the rest of the country. Zambia's problems, and there were many, kicked out every rung on society's ladder. When our neighbours were subjected to a carjacking at gunpoint, we couldn't simply up and move to a better part of town. This was the better part of town.

My parents had come to Zambia because circumstances and politics would permit them no nearer to their native countries. In South Africa, the white minority government was retreating further and further into a siege mentality as knuckleheaded as any generated during the Boer War, and destined to last a good deal longer. Rhodesia remained under the scarcely less odious rule of Ian Smith and his coterie of what, since their unilateral declaration of independence from Britain in 1965, were effectively freelance colonists.

At the time of writing this, Smith is still with us. What's more, he is looked upon in certain circles as a former statesman. This is a hall-of-mirrors distortion, in which a corkscrew figure is rendered upright by a twisted glass. One need not damn the motives of every Briton in Africa to recognise that Rhodesia's minority regime incarnated all that was venal, loathsome, mean-spirited and indefensible about white rule. It was a coterie of crackpots and gangsters, and the fact that Smith and his kind have given way to madder crackpots and bigger gangsters doesn't alter that one whit.

What peace my parents had known in Zambia was evaporating, and fast. Social upheaval had finally become more of a threat to family life then than their own third-born. They knew when to take a hint.

Earlier in the year, we had packed ourselves into our Volvo 145 estate and speculatively set forth on a north-easterly bearing: our destination, Nairobi, the capital of Kenya. Those 1,100 miles each way, plus an end-to-end tour of Kenya itself, took in several roads the existence of which was well-nigh illusory. Often they were defined not by the presence of a track, but by the absence of obstacles larger than a car. The timing of this jaunt was a small masterpiece of cunning. Our progress coincided precisely with that of the Intertropical Convergence Zone, a migratory band of low pressure, which hurls torrential rain up and down the continent.

Still, to our yearning eyes, Kenya lived up to its reputation as one of Africa's brightest jewels. We liked it so much we brought half of its topsoil back with us, adhering to every cranny and crevice.

Come September, our minds were made up. We emptied the collapsing cupboards and disintegrating shelves of our Mulungushi home. We shook the termites out of our clothing and bed linen. We packed up a few keepsakes, including a traditional witchdoctor mask, which would accompany us each time we moved house and scare the bejesus out of me for years to come. We bade goodbye to our friends and neighbours, foreigner and Zambian alike. And with a collective sigh of relief, we headed off to a new home.

I was thrilled, of course. Packing up and going anywhere was an adventure for me. I couldn't know that, to my parents' minds, we were moving in the wrong direction.

'When will we be coming back to Zambia?' I wanted to know.

'Twenty years too soon, whenever it is,' said my father.

'Will we have a house in Kenya?'

'No, we're all going to sleep in the car,' said my brother, who at ten was already proficient in sarcasm.

'Oh,' I said. That sounded all right. I often slept in the car, although not while it was stationary.

'Don't even joke about it,' said my father. 'If that boy goes to sleep in the car ever again, I want whoever's nearest to wake him up immediately. Poke him with a stick if you have to.'

He and my mother lit up cigarettes, and he rested his arm out of the driver's side window and tapped on the door, humming a song he was fond of, something about being back on the road again.

The wind blew cigarette ash in through my window, so I wound it up and watched the enormity of the plains roll by. 'M.M.B.A.', it was called by those who spent much of their lives driving through it: 'Miles and miles of bloody Africa.' For once, I felt as small as I really was.

chapter four

Wamagata Road

I WAS FIVE when my family settled in Wamagata Road. Within a month I had been attacked by raptors, set upon by dogs, assailed by drunks and run over by a bicycle. It was business as usual.

The raptors that attacked me were kites, a variety of hawk. I was standing at the roadside when I felt a sudden rush of air behind me, and a sharp sensation raked across my scalp. I looked up to see a kite shooting skywards with a clump of my hair clutched in each talon.

'Awk!' I said, and clapped a hand to my head. It came away bloody.

'Awk!' said the kite, circling around for another dive.

'Awk!' added another kite, shooting towards me from the front.

'Awk!' I said again, and dropped into a ditch as the bird whistled over me by inches.

I had no end of trouble with kites. They snatched my sandwiches from out of my hands at school, and on one sunny afternoon, took my French teacher's lunch. I was carrying a plate across the playing fields to the squash courts, at his instruction, when a kite swooped down and snaffled his chicken. He thought I'd eaten it myself and I couldn't convince him otherwise.

But that was many years later. When I came under direct aerial attack in Wamagata Road, I lay low until the birds had flown away then scuttled home in a blue funk. That fear may have been what set the dogs off. I had a pack of them yowling and nipping at my heels by the time I slammed the gate behind me.

Wamagata Road, part of a township called Woodley Estate, was a thin, rutted strip of tarmac little more than three hundred feet from end to end. It served two dozen or so detached, single-storey houses, each fenced and hedged in from its surroundings. The affluent centre of Nairobi didn't peter out here; it simply stopped. Wamagata Road was the border. The end of the street, where our house occupied its quarter-acre enclave, faced on to a patch of waste ground, across which lay the slums of Kibera – a shanty town of more than half a million souls.

Around the corner and across the road stood the shanty town's shanty mall, a riotous assembly of rickety kiosks, makeshift taverns and every imaginable variety of *jua kali* workshop. *Jua kali* – literally, fierce work – meant repairs conducted in the open air, under an unforgiving sun. A practitioner of *jua kali* was known as a *fundi* – an expert, a craftsman, although this designation tended towards the sarcastic. Most *jua kali fundis* were noted for enthusiasm rather than finesse. Their standard approach to fixing something was to hit it repeatedly with something else until one or other item gave in. That said, certain of their number were capable of amazing lo-tech ingenuity. Anyone who has watched the film *Apollo 13*, in which astronauts patch up their malfunctioning spacecraft with chewing gum, spittle and string, has seen a fine example of the *jua kali* principle. But a first-class *fundi* would have done better. Given ten bob, a few beers and a monkey wrench, he'd have had that capsule back on earth in jigtime.

The clamour and babble of this tumbledown bazaar drifted in over the tall hedges to our back garden. It had an allure that no small boy could resist – not even me, already possessed of a powerful aversion to crowds. At first, I wandered the edges of the marketplace and fixed upon a shack on the nearest corner which sold sweets for ten cents each: brown or black toffee chews with an elephant logo printed on the wrapper, stored in big glass jars.

Mr Moses, the shopkeeper, was an affable sort who always called me, with mock solemnity, 'Mr David'. Kenyans are by and large a very friendly people, and they like children. Good thing too. At the time, the average Kenyan family had eight of them.

'*Jambo*, Mr David. *Tamutamu ngapi?*'

How much candy did I want? How much had he got?

The Kenya shilling – a 100 cents – exchanged at around 20 to the

British pound back then, so ten cents was worth half a penny. Round, chalky sweets were only five cents a go, so you got twice as much sucrose for your coppers, but when they failed to dissolve excitingly in water, I lost interest and thereafter stuck to the more deluxe items. They in turn stuck to me, as well as to my clothes and to everything I handled. After a visit to the market I was a walking gluepot. It didn't take Sherlock Holmes to deduce where I'd been. Most of my route was still clinging to me.

* * *

DRUNKS WERE a regular hazard as I went to and fro. They would emerge from the drinking dens at the back of the market – the shacks with blankets thrown across the entrance to cloak the debauchery unfolding within – pie-eyed on home-made beer or a corrosive brew known as *changa'a*. Bathtub gin was mother's milk compared to *changa'a*. This toxic moonshine was rumoured to make imbibers see triple, at the very least. Blindness and brain damage awaited those who survived the walk home. *Changa'a* drinkers were routinely struck by vehicles while lurching along the roadway or, more often, lying in it, prostrated and burbling.

At night, the muddy wasteland between the market and Kibera became a hunting ground for bandits, who preyed on the luckless sots. From suppertime to the small hours, terrible screams would well up from the darkness.

'Shouldn't we do something?' my mother would fret, remembering all too well her own ordeal in Livingstone. But if my father moved to the door, she would stop him. 'You're not going out there,' she said. 'Not unless you want me to bring these three kids up on my own.'

There was no point in calling the police. If they turned up at all, it was always far too late. Out of habit, they pretended to take a statement.

POLICE: 'At what time did you hear the shouting?'

MY MOTHER: 'Three hours ago. When we called you.'

Then they apathetically waved their torches in the vague direction of the long-vacant crime scene, and drove back to the station, knocking down a few stray inebriates on the way.

There were fewer drunks roaming in the daylight hours, but I attracted them all. A tiny white boy wasn't that strange a sight, yet in these men, I kindled an inexplicable fascination. It may have been because I moved. Or maybe not. They also appeared fascinated by tree stumps, road signs and their own fingers.

'*Ntoto! Kuja hapa!*' they bellowed at me. ('Hey kid! Come here!') The drunkest of the drunk could be identified by the fact that they called me '*watoto*' – the plural form – under the impression that there were several of me.

My Swahili was never better than rudimentary, thanks to the typical idleness of the anglophone who finds himself among people who have made the effort to master his own language. But that much I understood. And I wasn't about to *kuja* anywhere near one of these haywire soaks, let alone *hapa*. Whatever was on his mind, he could communicate it just as well from a distance. Seeing my disinclination to come to him, he would make a beeline for me. A *changa'a* tippler's beeline involved a great deal of walking sideways, backwards, in a zig-zag pattern and directly downwards into the ground. After watching this for a while, I would go and find something else to do.

As for the bicycle that hit me, it was the archetype of Nairobi's heavy, creaky, one-speed, standard mode of transport. The black paint alone must have weighed several pounds. The sardonic Kenyans dubbed this machine the 'black mamba', after the world's swiftest snake. It might have proved equally deadly had it not been so slow. It bounced me into the roadside drainage ditch, a location I was now getting fairly well accustomed to. The rider was contrition itself, and not in the least bit drunk.

'I did not see you,' he apologised. 'You are very small.'

I told him not to worry. 'I'm all right,' I said. 'It's not so bad in there. I was in there this morning. Some birds hurt me.'

He didn't seem at all surprised. Either the birds had acquired a reputation, or I had.

* * *

EARLY ONE Saturday evening I was sent to the *duka* – the shop, in this case my favourite corner kiosk – on an errand. We were out of paraffin or flour or light bulbs – some domestic essential, at any rate. I was given a 20-shilling note, more money than I had previously guessed existed in the world, and entrusted to the care of one Judy McLean.

The McLeans were an American family who lived over the road, and with whom we had struck up a neighbourly relationship. My father and Gerald McLean were both whisky aficionados, in as much as they knew whisky was the brown drink, and liked it. Judy was a few years older than me, and took me on as a sidekick. If she had a silly joke or trick that needed an audience, or simply wanted to order me around for the hell of it, I was game. I was a remote-control homunculus, ready to act upon her whims, which might involve having me jump into bushes, or run around with my eyes shut, or pretend to be invisible, something at which I'd gained plenty of practice to date. I already had a big sister, but there was no way I was going to be that obliging with her. She could find her own pet biped.

So Judy walked me to the *duka*, where it transpired that whatever it was we had run out of, they had run out of it too. Having come out on a mission to spend 20 shillings, I was not about to be thwarted. I handed over the loot to Mr Moses and came home with so many sweets that Judy had to help me carry them.

'For crying out loud,' shouted my father, doing just that. It was a phrase he often employed, particularly in reference to me, followed by the time-honoured threats of knocking heads together, even when mine was the only head in sight. I think my mother had encouraged him to use 'For crying out loud' in place of 'For Christ's sake', and he managed to make it sound like the bloodiest of oaths. He fumed at me for a while, then turned his fire on Judy.

'How could you let him do that?' said my father.

'You just told me, walk him to the corner,' said an unrepentant Judy. 'You didn't say anything about not buying candy.'

'I didn't tell you not to sell him to a travelling circus either!' my father said. 'Would you have done that too?' Judy's face lit up at the thought; she would have done exactly that, without a second's hesitation. She obviously regretted that the opportunity hadn't come up, and I'm sure she kept a close eye out for it thereafter.

'Just because you have some money doesn't mean you have to spend it all at once,' said my sister, who was at that age when girls most enjoy being loudly sanctimonious. This was news to me. I'd never before been in charge of so much money that I couldn't spend it all at once and eat the spoils in 15 seconds flat.

Ordinarily, I would have made a rebuttal – something along the lines of 'Shut up shut up shut up', which had served as an iron-clad argument in previous inter-sibling debates – but I sensed this was a good time to say absolutely nothing to anyone about anything. Eventually the shouting died down, all other children were cleared out of the lounge, the sweets were put away far beyond my reach, and I was given a Stern Talking To.

My parents sat on the sofa and I stood in front of them, hands behind my back, rather like the boy facing his inquisitors in the celebrated Victorian oil by William Frederick Yeames, *And When Did You Last See Your Father?* Unlike the boy in the painting, I knew exactly where my father was. That was the problem – that, and his expression. Even my mother looked furious, which normally she couldn't do if you paid her.

The Stern Talking To proceeded as far as the words, 'Do you know why what you did was wrong?' I hadn't the first clue why what I'd done was wrong, but I suspected this was not the answer they were looking for.

'Yes,' I replied, gravely.

'Yes, *what?*' demanded my father.

I racked my brains over that one. I stood there in silence for a full minute, under my parents' twin basilisk stare, trying to remember something that went with 'Yes'. Finally, I gave up and went with the answer I first thought of. 'Yes. . . please?'

They were still laughing when I crept through the drawn curtains, out of the French windows and escaped into the twilight.

The following week each child in my class at St. Michael's school was instructed to draw pictures of his or her parents, and write an accompanying description. My mother, who worked at the school, had her attention drawn to my work by several fellow teachers, all of whom seemed very keen that she should see it. Beneath a portrait crafted with standard five-year-old expertise and a fresh set of crayons appeared this summary: 'My dad has red eyes. He gets very cross and has a hole in the top of his hair.'

'That's it,' said my father, when he saw the drawing. 'I'm not coming to any more open days until he's at secondary school.' He was as good as his word.

chapter five

To Hell and Back in a Big White Car

'SIX YEARS old,' said my mother, 'is too young to go on safari to Lake Turkana.'

I was desperate to go on safari to Lake Turkana. I didn't know where Lake Turkana was, but my father was going, my brother was going, and it was important to me to be one of the menfolk. I hadn't missed out on a family adventure yet. That was what had my mother worried. She felt that there was a limit to the amount of adventure one little boy should be subjected to. I didn't. Nor did my father.

'Oh, come on, Mavis,' he protested. 'We've taken him on much harder trips.'

'And look what happened,' said my mother. 'What will you do if he gets sick, three days' drive from Nairobi?'

'Call in the flying doctor,' said my father. 'But nobody's going to get sick.'

He was right about that much. An awful lot else went awry on our 1974 Lake Turkana excursion, but nobody got sick. In terms of inconvenience relative to achievement, this particular safari may have set a record of some kind.

I'm not claiming a place for it among the most disastrous treks ever undertaken. Unlike the ill-fated Donner Party of 1846, Scott's doomed Antarctic enterprise, and Captain Cook's voyage to the South Seas, we made no history, and suffered no fatalities. The only thing that perished on our expedition was a pack of lamb chops. We weren't obliged to turn cannibal, or done in by the elements, or waylaid by angry tribesmen. The tribesmen couldn't have cared less about us. But sweet Jesus, it was a woeful affair.

In 1974, Lake Turkana was a year away from being renamed after its local population. Since 1888 it had been officially known as Lake Rudolf – a name bestowed on it in honour of the Hapsburg crown prince, by a party of Austrian explorers who, I'm guessing, had a better time there than we did. Had the new name been down to us, Lake Buggerit might now be a feature of any reliable world atlas. This was the trip when it became clear to me that I could get into things over my head. I had spent my short life to date getting into things over my head – usually bodies of water – so you could argue that this realisation was well overdue.

* * *

LAKE TURKANA stretches over 150 miles to Kenya's northern border, and juts a further 30 into Ethiopia. It spans only 37 miles at its widest point; a long, narrow lake once mistakenly thought to be the source of the Nile. In fact, it has no outlet other than evaporation, and plenty of it. Nicknamed the Jade Sea because of the light green algae upon its surface, it is unnervingly beautiful. All the more so for being surrounded by the vast and ungodly desert terrain of the Northern Frontier District, a region so inhospitable that it has bred, in the Turkana tribe, one of the most rugged races on the pockmarked face of the earth.

Turkana is uppermost in a trail of Kenyan lakes set within the biggest scar on the planet: the Great Rift Valley, which runs thousands of miles along the eastern side of the African continent. On this scale, the Grand Canyon is no more than a scratch. So vast is the Great Rift that only near the edge do you sense you're in a valley at all. It contains mountains from the peaks of which you still can't see its sides. It is a geological colossus, an incomprehensibly immense agglomeration of vulcanism and tectonics, of calderas, hot springs and volcanoes both dormant and extinct.

The Great Rift has defined and dominated life in modern Kenya. Most major cities develop as hubs, on waterways or trade routes. Nairobi exists only because it was the site where imperial chutzpah was halted, briefly, by a gargantuan physical obstacle.

In 1896, British East Africa extended westward from the Kenya coast to Lake Victoria and Uganda. What lay between was a matter of conjecture. To open up this territory, the British East Africa Company decided to build a railway across it. Soon to be aptly dubbed 'the Lunatic Line', the scheme began in the port of Mombasa and crawled inland at an initial pace of 24 miles per annum. Once it had overcome a hitch on the dusty plains of Tsavo, where lions took to snacking on that part of the workforce spared by disease, the line made splendid progress until 100 miles south of the equator when it hit, in quick succession, a sizeable swamp and the upper edge of an even larger escarpment. The latter proved to be one side of the Great Rift. The former became, by default, a railway terminus, then a town, and eventually the nation's capital.

The problem of how to get the train carriages onto the floor of the Rift was solved by loading them individually onto trestle cars, which featured one axle level with the flatbed and the other on 20-foot shafts, so that the cargo remained horizontal. The trestles were then lowered on ropes straight down the 45-degree slope. If this strikes you as confusing, intricate and laborious to the point of derangement, then you have grasped the spirit of the entire project.

The Lunatic Line was a great success. It achieved all of its stated aims, triumphed over received wisdom and proved its many and eminently sensible critics wrong as wrong can be; leading one to the uncomfortable conclusion that slap-happy ideas may be right as often as not.

Our trip to Lake Turkana was one such idea that may, with hindsight, be filed under 'not'. When you plan an expedition to one of the world's wilder places, you must consider carefully what – and who – you bring.

On the plus side, we had a seasoned safari veteran: my father. He had driven around most of sub-equatorial Africa in his time. We had two insulated coolboxes of fresh food, and two bottles of whisky. Our vehicles measured up to the task. One was a short-wheel-base Toyota Land Cruiser. The other was the new Range Rover with which my father had replaced the Volvo estate. The Range Rover boasted all the power and comfort lacking in its more basic cousin, the Land Rover. Also, it was fitted with a gizmo called a differential lock, which prevented the wheels from spinning when the car was mudbound. My father had spent many a glad hour on the wasteground that separated our home from the slums of Kibera, steering the Range Rover into the stickiest patches he could find, making sure it was thoroughly bogged down, then engaging the differential lock and easing the car onto solid ground again. He never tired of it.

Our party also included Gerald McLean and his teenage son Ted; our friends Simon and Elina Morse, a young couple; a pal of theirs called Diane; and the remaining male Bennuns. My brother and I were used to being dragged around the less accessible parts of the tropics. The McLeans were hearty Californians who boasted of the pleasure they took in camping. Elina worked as the local representative of a tour company based in her home country, Finland. As far as she was concerned, any holiday – a fortnight up a flagpole, say, or digging her way to the earth's core – would be pure luxury, so long as it didn't involve two gross of Scandinavian steel-workers in the grip of aquavit-induced dementia. Simon was happy to go where Elina went. Diane . . . Diane wasn't happy about anything. Nor was Diane likely to become happy about anything. Diane, it is fair to say, was a miserable cow.

Diane didn't see why she should ride in the Land Cruiser, which her friends the Morses had borrowed for the journey, when the Range Rover had nicer seats. Diane didn't understand why it had to be so hot, and so dusty. Diane was uncomfortable. Diane was tired. Diane was sure the whole thing could have been a lot better organised. Diane, remarkably, managed to accumulate and express all these grievances before we had left Nairobi. But Diane was just warming up. Once we got going, so did Diane.

* * *

OUR ROUTE took us north through the White Highlands, a region of prime farmland on the Equator settled by British ranchers. Nairobi, at 5,500 feet above sea level, was considered temperate by Kenyan standards; up there the air was cooler still, and the smooth, undulating hills could pass for a voluptuous variation on the Sussex Downs. We passed through the country's highest town, Nyahururu, and on to Rumuruti, where the tarmac road and the greenery come to an end.

The descent into semi-desert takes a matter of minutes, and feels like switching continents. The heat grows by the second, all but palpably; the atmosphere thickens and dries; the wide acres of pasture shrivel into slack reddish dust, sparsely vegetated by clumps of thin grass and dotted with tiny trees in the branches of which, every so often, you may spy a goat. This curiosity had first been observed by my sister, on a previous outing, when she was nine.

'I just saw a goat in a tree,' she said.

'No, you didn't,' said my father.

'I *did it!* I did see a goat in a tree,' protested my sister, much as Tweety Pie might assert the presence of a Puddy Tat.

'It must have been a bird,' my father said.

'It was a *goat,*' Lesley shouted, blinking back furious tears. 'I know what a bird looks like. It was a goat. It had four feet and it was eating the leaves.'

'With its feet?' said my brother.

'Maybe it was a very big bird,' said my father.

'Maybe it was a gryphon,' said my brother, whose erudition was matched only by his capacity for stirring up trouble.

'It wasn't one of those,' wailed my sister, who had no idea what a gryphon might be, but knew it wasn't a goat in a tree. 'It was a goat in a tree.' And, to my brother's satisfaction, she burst out crying.

Before long, of course, my sister was proved right. We all saw goats that had climbed into the trees to forage, the ground giving up as it did scant sustenance. And every time we saw one, she would point and cry exultantly, 'See? See?!' This habit finally tailed off sometime around 1987, when she was 23. One attribute common to all members of my family except my mother is a fondness for making a point.

By the time of our Turkana expedition, treebound goats were no longer a novelty to us, but Gerald and Ted McLean, in our Range Rover, were fascinated. We stopped so they could take some pictures. The Morses' Land Cruiser pulled to a halt a few yards behind us, and Simon

Morse stepped out of the driver's seat, his face like a Kabuki mask with a floppy-brimmed hat on. As his door opened, Diane's voice came sharply into range, as if a radio dial had been swivelled to her exact frequency.

Diane wanted to know why we were stopping. Diane wanted to know how long she was going to have to sit in the middle. Diane wanted to know what that goat was doing in a tree. Diane's underpants were sticking to her nether regions, which despite all reasonable assumptions to the contrary ought, Diane believed, to be a concern for persons other than Diane. Diane was annoyed because Simon wouldn't answer any more of her questions. Diane felt that somebody should tell Max that she suspected (despite being no better acquainted with the local geography than a carp is with needlepoint) he had taken a wrong turning back there.

Through the windscreen I could see Elina nodding sympathetically, with a patience born of shepherding countless drunken Norsemen through 14-day safari packages.

'I swear,' muttered Simon, 'if sunstroke doesn't get her, I will.'

A hot gust swung his door shut with a *thunk*, and Diane's monologue, muted but by no means concluded, was lost to the wind. Simon looked at the incongruously arboreal goat. 'Want to swap places?' he said, loudly. The goat, chewing all the while on a leathery acacia leaf, glanced sideways at him for a moment, then returned its attention to the thorn-studded branches. A dumb animal it might have been, but it wasn't that dumb.

The road to Maralal, our intended stopover for the night, was rough and rutted. About 25 miles out of Rumuruti we felt the unmistakable judder that indicates a flat tyre. We pulled up and got out to take a look. The tyre wasn't merely flat; it appeared to have been mauled. Chunks of the rubber were peeling off and flapping against the wheel arch.

'Shouldn't have bought retreads, Max,' said Gerald McLean to my father.

'I didn't,' said my father, irritated. 'This whole set of tyres is brand new. They came with the car.' We set about changing the wheel, my father taking heart in the thought of what he would say, upon our return to Nairobi, to the dealer who sold him the Range Rover.

Half an hour's driving later, we again sensed that slight but disheartening tilt in the car's axis, and through the window came a noise – 'flubba-flubba-flubba' – that could only be another flat tyre. This was odd. We averaged less than two punctures a trip. Now we'd had two in 20 miles. The sun was already close to the western horizon as we jacked up the chassis and bolted on the second spare wheel.

The third flat came soon after, in the early twilight. This time, the tyre hadn't come apart; it had permitted a long acacia thorn, of the type that usually splintered beneath our wheels, to pierce straight through the tread and poke a hole in the inner tube. There was now no option but to dig out the puncture repair kit, manhandle the tyre from its hub – a pig of a job – and rotate the reinflated tube in a basin of water, looking for bubbles. Having patched the hole, we waited for the glue to dry, then remounted the tyre on the hub – a job which turned getting it off the hub in the first place into a fond and rather wistful memory – and set off on our way; the entire procedure being effected to the accompaniment of an aria, both *forte* and *accelerando*, from the lungs of the ill-used but strangely vigorous Diane, entitled 'Oh, Why Didn't Anyone See This Would Happen?'

* * *

IT WAS DARK when we pitched up at the Maralal campsite, which was distinguished from the remainder of that desolate district solely by a ring of stones that served as a fire pit. Leon and I unloaded the back of the Range Rover. A canvas sack hit the ground with a reassuring clang; we had not, as we had once discovered 200 miles from the nearest alternative shelter, forgotten the tent poles.

The bulk of the remaining cargo belonged to the McLeans. Gerald and Ted had brought four bags apiece, each one fatly protruding with enigmatic lumps. What could they possibly need that badly in the Northern Frontier District?

As the tent poles came rattling from their upended sack, Ted approached us carrying a kettle and a flex with a two-pin plug fixed inside a travel adaptor. 'Uh, where's the electric hook-up?' he said.

We looked at him for a while.

Ted assumed our bafflement stemmed from a failure to recognise a kettle when we saw one. 'I, uh, thought I could make us all some coffee or tea,' he explained, gently, in the tone one might use with a rather slow-witted toddler to account for the death of a hamster.

We looked at him a little while longer.

'Ted,' said Leon at last. 'Where did you last go camping?'

'Yellowstone Park,' said Ted.

We were interrupted by Gerald, carrying a large, fleecy towel that must have taken up an entire rucksack itself.

'I missed the sign for the showers, it's so dark,' said Gerald. 'Did you see them on the way in?' We stopped looking at Ted and instead looked at Gerald. Gerald and Ted looked at each other.

'Does this mean we, uh, can't use the hairdryer?' said Ted.

Our tent was a blue, rotund item that rose to a single peak at the centre, and was therefore referred to as the Circus Tent. It had a self-enclosed inner sleeping compartment made of cloth, which hung from the frame and was customarily occupied by the younger campers: in this case, Leon, Ted and myself. The adults – Gerald and my father – slept in the outer portion on a groundsheet. We all used inflatable mattresses, but even so, it was advisable to check the ground very carefully before the tent went up. If you found yourself lying on a rock or, worse, a root, you were stuck with it until daylight.

We had not checked the ground carefully. In our weariness, and our desperation to get the tent up, we had not checked the ground at all. The strongest-willed of fakirs could not have passed the night comfortably in that tent; he would have longed for his bed of nails as anyone else might hanker after box-springs and goosedown. Our only hope was that fatigue would prevail over discomfort, which it did.

We could also be grateful that we were not sharing quarters with Diane. From the Morses' tent – the more traditional triangular variety, sewn from olive-green canvas and slung on heavy, wooden poles – her recital of the plaintive ballad, 'It's All Your Fault That I'm Suffering', persisted dimly late into the night, until it was drowned out by my father's powerful snores and I fell asleep.

The next morning we ate a basic breakfast and repacked the vehicles, bound for South Horr and then Loyengalani on the east side of the lake.

Here the road was so rudimentary as to vanish for stretches where it climbed through staircases constructed by nature from volcanic rock. The cars were up to the task, but the Range Rover's tyres were not. All four were partially shredded by the end of our journey. We had no choice but to continue on them – slowly. The problem, we would later discover, was that the Range Rover was designed for the country estates of the British upper classes. Its tyres were the softest of radials, ideal for the well-cushioned pastures of the Home Counties but less well suited to lava and three-inch thorns.

As it was, I lost count of the number of times I watched my father, stripped to the waist in the baking desert air, turning a tube through a basin of water while issuing an even stream of curses fit to make a docker blush.

* * *

SIMON AND Elina were thrilled when we arrived at Loyengalani. They were insistent that we should stay as long as possible. Our campsite was blessed with a spectacular view across the shimmering lake. That was all it was blessed with. The local authorities had resolved to place the site on a bare hilltop, the most exposed patch of ground in the vicinity – which, with so much to choose from, must have taken some finding. There was no escape from a heat which could, without fear of exaggeration, be described as infernal. Nor could one shelter from the wind, continually blowing either onto or off the lake, kicking up dust and grit like a tireless beach bully. You might have hoped the wind would take the edge off the heat, but each gust was the breath of a furnace; if anything, the air was less scorching during its rare moments of stillness.

On the campsite floor, there was no trace of vegetation. The hardiest of grasses had nothing to cling to here. No living thing could endure bar selected insects of quite dismaying appearance. Not that we needed to worry about those: the scorpions kept them in check. Everywhere lay sand and rocks; although, by way of comparative luxury, the authorities had ensured that the ratio of sand to rock was slightly higher than on the surrounding terrain. Also on the plus side, more sand was blowing into the campsite all the time, the wind not yet having built up sufficient force to pelt us with rocks.

The tents went up quickly, before the metal poles became too hot to touch. Building a fire seemed an irrelevance, although it was waggishly suggested by Simon that doing so might cool the air a little. Still, we needed to cook our chops. Gathering fuel was quite a task. Scouring the ground for half a mile in each direction yielded up more, weight for weight, in scorpions than it did in the meagre, shrivelled remains of a few trees that had given up the struggle midway through the Pleistocene epoch. Simon, who was full of bright ideas, proposed we burn the scorpions. We agreed, on condition that he be the one to gather them.

Through the skilful use of paraffin, canvas windbreaks and swearing, we succeeded in setting light to the wood. We dug the lamb chops out of the coolbox and set them on the grill. One of the whisky bottles began to circulate among the adult campers. By the time the chops were cooked, a few minutes later, half the contents had gone. By the time the chops were eaten, the bottle was empty.

'You know,' said Simon, gnawing at the last of his dinner, 'we have to be careful to keep these bones together and throw them well away from the campsite.'

'Uh-huh?' said Gerald. 'Why?'

'Hyaenas,' said Simon, putting down his chop and picking up the whisky. 'The hyaena,' he said, between gulps, 'the hyaena has the strongest jaws in the animal kingdom. It can crush the shell of a tortoise with a single bite. A lion can't do that . . . 'He leaned in meaningfully towards Gerald. 'A leopard can't. . . but the hyaena can. It crunches bones just like *that*.' He bit down firmly on his chop, which did not give way. 'Erm,' said Simon. 'Ow. But that's just what I'm talking about. No problem for a hyaena. And they're scavengers. They smell the bones, they come into your camp, and when the bones are finished,' and here he brought the whisky bottle down in the sand with a small, muffled *whump* for effect, 'they . . . start . . . on . . . your . . . *feet*.'

With each word, Gerald's face grew paler and his eyes wider. Attention was diverted from his unease by a lively new air from Diane, entitled 'How Could A Girl Like Me Come To Such A Pass?'.

'I'm going to turn in,' said my father, in a voice that implied it had come down to either that or braining Diane with a lump of lava. The interior of our tent had little to recommend it over a Dutch oven, so we dragged the mattresses outside, checked for scorpions and over-sharp pebbles, and – having flung the chop bones far into the distance – bedded down under loose blankets in the open air. Between the heat, the whisky and the chops, everyone quickly slumped into a state less sleep than stupor.

Although the sky was clear, the moon was new, and it was very dark. When the screaming began, around midnight, nobody could see what was going on.

'Ahhhhh! Ahhhhhh! *Ahhhhhhhhhh!*' the screams rang out. 'Get it off me! Ahhh! Help me! Oh my God! It's eaten my feet! Jesus Christ, get it away from me!'

A torch clicked on and the beam swung around in the darkness, momentarily illuminating one astounded face after another, until it lighted on the features of Gerald McLean, contorted woodcut-fashion into a monotype of pure horror.

'It's a hyaena,' croaked Gerald. 'A hyaena was eating my feet!'

By now two or three more torch beams were playing upon the campsite. One of them caught, and held, something; the others joined it. Scurrying into the distance, its tail between its legs, was a mongrel dog about the size of a half-starved spaniel. When the torchlight hit it, the mongrel turned to face us, revealing as pathetic and mangy a creature as ever took to its heels with a whimper. Cringing, it paced backwards and away.

'*Ahhhh!*' Gerald keened. 'Get rid of it!'

We threw some stones towards the dog, which slunk off into the darkness. Then we threw some more stones in the direction it had taken; we had so many of the damn things, why not?

'It got my feet,' moaned Gerald, who plainly reckoned himself a man trembling upon the lip of oblivion. A torchlit medical inspection by my father revealed that Gerald's toes had been slightly licked.

The wind was whipping up now, and the flying sand began to sting. We retreated to the tents and tried to go back to sleep. We had no chance. A full-blown sandstorm had come upon us. It wrestled the Circus Tent's pegs from their friable moorings and swept the canvas into a snapping horizontal sheet six feet above our heads, held only by its fastenings to the poles. The entire tent threatened at any moment to lift off and, like some great, gaunt, suicidal stork, fling itself wholesale into the lake. Leaping about in the dark, we were a crew of blind roustabouts. We hammered the pegs back in as deep as they would go, and loaded the edges of the flysheets with rocks, which for the second time that night had proved surprisingly useful.

It seemed only moments later that we were woken by a sunrise as jarring and abrupt as cannon-fire. At breakfast, we were all somewhat subdued, except for Gerald, who was very subdued indeed. Even Simon and Elina had misplaced their enthusiasm. We could not face the prospect of loitering in the campsite all day, but the Range Rover's tyres were in no state for recreational driving. To pack up and go home so soon would be an admission of defeat.

'What do people do around here?' said Simon.

'They fish,' said my father.

* * *

ELECTING TO risk the radials, we drove down to the town of Loyengalani. Here was a place where the passing of time might be best represented by Salvador Dali's melting clocks. Most of its denizens looked equally malleable. The heat and the ennui were enough to sap the human spirit within minutes, let alone a lifetime.

There were only three commercial establishments in Loyengalani. One was the Oasis Lodge hotel; the second, a ramshackle *duka* staffed by a chap listless even by local standards. At some point in his tenure he had become fused with the counter of his shop, and it was all he could do to peel away a finger and gesture directions towards the third business concern: a boat-and-tackle hire service.

The lake hosts a crocodile population, which is not only the world's most numerous, but also one of the best fed. The reptiles are huge and fearsome, and it didn't take us long to find out why. The water was also full of giant Nile perch, which shared in the region's general *joie de vivre*. For these fish, any opportunity to end it all could not come too soon. With the benumbed sluggishness which characterises deep depression, they bit mopishly onto our hooks, and having done that much, would do no more. They neither resisted nor yielded, but drifted disconsolately on the end of the line until hauled into the boat. For all the fight they displayed, we might as well have been dragging aboard large sacks of canned tuna.

Canned tuna would not have posed the problem that now faced us. Just one of these leviathans would have fed us for a week, if we'd had any way of preserving it. By lunchtime, several hundredweight of fresh fish was piled up in the boat.

'What the hell are we going to do with all of it?' said Simon.

'Can't we keep it?' I said helpfully.

'Where?' said my father.

'In the tent,' I said, as if stating the obvious.

A silence followed at the savoury thought of a close, airless tent full of very warm fish.

'We could give it to the El Molo,' said my brother.

The El Molo are 'the people of the lake'. They are not to be confused with the Turkana, and there is little danger of anyone doing so. The harshness of life hereabouts, which has so toughened the Turkana, has registered the opposite effect on the El Molo. They are Kenya's smallest tribe, and by far its most downtrodden and degraded. That a few hundred of them survive at all is largely due to the attentions of foreign altruists, who find it insupportable that an ancient culture should be allowed to die. They are certainly more impassioned about it than the El Molo themselves, who appear dismally apathetic as to their own fate. Aid which might have bolstered a more vigorous people has simply eliminated in them the last, feeble vestiges of self-sufficiency. They have a lot in common with the Nile perch on which they forlornly subsist.

Thus, when we drove up to the El Molo's huts with a carful of the stuff, we could not give it away. A few relatively dynamic souls turned and ran at our approach. Most just sat where they were and ignored us, much as they ignored the flies that buzzed around their faces. Those who would speak to us expressed an attitude which may be summed up as, 'Dear God, please, not more fish – not ever again.'

Our next stop was the Oasis Lodge.

'Certainly,' the manager told us. 'We'll take your fish. . .'

'Great!' said Simon Morse. 'We'll unload it for you.'

'. . . but only,' the manager went on, 'if you come back here tonight and eat it. Dinner is only four hundred shillings per head for non-residents.'

Four hundred shillings in 1974 would have bought dinner for the lot of us in one of Nairobi's fancier restaurants – had we only been in Nairobi. And Lord, did we wish that we were in Nairobi.

'But –' Simon began.

'That's fine,' said my father quickly, staring hard at Simon.

We left the fish and left the Oasis Lodge; to my knowledge, none of us has been back there since.

That night, the second bottle of whisky was soon dispatched. One of the more sober adults opened up the coolboxes to discover that the lamb chops had developed a green film to match that of the lake itself.

'Let's go home,' said Elina. 'Now. Let's just pack up and go.'

'It's eight o'clock at night,' my father said.

'I don't care,' said Elina, who only 24 hours earlier had been determined to stay indefinitely.

'She's right,' said Simon. Diane, for once, was silent, although her face was suffused with a punchable smugness. Simon and Elina had to be physically restrained from packing up their tent.

'You know,' said Gerald, who was at last getting into the safari spirit, 'if you scrape this slime off the chops, they cook up just fine.'

Gerald and my father ate the chops, which did them no harm at all. Everybody else had baked beans.

The following morning, a new mission was decided upon. Whisky. That was one thing everyone over the age of 18 could agree on. The party needed whisky.

'Diane won't make it through this trip without more whisky,' said Simon, *sotto voce*, to my father.

'I didn't know she was drinking it,' my father said.

'She isn't,' said Simon. 'But if I don't get a new bottle of whisky, I'm going to kill her with this empty one.'

The Oasis Lodge was out of the question, and had the Loyengalani *duka* ever stocked any kind of liquor, the proprietor would long since have swallowed the lot and chased it down with rat poison.

We struck camp and headed east, via North Horr and through the

Chalbi Desert, on to Marsabit National Park, stopping in at every shack, hut and hole in the ground in the quest for whisky. We would have had better luck trying to buy a cut-price iceberg.

At last, at Marsabit Lodge, the management agreed to sell us a bottle at bar rates. What the Oasis Lodge had been denied, the Marsabit Lodge exacted. Our kitty was now all but empty. We had just enough cash for petrol, and no option but to return home the next day.

As we drove out of Marsabit, I was faced with one of the most ravishing sights of my life. Overnight, the Chalbi had soaked up a very rare dousing of rain. Inches of it. The ground, which had been baked bare and yellow-brown, now shone blue to the horizon. Tiny flowers had erupted from every crack in the parched surface. It would have been worth a dozen more and greater tests of endurance just to see this.

The five figures who tottered from our Range Rover back in Wamagata Road were caricatures of the gung-ho wayfarers of nine days before – parched, sunburned, mantled with dirt, physically and spiritually spent.

'How was it?' said my mother.

'It was quite something,' said Gerald McLean.

'It was, uh, something else,' said Ted.

'I want a shower,' I said, for what may have been the first time in my life.

'I thought it was a wonderful trip,' said my father. 'I'd do it again like a shot.'

Simon Morse stopped by later that evening with news about Diane. She had moaned throughout the entire trip, and had declined to make any kind of contribution – cooking, washing up, collecting firewood – aside from pointing out what everybody else was doing wrong. Now she was refusing to pony up her share of the expenses.

'I'll cover for her,' said Simon. 'The way I see it, it's a small price to pay for not sharing a car with her any more.'

'We should have left her behind in Loyengalani,' said my father. 'We'd have been doing civilisation a favour.'

'It wouldn't have been fair to Loyengalani,' said Simon. 'I don't suppose you've got a drop of whisky around the house?'

'David, pour Simon a whisky,' said my father. 'No, not that one. The good one. Now put it down. You can't have any. Next time we go,' he told Simon, 'it should just be you, Elina and I.'

Simon, mid-swig, began coughing. I recognised his appalled and incredulous expression. I had often seen it on my parents' faces, directed at me.

'I was thinking of when the rains have gone. . .' said my father. But Simon was already looking at his watch.

chapter six

Black Belt Jones and The Gnome-Mobile

THE METROPOLE cinema in Adams Arcade could not fairly be described as a fleapit. That would be to exaggerate its custom. I don't think I ever once saw a flea in there, let alone any other patrons on whom fleas might conceivably have fed. Between 1974 and 1977, I single-handedly supported the place. Considering that I bought my tickets on a child discount, the cinema must have had very low overheads.

Adams Arcade, although only five minutes' walk away, differed from Kibera market the way a marching band differs from a riot. It may have been slightly down at heel, but the arcade was a solid, genteel shopping centre, in which businesses were to be found where you last remembered seeing them. Their premises were not movable on a whim. There were no shebeens, no roving dipsomaniacs, no *jua kali* mechanics walloping merry hell out of a wheel hub with a lump hammer.

The shopping centre described an L-shape, and its car park completed a rectangle. The arcade was built on a slope, so that an understorey gradually emerged as you walked down the hill. At the lower end of the car park stood a curious piece of public art: a large, Henry Moore-style abstract sculpture, all curves and holes, which doubled up as a slide for the neighbourhood children. When I wasn't in the Metropole, or trailing my mother around Woodley Grocers, or keeping a sorely begrudged appointment in the barber shop, I was slithering down the artwork, gleefully helping to wear it ever smoother with my shorts. But more often than not, I was in the Metropole.

The cinema stood on the upper storey, at the crook of the L. As well as the auditorium, with its creaking fold-down seats of an indeterminate shade that might once have been burgundy, it housed a bar, tucked away around a corner in the lobby. The management could normally be found in here. It beat manning the ticket booth. There was nothing to stop me walking straight through to the gallery, but I habitually put my head round the door of the saloon and handed over my three-shillings-fifty.

ME: 'One ticket for the royal circle, please.'

MANAGER (beer in hand): 'Thank you. You may go in. Tell the usher I said it was all right.'

ME: 'He says –'

USHER (sitting next to the manager): 'That is fine, I also heard him.'

I instinctively sympathised with the bar-room regulars, who were doing in their own way what I was doing in mine – withdrawing from the uncertain outdoors into a hidden sanctum of shadows and obscurity. Their preferred means were stubby brown bottles of Tusker Export lager. Mine, *The Railway Children*.

If *The Railway Children* hadn't just finished a week's run at the Metropole, then it was about to start one. I saw it more times than I can guess at, and never understood it once. I had no inkling what was going on. A family lost their father and their money and went to live in the English countryside. That much I twigged after a dozen or so viewings. The house they were forced to occupy was big, if dusty, and looked quite similar to many of the grander residences in Nairobi. So were they poor or weren't they? What were they doing down by the train tracks all the time? Who was the fellow in the tunnel with a broken leg? How did the nice old gent on the train fit in with any of it? I was, and remain, mystified.

By rights, the image of Jenny Agutter waving her knickers on a stick should skulk the corridors of my adult psyche as a fully evolved and distastefully tawdry fetish. But it doesn't. Jenny Agutter, bloomers or no, stirs neither my longing nor any more corporeal part of me. My pulse does not quicken at the sight of Edwardiana. I have never been tempted to revisit the movie, not even to find out what it was actually about. The truth is, I watched it because it was there. If the Metropole had screened Russian arthouse cinema, or the œuvre of Jerry Lewis, I would have watched that, and made about as much sense of it.

* * *

WHEN, VERY occasionally, *The Railway Children* was relieved from matinée duty, it was substituted with a live-action Disney feature of similar vintage and lucidity. *The Gnome-Mobile* centred on some tiny people who lived in a Californian forest and had a run-in with some not-so-tiny people, which they eventually won. That was fine by me: the gnomes were no less plausible than those old-fashioned kids with their starchy collars and their fascination with trains. More to the point, neither film was remotely as odd as what went on outside the theatre, in my daily life. The Metropole was not my retreat into fantasy, it was my retreat into order. Here was a place where events happened in a predictable and well-worn sequence. A led to B, which in turn gave forth C, and by the later reaches of the alphabet, everything was neatly wrapped up and happily concluded. The fact that A, B and C through Z were altogether unintelligible to me made it no less satisfying. I was in the dark, literally and metaphorically, and I liked it.

There was a reassuring uniformity, too, about the newsreels that opened every programme. Modelled on the famous and now widely parodied Pathé News round-ups, this solemn series was titled 'News of Kenya', and consisted of a stentorian voice-over explaining what the president, Jomo Kenyatta, had been up to that week. It was the same as every week. He had visited a town or attended an event, and been greeted by traditional dancers. In a big news week, he had either left the country (seen off at the airport by the Harambee Dancers) or returned to the country (welcomed at the airport by the Jamhuri Dancers.) Mzee Kenyatta, to give him the respectful title due to a wise elder, could not leave home without being danced at. Sometimes he didn't leave home, and still got danced at, on the State House lawn.

After a spell of watching the gyrations, the father of the nation would join in for a few rather notional steps – he was, after all, around 80 years old, although nobody knew for sure – then augustly mount a podium from which he would deliver a short address. It invariably concluded with the slogan '*Harambee*' (unity) repeated several times and echoed by the crowd, emphasised with solemn shakes of his ceremonial flywhisk.

MZEE KENYATTA: *'Harambee!'*

SPECTATORS: 'Ey*!'*

MZEE KENYATTA: *'Harambee!'*

SPECTATORS: 'Ey*!'*

This call-and-response chant, which signalled the end of the newsreel and the beginning of a short interval, was my Pavlovian dog bell, triggering in me an impulse to go and buy an ice lolly.

ME: 'One Orange Maid, please.'

MANAGER: 'One shilling and fifty cents, thank you. Help yourself at the counter on your way back.'

* * *

THE COSY sense of continuity in my movie-going was dissolved when one day I turned up too late for the matinée, bought a ticket anyway, and found myself watching a movie with the promising title of *Black Belt Jones*. The only Jones of my acquaintance was an undersized and rather diffident lad at school; if he or someone much like him was secretly a kung-fu master, I wanted to know about it.

This Jones, the one with the black belt, was something else again. For a start, he was American and he was black. I had met plenty of Americans; in Nairobi they almost matched the British in numbers. And as for being black, this was the norm. It was *wazungu* like me, the whites, who were out of the ordinary. But black Americans? Who knew kung-fu? And took on the Mafia (whatever that was)? Where was this guy when the gnomes needed him? The world outside Kenya was suddenly revealed as much wider than either of my routine cinematic immersions had led me to suspect. It had crime, corruption, injustice, inequality, racism and misery in it. So too did Kenya, and then some; but typically, I had failed to see it all around me. It took what I now know to be a third-rate Blaxploitation flick, filmed from the underdog's point of view, to drum into me some awareness that human life was a lottery in which I had drawn a winning ticket. Like all lottery winners, I was not in the slightest bit deserving of my luck. Nor, it now struck on me, were the losers.

Black Belt Jones's hair was another revelation. This was Africa, 1976, but nobody around here wore an Afro. The only person who came close was my brother Leon, and even he was a year or two away from developing the sort of magnificent homegrown busby more often seen on funk-band percussionists with names like Rooty-Toot Starchile. You didn't come across people who looked like Black Belt Jones, not even in the advertisements that preceded every screening. And these were strange enough in themselves.

Some of the clips had been made specifically for the African market. The cigarette ads struck the unlikely aspirational tone of cigarette ads everywhere. They featured immaculately groomed black Africans, in lightweight suits or shimmering cocktail dresses, savouring a lifestyle which was at best improbable, and cigarettes which were, by contrast, readily obtainable. 'Three Fives! State Express,' purred a sleek, Afro-baritone. 'The very special taste of success.' 555 State Express could be purchased singly at Mr Moses's Kibera kiosk, but I had yet to spot any pin-sharp executive types queuing up to restock their slimline silverette cigarette cases. Still, it was only a matter of time before they saw the ad and got the message. Assuming they didn't instead opt for Embassy,

which associated itself with air travel, leather briefcases and gold fountain pens. '*Embassy,*' shrilled a delighted chorus, as the images glid by,

> *The smooth way to go to places*
> *It goes with the finest of faces*
> *It's the cigarette*
> *Today's people get*
> *When they're on their way in the world*
> *It's Embassyyyyy. . .*

Embassy made a pretty good argument, I thought. The 555 smokers
had a glass-topped coffee table to sit around, and that was splendid, but
the Embassy crew were too busy jet-setting between first-class airline
lounges to sit around any kind of table at all. Maybe they even worked in
an embassy. I'd met quite a few people who worked in embassies, and
while presentable, they weren't nearly as elegant as these ambassadors of
tobacco. Presumably, they'd been smoking the wrong brand. When I later
plotted, along with my friend Alan Forrest from up the road, to buy two
cigarettes from Mr Moses and smoke them behind a hedge, it was
Embassy we plumped for. They were foul beyond description.

Once *Black Belt Jones* alerted me to the fact that America had black
people in it, I realised I had all along been watching a hitherto unidentified second strain of advertisement, borrowed from the black American
market. Cosmetics and lotions were the focus here, with a suggestion,
never openly stated but obvious even to a very young white boy, that they
would leave the user paler and thus comelier. A parade of light-skinned
lovelies – again, unlike anyone I knew in Nairobi, where black meant
exactly that – testified to the virtues of product after product. Creams,
pomades, unguents; elixirs to straighten your hair, to curl it again, to shine
it, relax it, teach it fluent Spanish in nine easy lessons while you slept.

'Take a look at this face,' invited Lux Beauty Soap's burnished
spokesmodel. 'Closer. What do you see?' I saw that she had a large mole
on her otherwise flawless cheek. Was this the work of Lux? If so, was it
wise of them to draw attention to it in this way? Surely Kenya's female
cineastes would instead favour Princess Patra, which not only pressed a
claim for 'international beauty' – far preferable to the ordinary, localised

sort – but moreover promised, in a lilting soprano, '_the touch of soft caress_' while it was about it.

For full-blown bewilderment, nothing – not even _The Railway Children_ – could match a third variety of commercial: those drafted in from abroad without a thought for their intended audience. I watched nonplussed as the powers of Lucozade revived an ailing English tyke wearing a football scarf. Of course he was hot and dehydrated – anyone could tell you football and scarves didn't mix. Even a shirt was too warm for football on most days. But not in the alien landscape where One Hundred Pipers Scotch whisky was guaranteed to conjure up a bekilted bagpipe horde caterwauling their way through a thick fog the instant the glass touched your lips. No wonder my father favoured Johnnie Walker red label, as did everybody else south of Cairo. That confined its assault to the tastebuds, and left your ears alone. (My father had once bought a bottle of purported Scotch in South Africa. The label read: 'Very fine old Scottish whisky, distilled in the cellars of Buckingham Palace by King George VI, God bless him.' After that, Johnnie Walker red was nectar.)

Omo washed whiter and it showed, on a pair of matching floral dresses, one of which had been Omo'd to a sheen brighter than the naked eye could withstand, while the other had been laundered in potash and ditchwater. According to a manly country and western ditty, wherever wheels were rolling, no matter what the load, the name was known as Firestone, where the rubber met the road. If you were going to go somewhere, British Caledonian Airways suggested you do so with them. Their stewardesses, it was hinted, were very obliging.

Not being in the market for any of this stuff, I let the adverts wash over me, absorbing them through a combination of repetition and osmosis. They became as much a part of my familiar cinema experience as the films themselves, until the day Black Belt Jones karate-kicked a hole in my complacency.

It was dark when I walked home, and I was greeted with the mixture of relief and annoyance so familiar to wayward children fortunate enough to be part of a family that cares what happens to them. My parents weren't happy about my wandering around after sundown. Given my track record, this was fair enough.

My sister instantly rose to her habitual pitch of indignation when she discovered I had watched a movie of such depravity. Particularly as she wasn't allowed to.

'That film has a '15'-certificate,' she protested to my parents. 'You wouldn't let me go and see a '15'-certificate film.'

'Do you want to?' said my father.

'It's on again tomorrow,' I put in, helpfully.

'No,' she sniffed. 'It's disgusting.'

'How do you know?' I said. 'You haven't seen it.'

'I know what those films are like,' said my sister.

I reassured everyone that I wouldn't do it again, and that *Black Belt Jones* had in no way corrupted me. Which was true. *The Railway Children*, however, did prove to be a malign influence.

'I think,' my mother told me, 'that you should spend less time in that cinema.'

So instead, I spent more time with Alan Forrest from up the road. We took to playing on the nearby train tracks in Kibera, testing who could loiter longest in the path of oncoming locomotives. He usually won.

chapter seven

Rodeo Robert's Dancing Chickens

IN 1974, WHEN I was six, our neighbours the McLeans left Kenya and my family moved across Wamagata Road into their house, which was bigger than our old one.

My parents hired a man to look after the house. Such servants were usually known to their employers by the term 'houseboy'. At school, I would hear children my age complain that 'the stupid houseboy' – often a grown man before they were born – had failed to wash and fold their PE kit. This struck me as wrong even then. I was in no way averse to having work done for me. I simply saw no purpose in insulting the people who did it.

In Nairobi, everyone had servants. I don't use 'everyone' in the ex-colonial sense of 'everyone white', the implication being that everyone else is no one. Everyone had servants. The servants had servants. It was common for even the poorest Nairobi families – and it is a measure of African poverty that the families of household servants did not necessarily number among these – to engage an *ayah*, a nanny, to look after their children. Usually the *ayah* was an older child, no more than twelve, maybe a relative sent to the city to earn her keep. When she wasn't minding the kids (there were invariably a lot of kids; the Kenyan birth rate was on its way to becoming the highest in the world), an *ayah* could often be seen struggling homewards underneath a bushel of firewood twice her own size.

Kenyan men did not do housework in their own homes, but the majority of servants paid to keep house by the affluent were male. Obisa had turned up one day on our doorstep looking for a job, having travelled from his home in Nyanza province, in the west of the country, by Lake Victoria. He may have been forewarned about the bizarre habits of the *wazungu*, because no matter what occurred, my family never seemed to alarm him. I had to admire his composure. My family certainly alarmed me.

Obisa was a droll, talkative individual, with a relaxed approach to life. The only time I saw him really excited was when he noticed that the kitchen contained an electric kettle personalised for my father: on the inside, near the brim, embossed in capitals, was the word 'MAX'.

Little else would faze Obisa. When the chickens in our backyard coop stopped providing us with eggs – or 'axe', as he called them, leading to some temporary confusion, as our Swahili was on a par with his English – he advised us that this must be because of the *fira*.

'What *fira*?' said my father.

'The *fira* is take the axe,' said Obisa. 'I show you.'

My father picked up a torch and followed Obisa to the chicken coop. Obisa swung wide the door and my father peered inside. A large hooded cobra reared up, jaws agape, fangs unsheathed, and sprayed twins jets of venom directly at my father's eyes. He stumbled back with poison streaming down the lenses of his spectacles.

'*Fira*,' said Obisa, matter-of-factly.

Those chickens were the bane of my home life. To keep the chickens happy, and the egg supply forthcoming, we also owned a *jogoo*, a cockerel, a ferocious red brute only half a head shorter than I was. It was the most aggressive animal I had ever seen, propelled by some atavistic impulse from the days when birds ruled the planet, an era it evidently nursed hopes of reviving. Its plan was to visit havoc on its enemies from the ground up, starting with the smallest adversary it could find: me.

When, playing on the lawn, I heard the hens scratch and cluck their way around the corner of the house, I froze, knowing the *jogoo* must follow. My eyes darted this way and that, sizing up the distances to possible places of refuge. The back door was nearest, but that way I would risk crossing the path of the *jogoo* as it stalked the chickens, haughtily weighing up which one to ravish next. Backwards and up a nearby tree was an alternative escape route, but no more satisfactory. How would I get down again? That *jogoo* had a true hunter's patience, and a proven willingness to keep me up there indefinitely as it strutted around the trunk, issuing the occasional triumphalist squawk.

Once or twice, when the *jogoo* had me treed, it had taken a good run up and flapped its way into the lower branches, delivering a few solid pecks to my shins before plummeting back down to earth. That took a lot out of the *jogoo*. It wouldn't jump a hen for at least a quarter of an hour afterwards. But the *jogoo* held this sacrifice to be worth it.

My final option was to make a dash for the front gate, bringing down upon myself the humiliation of having the entire street howl with mirth as I fled, pursued by a screeching crimson featherstorm. That's what I usually chose to do. I feared disgrace, but I feared the *jogoo* more. And it wouldn't follow me far onto Wamagata Road. The *jogoo* didn't like to leave its hens unattended, in case some other bird attempted to inseminate one of them. I doubt if any other bird would have dared.

When we learned about the spitting cobra in the chicken coop, my fondest wish was that it might slay the *jogoo*, but no such luck; it was the snake that perished, at the end of a spade, while the *jogoo* swaggered on. I also had high hopes for a mongoose, which, instead of following the lead of Rudyard Kipling's noble Riki Tiki Tavi and dispatching the cobra, had followed the lead of the cobra and taken to menacing the local poultry. Unfortunately, the craven rodent never went near the *jogoo*, and I don't suppose I can blame it.

Obisa was my sole protector from the *jogoo*; frequently, and with great amusement, he gathered up the indignantly clamorous rooster and deposited it sufficiently far away for me to make a break for it.

* * *

AFTER A while, Obisa was joined by Robert, who took on the role of *shamba* man, responsible for keeping up the grounds and looking after livestock.

Robert could not have been more different from Obisa. He was taciturn where Obisa was garrulous, introspective, a worrier, and a family man. Obisa had a wife and children, but they lived in Nyanza. While in Nairobi he kept company with a series of girlfriends. Robert's family lived with him. His wife, Esther, took on duties as a laundress to supplement their income. She was a dreadful laundress. Not through any lack of application: like her husband, she was dogged and reliable. But she could not be dissuaded from pegging the newly cleaned clothes, unwrung and heavy with water, laterally onto the washing line.

Trousers and skirts sagged and broadened until they were fit only for obese midgets, a species of endomorph that numbered zero in our household. Shirts stretched widthways, taking on the appearance of sails with sleeves. On a gusty day, while wearing an 'Esther special', one ran the risk of being caught up and blown off course, which could be dangerous when, say, walking beside a busy road. I began to develop incipient nautical skills – reflexively coming about, tacking windward and so on – merely by strolling around wearing T-shirts which Esther had transformed into spinnakers.

I didn't complain, because I knew that if I did, my parents would tell me to wash my own bloody clothes, and I didn't want to wash my own bloody clothes. Furthermore, I was relieved that Esther used a washing line at all, rather than trusting in the more customary African practice of draping wet laundry on the ground or across small bushes. This invited the attentions of the tumbu fly, *Cordylobia anthropophaga*, which would lay its eggs on the material. On contact with human skin, larvae would hatch and burrow into the epidermis, where they would happily feed upon their host, while livid boils began to fester upon the surface above them. If you put your ear to one of these sores – an action neither congenial nor prudent – you would swear you could hear party music and cheering. Eventually, the fattened parasite would crawl out to pupate. While this process was repulsive, it was at least relatively swift, taking little more than a week. We had houseguests who were less welcome and stayed for longer.

Esther and Robert had a rural robustness about them. When Esther delivered her fourth child, a boy, on a Saturday morning, my father went to assist at the birth. Half an hour later, he spotted Robert sweeping up near the chicken run.

'Robert,' he suggested, 'why don't you take the day off?'

Robert nodded thoughtfully and put away his broom. Had they still been living in the countryside, no doubt Esther would have returned to the fields that afternoon with the infant strapped closely to her breast.

The chicken run had just been restocked with a sisterhood of specially bred laying hens. These costly *kukus*, so ran the sales pitch, would pay for themselves in no time. To hear the dealer tell it, eggs – each and every one a hefty, flavoursome double-yolker – would come tumbling roundly out of the straw at a rate to rival that of a spawning codfish. These hens, he averred, simply could not stop producing, even if you slaughtered them, which is what we eventually did.

After gobbling up several sackloads of a choice grain blend priced by the troy ounce and quoted alongside precious metals on the business pages of the *Daily Nation*, the chickens swelled to obscene proportions. When I walked past the coop, half a dozen beachballs trimmed in snow-white plumage would roll in my direction, bouncing off each other in their eagerness to cadge another handful of nourishment so costly it belied the term 'chickenfeed'. No Kobe bull was more extravagantly spoiled than these chickens. Had we hired a masseur for them, that would have counted as a minor item in our poultry-related expenditure. The egg yield was nil.

Within a few weeks, we deduced that the dealer had sold us not laying hens but capons. Robert, who had a chicken-sexer's eye for such matters, sombrely confirmed this conclusion. By now, the chickens were so enormous that it was a matter of eating them before they wised up and ate us.

Obisa had designs on the birds, having cannily directed their predecessors into his *sufria*, or tin cooking pot, but my father was adamant that our family should consume them.

'These,' he said, 'will be the most expensive chickens ever eaten. I've paid for them, and by God, I'm going to be the one to eat them.' They were delicious, and so they should have been. It's a pity that my father has never been very partial to chicken.

The capons gave way to hens endowed by nature with the capacity to lay eggs, although once more the yield was disappointing.

'Some are not laying,' said Robert. 'I will mark them.'

'How will you know which ones?' I asked him.

'I know,' said Robert, and borrowing a tin of silver enamel paint from my brother, who was a fan of Airfix model aeroplane kits and had once constructed an astonishingly realistic Sopwith Camel, he delicately embellished the toes of all those chickens who were earning their keep. The remainder shared the fate of the capons. The egg production did not falter. Robert was vindicated.

The chicken coop now had a vague air of the Radio City Music Hall about it. When you saw the birds wiggle their glittering feet in the dirt, you half-expected them to form a line and perform a series of synchronised high-kicks. Sometimes I would feign a lack of interest and look away, then wheel about sharply, hoping to catch them at it.

* * *

ROBERT MAY have been laconic, but he was a chatterbox compared to Japhet. Japhet was Robert's cousin; at Robert's request, my father had employed him as the caretaker at his office in Hurlingham. Japhet was a surly, silent character. What little he did say usually made you wish he hadn't. He was, nonetheless, an improvement of sorts on his forerunner in the job, Titus.

Titus had been cheerful, willing and quite mad. He was afflicted with acute schizophrenia, an appalling burden under the best of circumstances, and his hardly qualified as that. One night, having neglected to take his medication for several days beforehand, Titus trashed his living quarters with such thoroughness that he left behind no piece of debris larger than a fingernail. Conveniently for anyone wishing to make the comparison, he also left behind at least two of his own fingernails. Screaming bloody murder, Titus was dragged away by the police, and incarcerated in the psychiatric hospital at Mathari, a desperate and grim establishment from which it proved impossible to extricate him.

What happened to Titus was a tragedy. Japhet, conversely, was the author of his own misfortune, or at least its co-author; he had a little help. That he did not like his job, Japhet could not have made plainer. Nobody held that against him. It was not the kind of job anybody would like. He was not required to like it, or even pretend to like it – only to do it. Japhet carried disgruntlement to the boundaries of art. Sullenly leaning upon his mop, he might have been a sculpted study in dyspepsia, although such an effigy would have been likelier than Japhet to exhibit any sign of movement.

Japhet's downfall came in female form. He dispensed with his regular companion, Lady Friend, A, and acquired a new one, Lady Friend B. This was, without question, Lady Friend B's idea. Lady Friend B had any number of ideas, most of them involving Japhet, and she was not shy about making Japhet aware of them.

Whenever I happened by my father's office, I would overhear Lady Friend B explaining one of her ideas about Japhet to Japhet. Pretty much everybody in Hurlingham, and a fair few residents of neighbouring boroughs, could overhear Lady Friend B familiarising Japhet with the particulars of her ideas about Japhet. There were people on buses heading down Haile Selasse Avenue into the city centre, a good mile or more away, who could overhear Lady Friend B clarifying the finer points of her ideas about Japhet to Japhet. Lady Friend B's ideas about Japhet became a popular subject for public discussion, on those occasions when Lady Friend B took a well-earned break from expounding her ideas about Japhet to Japhet, and the public could hear one another speak.

'Why is that lady always shouting?' I asked my father. We had stopped off on the way to the shops one weekend morning so he could pick up some papers from his desk. Lady Friend B was, as usual, in full eruption. She was a natural phenomenon, a human Old Faithful who could be relied upon to fling noise and vapours into the atmosphere at regular and very closely spaced intervals.

I wasn't the first to ask. Several neighbours in Hurlingham had begun to wonder just how long Lady Friend B would be permitted to air her ideas about Japhet before my father decided it was unprofessional and unseemly to have her do so in the vicinity of a doctor's office.

'I don't know why she's always shouting,' my father told me. 'But even if Japhet isn't sick of it, I certainly am. Wait here a minute. It's time I had a word with him.'

While my father spoke to Japhet, Lady Friend B fumed in the

background, her countenance radiating all the fury to which she usually gave vent with sound. No sooner was that conversation done with, than Lady Friend B came up with her best idea about Japhet yet. This was a masterstroke, a scheme she doubtless considered foolproof – which, had you met Japhet, you would have known to be a key requirement.

Phase one of Lady Friend B's strategy involved Japhet seeking out my father on Monday morning and telling him that he, Japhet, no longer wanted to work. This Japhet did, in the manner of a conscript advancing into enemy range with even heavier fire at his back.

'Fine,' said my father. 'Don't work. Pack up your things and go away.'

Now Lady Friend B set in motion phase two of her brilliant plan. The next day, Japhet, Lady Friend B and two police officers arrived at the surgery and demanded an audience with my father.

'We are here on behalf of the Ministry of Labour,' said the senior of the officers. His underling jutted out his chin self-importantly. He had come along to demonstrate that the senior officer was sufficiently grand to be accompanied by a junior officer with no particular function, but he too wished to make it clear that he was here on behalf of the Ministry of Labour, even if he was not permitted to speak on behalf of the Ministry of Labour, or his boss, or himself.

'We understand that you have dismissed this man,' continued the senior officer, indicating Japhet, who was slumped rancorously in a chair, beside the complacent and self-approving Lady Friend B.

'That's absolutely correct,' said my father.

'You cannot just go about dismissing employees,' the officer admonished him. 'This man has certain rights. He is a citizen of Kenya, while you are a foreign national. There is a process set down by the Ministry for dealing with such matters. There will be tribunals to be attended, and compensation to pay. On what grounds did you dismiss him?'

'He told me he didn't want to work,' said my father.

The officer looked as if he had been punctured with a pin and all the air had rushed out of him. His subordinate flinched, instinctively sensing who would take the blame for this debacle when they returned to the station.

'Did you,' said the officer, turning to Japhet, 'tell the doctor that you did not want to work?'

'Yes,' said the surprised Japhet, unable to fathom what that might have to do with anything.

The officer grimaced wearily, stood up, bade my father goodbye, and left, his junior in tow. Japhet sat for a few seconds more, staring gloomily at Lady Friend B, waiting for her to tell him what to do next. But Lady Friend B, perhaps for the first time in her life, had nothing to say. Stupefied, she opened and shut her mouth like a guppy. Then, as if electrically triggered, she leapt up, bolted for the door and fled through the car park with a speed and sense of purpose that had not often been witnessed in any of Japhet's associates. Japhet followed, at a broken trot, never to be heard from again.

Even his cousin Robert had no sympathy for Japhet. Being puzzled at the turn of events (I was puzzled at almost any turn of events), I asked Robert what had become of his errant relative.

'Japhet has gone back to our *shamba*,' said Robert, referring to the family plot in the Kikuyu highlands. 'He is,' Robert sighed, 'a very stupid man.' And turning his back on me and on the subject of Japhet, he trudged away to feed the chickens.

chapter eight

The Great Migration

WHERE THE northern tip of Tanzania's Serengeti plain extends across the border into southern Kenya, the wide grasslands and low hills have been designated a game reserve and given the name Masai Mara, after Kenya's best-known and most picturesque tribe, the Masai.

The Masai, or Maasai – either is correct, but the latter is more commonly used – have shared the Mara with its wildlife since the year dot; possibly earlier. They are a lean and rangy people, subsisting as they do on a high-protein mixture of milk and cows' blood. To the Maasai, eating the cow itself would be akin to you and yours sitting down to a tureen of fresh, crisp banknotes. Livestock is wealth. As any sensible investor will tell you, you don't live off your capital.

Traditionally, the Maasai have followed two vocations: herding cattle, and stealing cattle. The second activity having been curtailed, although not extinguished, they now tend to concentrate on the first. A certain amount of freelance banditry persists among the Maasai, but no more so than anywhere else. Once, when my family was camping near Namanga, on the Kenya-Tanzania border, a gang of pre-teen Maasai tearaways raided our tent while we were out on a game drive and made off with our cutlery and our melamine utensils. They considerately left behind one fork, one spoon, one knife, one plate and one cup.

'Maybe,' said my mother, who always wanted to think the best of everyone, 'they think we take it in turns to eat dinner.'

More likely, they had no idea what the stuff was for, and appropriated it out of curiousity. As a rule, the Maasai are interested only in things which moo, or things which may be exchanged for things which moo. Cattle and cash, in short. Plastic dishes, however durable and attractive, are not a priority.

The Maasai tend to be self-contained and somewhat reserved. Which is not to suggest that they are unfriendly – far from it – merely that they have their own way of doing things. The opinions of outsiders are of no consequence to them, unless those outsiders fancy making them an offer for a spear, or for one of the resplendent glass bead necklaces so fetchingly modelled by their womenfolk.

These decorations were once the subject of a breathless study by an American academic – a young woman who spent many well-funded years researching her doctorate among the tribespeople, and became something of a Kenyan legend. She gushingly detailed the symbolic and mystical import held by each colour in the beadwork since the birth of mankind – which was, to be fair, an event local to East Africa.

Had she consulted a more conventional and less daring scholar than herself, she might have discovered that coloured glass was unknown in the region until the late Victorian era, when it was introduced by British colonists, and that the Maasai had until then possessed only plain white beads made from the shells of ostrich eggs. But she consulted no one except the Maasai, and the Maasai are a polite lot, unlikely to contradict a guest, particularly a wealthy one. The Maasai are very respectful of wealth.

AMERICAN LADY: 'So green represents the seasonal pastures on which your nomadic ancestors grazed their livestock for thousands of years, and for this reason it is woven next to the red that is the lifeblood of your herds and thus of your people?'

MAASAI LADY: 'Um, if you like.'

The Maasai are fine-looking folk, and accustomed to being gawped at. Often as not, they will gawp right back, and with good reason. While their own dark red robes are striking, the raiment of those who visit them is often ludicrous, as anyone may attest who has seen a fully equipped battalion of tourists descend upon a Maasai *manyatta*, or encampment.

Maasai men generally confine fanciful decorations to their earlobes, which they may distend with successively larger wooden pegs until the skin is drooping upon their shoulders. We used to look forward to catching a glimpse of one chap in Namanga, who lived in a ditch by the border post, inside a shack made entirely of empty tin cans, and who hung his leftover building materials from his ears, lending him the appearance of the rear bumper on a newly weds' limousine.

The Tin Can Man was something of a theatrician. When a car drove past, he would jump out through the hole which served him as a door and stand in the ditch, wobbling his head and a flaunting an assortment of cans which he had tied to a stick, all the while gabbling in a language which, while I can't swear it wasn't Maasai, I suspect may have been as originally and uniquely his own as his taste in decor.

We would wave back at him. '*Jambo*, Mister Tin Can Man,' I would call out. He liked that, so far as I could tell.

In terms of adornment, even the Tin Can Man couldn't compete with the camera-festooned sensations we regularly encountered on our game drives: improbable, whirring medleys of viewfinders, lenses, light meters and video recorders, enclosing – presumably – a human form somewhere deep within.

Nowadays a cheetah can't step out of the long grass without being surrounded, paparazzi-style, by a knot of vehicles, while dozens more bump hastily across the plain to get in on the action. Behaviourally speaking, it's very similar to the way vultures gather on a freshly sighted corpse. But when I first visited the Mara as an eight-year-old, in 1976, we could drive around all day without catching sight of another human being. It was just us and a million or so wildebeest.

* * *

THE WILDEBEEST were migrating, which is what wildebeest do. Towards the end of June, they head north from the Serengeti, in search of fresh grass. Grass is one thing the Mara isn't short of. To reach it, the wildebeest ford the Mara, Talek and Sand rivers in their thousands. They don't want to. The wildebeest at the front dig in their hooves and teeter on the high banks, issuing the plaintive combination of bleat and grunt which serves as a wildebeest's sole form of expression. They emit it when grazing, when stampeding, when drowning. Wildebeest are not bright.

'*Hnnnh!*' the wildebeest closest to the river will complain, as they skitter backwards on spindly legs, away from the water. '*Hnnnh!*' answer the animals behind them, lurching forward as several thousand more wildebeest press in behind them, all of them with a '*hnnnh!*' to contribute. The frontmost wildebeest are right to be afraid. There is a strong chance they won't survive the crossing. During the migration, the Mara's many crocodiles don't bother to hunt. They simply wait for the banquet to fling itself into their open jaws. Frequently, wildebeest that do make it across the water still perish, having failed to scramble up banks as steep and muddy as the ones they plunged down on the other side. Wildebeest really are not bright.

The crossing itself is mayhem. Dust, death, panic. A frenzy of thudding hooves, desperate splashing and snorting, *hnnnh! hnnnh! hnnnh! gurgle. . . hnnnh!* To be caught in it, on the riverside, is both terrifying and exhilarating. Hundreds of wildebeest come thundering past or around you, a typhoon of mass animal idiocy and instinct. If you don't flatten yourself against a vehicle, or shelter behind a tree, you too might well end up in the middle of the Talek. That's what happens to many of the zebra and topi (a large, dopey antelope with bluish hindquarters), which get swept up in the migration and doubtless start to regret it around 20 feet into the water.

The aftermath sees bloated grey corpses, too many to count, certainly too many for even the crocodiles to eat, floating with a grisly equanimity down the sluggish, twisting rivers. In October, the herds come back the other way, heading south for the Serengeti, and do it all again. Wildebeest are not at all bright. But they are hungry.

Just as the wildebeest return every year, so did we. We never missed a migration. Often, like the wildebeest, we would come twice in a summer – which as a season is merely theoretical this close to the equator.

The journey to the Mara was neatly divided into two sections by the town of Narok. To reach Narok from Nairobi, we would head west, up the Kikuyu escarpment and down into the Rift Valley, past the dormant, fraternally homogenous volcanoes of Longonot and Suswa. The floor of the Rift here is not flat; rather, it consists of giant longitudinal ripples, undulating into the distance, on which the daylight falls in a series of strips too broad for the gaze to encompass, alternating pale, grey-green illumination with dark, grey-green shadow. Along the fractured surface of the narrow tarmac road our car would rise and drop like a fishing bark nosing through great swells and waves. This was the easy part of the ride.

At Narok, an arid, dirty little town with something of the spaghetti western about it, we would pull in to refuel at the Shell petrol station. There was a toilet you could use for a 50-cent piece dropped into a box on the door. In a hatch cut into the garage wall sat the proprietor, a tiny, ancient Indian man. He looked 103 when I first laid eyes on him in 1976. When I last saw him, over a decade later, he didn't look a day older, although it's hard to imagine how he could do. For all I know, he's still there, and still serving up soft drinks and home-made samosas through the hatch. The samosas were cooked up every morning by Mrs Proprietor – she was notably younger than her husband, being around 80: it was a November-to-December match. We would usually buy whatever he had left, to fortify ourselves for the next part of the drive.

From Narok to the Mara's Musiara gate is the same distance again, and would take us more than twice as long. Turning southwards, we would clatter along the dirt road, a long plume of dust marking our progress. The trick was to drive just fast enough to prevent the dust overtaking your car, but not so fast as to fracture any of the larger bones in your body when you flew over a small hillock, into a crater on the far side and out again, in the passage of half a second. It was always advisable to wear a hat, not just because of the heat, but because it dampened the impact between your head and the roof of the car.

We drove with the windows open. Upon sighting another vehicle heading towards us, we would all cry out, 'Car!', and urgently crank the windows up. As the other car drew near, you would see its occupants doing the same thing. Occasionally, when we met a car unexpectedly on a bend, there would be time only to register its passengers' collective expression – a mixture of shock, self-pity and resignation which exactly mirrored our own – before the cabin filled with dust so dense the air struggled to carry it. Fortunately, the bumps would soon shake the bulk of it loose, otherwise we would have spent the remainder of the journey as a rejected sketch for a Wacky Races cartoon – a mobile sandpit with several sets of eyes peering tetchily from the upper layers.

The country was low-set scrubland around here. Prickly pear cacti speared past stubborn little shrubs, which clutched onto the unsettled soil. Occasionally, we might spot a dik-dik – a highly strung antelope the size of a large cat, with horns like pencil-points – gnawing at the paltry foliage. You rarely saw a dik-dik for more than a few seconds, particularly if its appearance coincided with that of a passing Land Rover, and you were too distracted to roll up the windows.

*   *   *

WHEN THE Esoit Olololo escarpment appeared in the distance on the left, it signalled our arrival on the Mara plain. Where the ground was not littered with smallish rocks, it was covered with short, even grass and stunted acacia trees. Here we usually stopped to swill the dust out of our mouths with water – although a thin but unignorable coating always clung muckily to the upper palate – and empty our bladders. This could not be accomplished with any privacy. The nearest thing to hide behind was the Esoit Olololo escarpment. The men would simply walk away from the car and turn our backs; the women had to crouch behind the car one at a time while everyone looked in the opposite direction until otherwise instructed.

From here we trundled downhill, into the *nyika* grasslands, to the gate, where, depending on their mood, the game reserve's officials might or might not be waiting to take our entrance fees. If not, we pushed straight on to our campsite, which lay a few dozen yards from the Mara River. We dipped carefully in and out of Python Gulch, a gaping four-foot ditch cutting across the track, often brimful of water, named by us for the 15-foot snake that had made its home there.

On that earliest visit in 1976, Python Gulch was flooded. My father halted the car.

'I'm not driving through that until I know how deep it is,' he said. 'We could flood the exhaust.'

He stepped into the water. There was a single, sudden splash and he vanished as dramatically as a conjuror's lovely assistant, leaving only his straw Panama hat bobbing on the murky surface, a guinea-fowl feather stuck jauntily into the band. The sides of Python Gulch were fairly steep.

Once we had retrieved my father from the gulch, and identified a more accessible crossing, we followed the track into the line of trees along the water. We pulled to a halt in a glade surrounded by creeper-laden branches, from which indignant monkeys scattered, shrieking.

It was a large camping party that year: two cars' worth of people, in four tents of varying sizes. We set to work, clearing sticks and stones from likely patches of ground. Within the hour we had the tents up, and had just begun collecting firewood when we heard the low-pitched whine of a four-wheel-drive vehicle throttling off and on along the winding track through the trees.

A Toyota Land Cruiser pick-up drove into the campsite. Its chassis bore the logo of a hotel that controlled bookings hereabouts. In the back squatted a quartet of local men wearing rangers' uniforms. From the driver's seat, a stiff, stringy white man in an ill-cut safari suit descended with the unmistakable bearing of a petty official asserting precedence in his own domain.

'I'm Cecil Pith-Vinegar,' he declared. 'Chief ranger for this area.'

'Max Bennun,' said my father, and stuck out his hand. Pith-Vinegar ignored it.

'And just what,' he demanded, 'is going on here?'

'We're pitching camp,' said my father, very slowly and clearly, keeping hold of his temper like a man clutching at his hat in a sudden gust of wind.

'You have no business being here,' Pith-Vinegar snapped prissily from beneath what remains, despite close competition, the least likeable moustache I have ever set eyes upon. 'You'll have to pack up and leave.' Waving aside a small stack of receipts and confirmations which indicated we had every business being there, he gestured at his embarrassed subordinates, who tried to look in any direction but his, and told us, 'If you're not gone by tomorrow morning, just remember ... *my men have guns.*' He climbed back into the cab, his knees flashing white in the waning sunlight, and reversed briskly out of the campsite, ignoring the low branches, which slapped against the exposed heads of his rangers.

The notion that this truculent ninny might have a family of five – and their companions – summarily shot for camping so intrigued us that we drove over to the hotel for a sundowner and a word with the ninny's boss, whose wife happened to be a patient of my father's. It was remarkable – and remarkably useful – just how many wives of bigwigs happened to be patients of my father's.

The boss was furious. 'That man,' he seethed, 'has no more notion of how to deal with the public than. . . than. . . a *puff adder.*'

A nickname was born. The Puff Adder was the kind of Englishman who in his home country would have become celebrated among traffic wardens as the traffic warden's traffic warden. Here he had his own staff, and a minuscule nugget of authority rattling around in his otherwise vacant brain-pan like a pea in a whistle.

Over the next few days we crossed the Puff Adder's path on three further occasions. Each time, he bristled, reddened and glowered impotently at us through the windscreen of his pick-up, while, hunkered in its open bed, the rangers grinned and waved.

* * *

I WAS sharing a tent with my brother Leon and an affable young Canadian fellow called Brad. There was no more space in the campsite's main glade, so we pitched the tent on the far side of the tree-line, facing on to a broad patch of *nyika*. There you could sit on a folding chair under the awning and from 50 yards or so watch zebra, waterbuck and buffalo mosey across the grass on their way to drink at the river.

You could also, it transpired, wake up with a start to the swelling thud of galloping hooves in the wee hours of a moonlit night, and watch through the netting window as a lioness brought down a wildebeest five feet away from your nose and began, with audible gusto, to devour it.

A voice came from another tent behind the trees. It was my father.

'What the hell was that?' he said.

The three of us looked at each other. Thus far, we guessed, the lioness might have our tent figured as an unusual variety of bush. If the bush started talking, the lioness might develop other ideas. And while a hungry lioness is dangerous enough in the first place, a hungry lioness with ideas might turn out to be considerably worse.

'I'm going to see what the hell that was,' said my father, loudly, to the other occupants of his tent.

'*Dad!*' I hissed, in a rasping whisper which I hoped would carry through the night air.

The crunching sound outside stopped.

'*Shhh!*' said my brother.

I heard a zip opening.

'Dad,' I said, in a clear voice. 'Stay in your tent. There's a lion out here.'

'Not any more,' murmured Brad. The lioness, which did not approve of mealtime conversation, had dragged its kill behind a nearby bush. Now we had no way of knowing what it might be doing.

'Everybody stay in their tents!' said my father. 'Go back to bed!' he added, and went back to bed.

In our tent, we sat, silent and awake, until first light, when two things happened.

The first was that we heard the Range Rover door slam. My father had made a dash for the car. He started the engine and let it idle for a minute.

The second was that we heard another noise, one we could not identify, and which perturbed us all the more for that.

'*Hrooosh!*' went the noise.

Terrified, I forced myself to glance through the netting. The sun appeared to be rising, in an immense blaze of orange, ten feet behind the bush concealing the lioness.

'*Hrooosh!*'

The sun surged upwards, revealing itself to be of a light-bulb shape, about 30 feet across, with a large basket depending from its underside. It was a hot-air balloon. In the basket stood a trio of American tourists, accompanied by an Englishman in khakis, who announced, in the plummiest of tones:

'Ey say! It sayms to bay a layon!'

'And it's eating something!' said one of the Americans excitedly.

The gigantic orange light bulb started to dip slightly, and from the middle of the basket a flame leapt up.

'*Hrooosh!*' The light bulb climbed once more.

I poked my head out through the flap of our tent, and saw the Range Rover easing around the leaves behind us. The plummy Englishman looked down at me without curiosity, as if I were a commonplace article of fauna unworthy of further notice and bringing his balloon safari directly over our camp were no different to hovering above a colony of baboons.

'Hey!' said my father, leaning out of the car window. 'What do you think you're doing?'

'Neow don't geyet exceyted,' drawled the Englishman. 'Way're looking at the layon.'

'Helloo!' called out an American woman.

'Get out of our campsite,' said my father to the Englishman.

They were interrupted by a blood-curdling growl as the lioness sprang through the bush, and landed in front of our tent. I jerked back inside so quickly I carried zipper marks on my cheeks for a fortnight. The lioness swung its huge head towards me. My father flung open the car door. 'Oi!' he yelled at the creature. It lunged back in his direction; he slammed the door shut and drove straight towards the lioness. It snarled, backed towards the bushes, then turned and loped away across the plain.

'Neow sey what yew've dawn,' grumbled the Englishman from 15 feet above us. 'Yew've fraytened it ite of here.'

'Bugger off!' said my father.

'Ey say,' said the Englishman.

'*Hrooosh!*' went the balloon.

'Byee!' called out the American woman, as she floated over the river.

* * *

THAT EVENING, as a convocation of vultures flapped around the remains of the wildebeest, our camping party began to drink. Adults, teens, kids, the lot. The grown-ups got themselves royally sauced. It wasn't planned. I think we all felt a little jittery. Even I made merry with a plastic beaker of hot buttered rum.

We had just said our good nights and headed for our sleeping bags, around eleven o'clock, when we heard another unfamiliar noise: an almighty crackling, like amplified machine-gun fire, which brought us stumbling from our tents, at once convinced that we were under attack from bandits or poachers, and that this time, it was the end.

The sound grew louder and louder. It seemed to be coming from around us, and then above us. As we looked up, the giant tree beside my parents' tent came sweeping earthwards, branches snapping, and smashed onto the ground, taking three or four smaller trees with it. It missed us, and it missed the tents, although it did put out the campfire. Had it fallen a few hours earlier, it might well have trapped both the lioness and the hot-air balloon in its upper branches, which would have made for an absorbing spectacle.

'Jesus Christ,' said just about everybody.

The tree measured four and a half feet across the base, not counting the roots, which were pulled up as it came down, and now pointed at the sky. Beside the newly-formed crater lay an enormous pile of empty bottles, which had been stacked against the tree over the course of the safari, most of them that night.

'I guess it couldn't take the weight,' said Brad.

We broke camp and went home the next day. We had intended to leave anyway, but there was an unspoken feeling that to stay any longer would be to tempt fate beyond endurance.

Once we were back on the plain, my mother and father lit up cigarettes. Leon, Lesley and I were engaged in a kiddie guerilla campaign to make them give up smoking. Blackmail, threats, sabotage – we were shameless. Skull-and-crossbone doodles would appear on their cigarette packets, along with slogans varying from Lesley's heart-tugging, 'Please stop smoking – we need our parents!' to my own succinct (and inadvertently slanderous to the arts and crafts movement) 'SMOCKING KILLS'.

My brother, as usual, was far and away the best at this sort of thing. He had obtained from somewhere a packet of tiny explosive devices each of which could be inserted unnoticed into a cigarette, detonating when the tip burned down to its level. His use of these was masterful. It was impossible to predict where he had placed them, or when they would go off. Once they were operational, so to speak, even he couldn't tell. So he had no way of knowing that my father's cigarette would explode just as we were passing through the gate, on one of the rare occasions it was manned.

'Christ on a crutch!' yelled my father, and slammed on the brakes. Our rear wheels slewed about in the dirt. From the gate behind us came the sound of rifles being hurriedly cocked. My father leapt out the car, his hands in the air. '*Pole, pole!*' he called to the men at the gate – *take it easy*. He walked back to calm them down.

'Oh, Davie,' sighed my mother, out of habit. 'I mean, oh, Leo.'

'For crying in a bloody bucket,' said my father, getting back into his seat. 'Don't you know how dangerous that is?'

'Not as dangerous as smoking,' said my brother, impassively.

Lesley and I began the complete, two-part, no-harmony rendition of *Joseph and the Amazing Technicolour Dreamcoat* with which we frequently occupied ourselves on long car rides. On the journey down to the Mara, we had been on our third recital by the time we reached the game reserve.

'I'm glad,' muttered my father, 'that I won't have to do this drive again any time soon.'

Early the next morning, he had to travel all the way back and sieve the campsite's topsoil with a tea strainer, square inch by square inch, until he found a gold earring my mother had lost.

* * *

AT FIVE o'clock in the afternoon of that same day, I was lying on my bunk bed reading a Billy Bunter novel. I owned several Bunter books, and it's fair to say I had missed the point of Frank Richards's fat cad. Bunter was looked down upon by his creator as a vulgar oik among the Greyfriars nobility. But to me, he was the hero of the stories, and his adversaries, the upright Famous Five – the gang whose companionship any schoolboy was supposed to yearn for – were a bunch of chortling bores.

Just as Bunter was clambering implausibly over a high fence, in flight from the stern Mr Quelch, something even less credible took place in my own bedroom. The walls began to tremble. The bedside lamp dimmed and died. The ceiling bulb shivered, dropped from its socket and shattered on the hard, red floor. The top bunk on which I was reclining joggled so violently that I had to cling on to the frame to avoid being thrown off. I knew that there could be only one force behind this upheaval.

'Leon!' I shouted out. 'Stop it. It isn't funny.'

But it wasn't my brother, whose powers as a prankster I held in such awe. It was an earthquake. It shook the house and cracked the tiles. It threw half the tableware in my mother's dining-room cabinet onto the floor, and scared our dogs so badly that they all ran away and one never came back. We were still clearing up by candlelight when my father returned from the Mara, covered in dust and holding my mother's earring between his forefinger and thumb, his expression darker than the lowering sky.

chapter nine

After the Earthquake

I WOULD HAVE been nine or ten when my mother chased me up a thorn tree with a ceremonial hippo-hide whip. What my crime was, I forget. My mother was, and remains, a woman of exceptional forbearance. I must have done something so obnoxious as to beggar belief.

Not that my mother intended to chase me up a thorn tree, or indeed to chase me at all. She intended to hit me. And tempting as it might be to portray myself as the innocent victim of outlandish abuse, it's simply not true. I have no doubt I deserved everything I got and more. Nor would I want readers to infer that I ran for fear of my usually patient mother's violent eruption of temper. I ran because it hurt. The whip, or *kiboko*, was a finely tempered thing, quivering and flexible. Even the thorny branches were less painful than the *kiboko* lashing my ankles.

I know of only one other instance when a member of my family climbed a thorn tree so rapidly, and he was being pursued by a maddened rhinoceros. A reel of Super-8 film shot by the quarry himself records the event. In it, a speck on the horizon rapidly assumes the growing and head-on form of a huge, horned, animate tank of a beast. Then the screen fills with a whirl of branches, sky, earth, limbs and the occasional overhead glimpse of snorting rhino. As a piece of cinema *verité*, it may not rank with *Rome, Open City*, but I mention it, by way of comparison, to illustrate the pitch of my mother's fury. Boy, was she angry.

The tree was one I had climbed and punctured myself on before. It stood in the back garden of the house we had moved to in 1976, when we left Wamagata Road. It was the nearest thing higher than my mother could reach. I fled out of the back door, galloped across the driveway, hurdled a weird, circular concrete plinth of mysterious purpose – perhaps it had supported a water tank, or provided the base for some gazebo-like colonial affectation – and scurried into the tree's spiky clutches as if they were the embraces of a nymph.

While my mother was swatting at my ankles, my father was in Canada. He had fallen in love with a Canadian nurse named Joan, and had left only a few months previously, not long after we had moved to the house. For this reason, he figures only vaguely in my memories of the place.

I recall hearing a thunderous wallop one evening, when I was reading in the lounge, and running into the corridor to find him flat on the floor, prone and spread-eagled atop a horizontal wooden ladder. He'd been trying to reach the water tank in the roof space when the ladder's feet slipped on the red stone floor which Obisa did such a fine job of polishing. He was winded and looked very surprised to be otherwise unhurt. It was much the same expression he wore when our dog Turly, an overweight and unbalanced black labrador, hurled itself full-tilt onto his lap as he sat in his new wheeled leather easy chair, and sent him rocketing back into the window bay at take-off velocity.

Add to that a few ugly marital barneys, sundry items of crockery splintering against the wall, and an overwhelming, unprecedented sense of things coming apart, and we quickly arrive at the night my mother called the three of us children into their bedroom to tell us that my father was leaving. I was nine. My sister was 13, my brother 14.

I felt a curious lack of shock. Perhaps I had guessed what was coming. The scene was one I had seen depicted again and again in cartoons featured in *Punch* magazine, to which my father maintained a surface mail subscription. The only aspect that truly surprised me was that our family should be involved in such a modern event as a divorce. Even my mother's words were already familiar.

'This doesn't mean your father doesn't love you. . .'

That was how the cartoon captions always read. When would we get to the funny part?

* * *

IN A BLEAK way, the funny part had already happened. My father's last two birthday presents to my mother had been, respectively, a beer tankard and a chainsaw. I watched him take the chainsaw to a fallen tree in the woods by the driveway. A tiny bat was suspended by its feet from a branch, vibrating to a blur with the buzz of the chain, but clinging on to its toppled home regardless. My father had also bought my mother a handsome set of Scandinavian stoneware crockery she coveted, just in time for Joan and Joan's then unsuspecting husband to eat off at a dinner party. Hindsight pieces these things together in a pattern.

The impact the divorce had on my mother remains outside my imagination even now. Her marriage, her family; these things made up the centre of her life, and they had been blown to dust. She had always possessed a certain style, a comforting composure. Slight in appearance, even more so in Biba dresses or bell-bottomed trousers, she had nonetheless embodied all the strength and calm that a child could want in a mother. Where my father's moods raged and ebbed, hers held steady and firm. When my father drove away from the house for the last time, she seemed – at least to my eyes, as she never had before – dazed and fragile. Despite her obvious efforts to hold herself together, the mildest breeze that stirred up in the garden might have seen her crumble on the doorstep.

My sister, too, was devastated. I had made a conscious decision to tough it out. I was a boy. I wouldn't cry. I didn't. But Lesley was sobbing her heart out when my father's car rolled away down the driveway. My mother held her, but looked shell-shocked, as if her daughter's pain, heaped upon her own, could add nothing to her sorrow. My brother remained, as ever, inscrutable.

We quickly adapted, as children will, to our new household set-up, and in a way that was far from helpful. My father's absence had left a power vacuum, which my mother was at first too shocked and hurt to recognise, let alone fill. Rather than support her, or each other, my sister and I embarked on a spiteful inter-sibling vendetta, which occupied a large proportion of our waking hours and served to make my mother's life even less bearable.

ME: 'Don't tell me what to do!'

MY SISTER: 'I'm older than you! You have to listen to me!'

ME: 'I don't care what you think!'

MY SISTER: 'Brat!'

ME: 'Bossy Boots.'

MY SISTER: 'Mum! He called me a name!'

ME: 'Well, she called me one!'

MY MOTHER: 'Oh, for crying out loud. I'll call both of you a name in a minute.'

ME: 'Which one?'

Why my mother didn't try to whack both of us with the *kiboko* on a regular basis still puzzles me. Even as I cowered from the blows – which is not that easy to do when you're up a thorn tree -- I knew I was receiving no more than my due.

After a while, my mother dropped the whip and let fly with a torrent of furious and well-aimed invective. A more compassionate or less selfish child would have found this unbearable. But it hurt less than the whip, so I didn't mind it as much.

I stayed in the branches until dusk, arranging myself around the thorns like the clumsiest monkey in the tropics. Then I climbed down, crept into the house, patched myself up with a square foot's worth of sticking plaster, and joined the rest of the family for dinner. No mention was made of the afternoon's events.

My sister's favourite record at the time was the soundtrack to *The Rocky Horror Picture Show*. When she had the lounge to herself, she would work on perfecting her 'Time Warp' dance. When she didn't, she would play the album anyway, as she did that evening. A parodic falsetto ballad titled 'Super Heroes' was grating from the speakers when my mother walked in.

'What's he saying?' asked my mother, catching a fragment of the lyric.

'It goes, "Down inside I'm bleeding",' my sister said.

'I know how he feels,' said my mother quietly, and she walked out of the room again.

* * *

WHEN THEIR parents divorce, it's said to be common for young children to suffer from bedwetting and nightmares. I was spared the bedwetting, but for a year or two afterwards I had nightmares in spades. It didn't cross my mind that the nightmares had anything to do with my parents' separation. Even today, I don't believe that was the case. I think I had nightmares because I was a nine-year-old boy who read too many horror stories.

'I'm scared of vampires,' I would say to my mother.

'There are no vampires.'

'How do you know?'

'Even if there were vampires, how would they get through the bars on the windows?'

'They turn into bats.'

'Don't worry,' said my mother. 'I would never let the vampires get you.'

Although I was far past trusting in parental omnipotence, this reassured me. I couldn't see how my mother would stop the vampires from getting me, but she probably knew something about vampires I didn't.

Following my father's departure, my mother was besieged by suitors. Initially, she kept them at arm's length. After a while, as she regained a little of her strength and poise, she began to at least consider the prospect of allowing another man into her life. According to the psychology textbooks, this should have made me jealous and disruptive. In the event, I wasn't in the least bit jealous, although my fear of vampires made me more disruptive than ever. It didn't bolster my mother's tentative receptiveness to courtship to have me materialise, more stealthily than Nosferatu himself, at all hours of the night, seeking comfort and protection.

'Dear God, man!' blurted one frustrated beau, sharing a brandy with my mother in the living room one evening. 'Don't you ever sleep?'

'It's the vampires,' my mother explained, leading me back to bed.

A gentle-mannered chap called Ian Kirk eventually found his way into my mother's affections. The wheels had come off his own marriage not long before. From what I could gather, his former wife was a creature of nightmare beside whom my vampires took on a quite cuddly mien.

'She's quite mad, you know,' was all Ian himself would say on the subject. My mother, who never had a bad word to say about anyone, was more forthcoming – although typically, she refused to pass judgement.

'She calls him up and threatens him,' said my mother. 'She told him to leave, so he did. And now she won't leave him alone. She keeps saying that she'll stop him seeing their children, but she won't tell him what she wants. She must be very upset. It's very sad.'

I was alone in the house one afternoon when the telephone rang. I had been taught to be both rigorous and immaculately polite when taking calls; in the days when my father still lived with us, an urgent message from a patient or the hospital might otherwise go adrift.

'Is Mavis Bennun there?' a woman's voice demanded, as if the act of saying the name was enough to scar its owner's tongue.

'I'm sorry,' I replied, 'but she's not here at the moment. May I take a message?'

It can't have eluded the caller that she was speaking to Mavis Bennun's young son.

'Yes,' she said, launching into what was plainly a prepared diatribe in which she enunciated each word with acid exactness. 'This is Candida Kirk. You can tell her that my children already have a mother, and that they don't need another one, and that if she thinks she can. . . '

'Please hold on a minute,' I said. 'I'll just get a pen.'

I found a pen and returned to the phone.

'Sorry to keep you,' I said. 'Would you mind starting again while I write it down?'

'Um,' said the caller, now sounding distinctly more hesitant. 'This is Candida Kirk. . .'

'. . . and your children. . . already. . . have a mother,' I added, carefully transcribing my words on a notepad. 'What came after that?'

'And they don't need another one,' said Candida Kirk, uncertainly.

'They. . . don't. . . need . . . another one. . .' I repeated, over the scratching of pen. 'Mm-hm?'

'And. . . and. . . ah, never mind the rest.'

'Thank you,' I said brightly. 'I'll be sure to pass that on to her. Goodbye.'

Candida Kirk never called back.

'What on earth makes her think I want her children?' said my mother, when I recounted the conversation to her. 'As if you lot don't give me enough trouble.' But for the first time in more than a year, she was smiling with her eyes.

chapter ten

Nairobi Snow

THE BUNGALOW we three children shared with my mother was not so much a home as a hotchpotch of oddities. Located on the eastern edge of the Langata district, it was enclosed by woodland and separated from Nairobi National Park only by a wire fence on the far side of Magadi Road. It had been built of grey stones in a faux-English-rustic style by someone who patently thought of architecture as an unnecessary and expensive fad, and opted instead to make it up as he went along. He had constructed it as an erratic series of annexes, so that almost every room had to be accessed via another. This was despite having to hand ample space to erect not one but several houses on a quite palatial model.

Most of this land had been left fallow, apart from a stretch of lawn to the west, where the greenery concealed a septic tank, and a seedy vegetable garden, quixotically planted at the front of the house for some, or perhaps no, reason.

At the rear – about a 100 feet away, beyond the bizarre concrete plinth and the tree I so speedily climbed when my mother came after me with the *kiboko* – stood an unsightly corrugated-iron garage. The garage was large enough to shelter many more cars than my mother's brown Toyota Corolla, although all it contained was a ping-pong table, a few crates, odd items of furniture, ironmongery and several nests of hornets, emissaries of which invariably stung my brother while we were playing table tennis.

ME: *Clack!*

MY BROTHER: *Clack!*

ME: *Clack!*

MY BROTHER: *Clack!*

ME: *Clack!*

MY BROTHER: '*ARGH! OW! Jesus H. Christ! Ow!*

BALL: *Bop-bop-bop-bopbopbpbpbpbpbpbprrrrrrrrrclick.*

ME: 'My point.'

Any invertebrate with venom and a grudge went after my brother. There was something about him that stimulated hostility in wasps, scorpions, spiders, centipedes and suchlike. Once, during the briefest of stops on a road trip, he wandered down to a riverbank and managed to get attacked by a giant, terrifying, scarlet-rumped insect hitherto unknown to science. Much as I sympathised, I was secretly glad that he drew their fire. That I came through two decades in Africa with a solitary bee-sting to show for it is almost certainly down to sticking close to him. That he elected to become a naturalist and spend most of his time in the Kenya bush, while I sat at a computer in Sussex and ventured out only for meals, is a fair measure of our relative fortitude.

Our parents' separation must have had an effect on Leon, but I was damned if I knew what. He devoted more attention then ever to his growing fascination with ornithology. He spent most of his time out of doors pointing his binoculars at trees and identifying small brown birds over great distances. 'It's a Great Gurgling Hag-Ridden Bullfinch!' he would enthuse, gesturing at something which I had taken to be a fleck on my cornea.

Woods and scrubland surrounded our property for acres in each direction. The house was strikingly isolated. In good weather, I used to wander for hours around this no-man's-land, now and then bumping into my brother as he stalked some mud-coloured blob with a name like Katzenjammer's Guttersnipe. His thatch of frizzy hair, which dwarfed even mine, and his thick-rimmed oblong glasses gave him a mad scientist look which I think he cultivated.

Above us, the rarely seen but often heard tree hyrax – a furry grey rodent which by some quirk of evolution is the least distant living cousin to the elephant – practised its gravelly shriek in the foliage. Porcupines rattled to and fro in the long grass. A clan of them had dug a burrow near our driveway and frequently charged at the cars of visitors, backing into the tyres and plugging them with quills.

Dogs would vanish into this semi-wilderness and never return. It was rumoured that leopards took them, dogs being the big cat equivalent of Twiglets. If so, the leopards spurned Martini, a preposterous mutt so named because his lineage spanned not only breeds but, I always suspected, species. I called him The Goat, because that's what he looked like. He was an unlovable animal. I don't know how we came to own him, but my mother insisted, out of pity, on keeping him; even when he jumped up and broke my upper left incisor with one of his hardier canines.

I would have been quite unmoved had leopards got The Goat. But despite our washing him whenever we could catch him, he always smelled so rank that even the hungriest of predators must have shied away from eating him. If he'd stopped moving long enough, he might possibly have been mistaken for carrion and consumed by buzzards. He was also a fertile breeding ground for a unique variety of flea that thrived on insecticidal pet shampoo. The parasites gambolled friskily in his bathwater, and I would not have been surprised to see them tossing pea-sized beach balls to one another.

THAT MY mother kept hold of her sanity in the days after her divorce is a source of wonder to me. As if looking after us was not taxing enough, she took on the job of headmistress at St Michael's and assumed responsibility for dozens more children. Then, whenever she came home from work, some new crisis would have developed.

It might be a water bill for 20,000 shillings – around 50 times the standard amount. That happened every few months. A computer malfunction was generally to blame, although in one instance it turned out that our account had been confused with that of Wilson Airport, Africa's busiest private airfield, a mile up the road. Sorting this out would require several visits to the water company, trying to locate a manager who was always 'just around' – that is, nowhere to be found. When, with tracking skills unseen since the heyday of the Sioux, my mother finally ran this character to earth, he would invariably warn of a five-week delay in clearing up the matter.

'I am sorry,' said the Just Around Man. 'The mistake has occurred because your name – you see here? – "Bennun", is so similar to "Wilson".'

'It isn't similar at all,' fumed my mother. 'And even if it were, next to "Wilson", it says "Airport".'

'Ah,' said the Just Around Man. 'We had assumed this was the name of your husband. Mr Wilson Airport.'

The only option was to pay the bill and wait for the money to be refunded. Otherwise our water would be cut off, and reversing that decision was harder than unfrying an egg.

Our water supply was periodically cut off for days anyway, but that was normally a problem across the whole district, when an engineer closed the wrong pipe and forgot about it, or a senior member of the ruling party, KANU, had the flow diverted to irrigate his *shamba*. When that happened, it was time to load the Corolla with every available *debe* (plastic water carrier) and fill them up at the house of friends who lived across town. A few weeks later we would return the favour.

Some householders became so frustrated that they had boreholes sunk into their land, to tap the water table directly, but this was not a practical option in a rented home. It would have been one more thing for my mother to worry about, and she already had plenty.

From time to time, opportunistic prowlers wandered down our driveway, but, finding the burglar-bars on the windows impregnable, they went away again. One man had a fair go at wrenching off a set of bars at one o'clock in the morning. With Obisa's help, we cornered him, then called the police.

'I am not a robber,' the man protested, unconvincingly. 'I was looking for Wilson Airport.'

'You don't work for the water company, do you?' my mother muttered, one hand over the telephone mouthpiece. 'Hello, police? We have a burglar here. . .'

'We cannot come to you,' said the policeman at the other end of the line. 'One vehicle is away and the other is not working. Can you come and collect us?'

'No!' said my mother.

The police arrived two hours later in a car with no headlights. 'We would have come sooner,' the sergeant told us, 'but we were in a collision with an animal outside the station. We think it was a cow. Fortunately, it was a small one.'

They put the prowler in the back seat and, with a sickening crunch, drove straight onto that cryptic cylinder of concrete in our backyard. The car was marooned, its wheels dangling freely on either side of the platform, while bits of suspension clanged lazily against the flat surface.

The sergeant leaned out of the passenger-side window. 'May we use your telephone?' he said.

My mother silently dropped her face into her hands for about half a minute. Then she turned around and went indoors to fetch her car keys.

* * *

MY MOTHER'S brown Corolla was berthed not in the garage but in a nearby barn. It was here that she reversed it over my new puppy. If my mother seems to be taking on something of an ogre-like quality, let me emphasise that both this and the *kiboko* incident were isolated and altogether out of character, and it really wasn't her fault. The puppy had been with us for a week. It was my tenth birthday present. I had named it Chui, the Swahili word for leopard, which was going it a bit. The tiny chap was pure mongrel and even then it was plain he would attain few, if any, of the noble hunter's qualities. As it was, we never found out. The famously reliable Corolla crushed him quite smartly.

I had never had much luck with pets, or their names. When I was six, my black rabbit, Peter, was savaged by a mongoose. The rabbit was succeeded by a hamster with the excruciating handle of Hamsterdam, who wasn't much luckier. He escaped, and was recaptured weeks later, minus a leg. By then we had given him up for lost. My parents were throwing a dinner party that night. I was lurking illicitly in a doorway, post-bedtime, to spy on the action, when I spotted Hamsterdam crossing the floor of the lounge, his gait weirdly uneven. This put me in a quandary; should I sound the alarm and reveal my forbidden presence, or go back to bed and let the rodent fend for himself? I didn't have long to decide. Even on three legs, Hamsterdam was a nifty mover.

'There he is!' I squealed and jumped into the lighted room, causing my mother to knock the coffee percolator off the sideboard and spill the contents over the hostess trolley.

'Thank God we found the little bastard,' my father had said, after Hamsterdam had been collared. 'I kept thinking I would wake up and find he'd chewed a hole in the waterbed.'

Hamsterdam's missing leg gave him a rather swashbuckling air, but he didn't seem to relish it. He returned to his cage only three-quarters of the hamster he used to be, and morosely ate himself to death with a surfeit of oats.

The brown Corolla which added Chui to my run of unfortunate pets was a replacement for a squat yellow Fiat 127. The 127 was a good little car, unlike its own predecessor, a nasty, woodlouse-shaped Fiat 850 coupé painted industrial orange. The 850 was so underpowered that it came to a halt on quite gentle hills, whining, grinding and spewing out malodorous fumes. The 850 was not much mourned when, unoccupied, it finally succumbed to gravity, slipped its handbrake, rolled down the side of a coffee plantation and slung itself autocidally against a gum tree.

The 127 had, in turn, met its end soon after my father's departure, when my mother gave my brother a driving lesson on the dirt driveway that circled the house like a noose. He steered the car smack into the dining-room wall. Quite how, or rather, why, we never figured out. How is easy to explain: he wheeled the Fiat sharp right until it pointed straight at the house. Then, by way of evasive action, he plunged his foot onto the accelerator, ensuring that what might have been a gentle bump became a full-on wreck, complete with smoke, crumpled metal and shattered glass – or Nairobi Snow, as it was known locally.

My mother, as usual, was forgiveness itself. 'It could have happened to anyone,' she told my brother, who was so galled by his blunder he had stopped talking altogether. 'Look, if you want to make it up to me, why don't you get rid of those hornets in the garage like you always say you will?'

The following day, Leon and I dressed ourselves in the thickest clothes and gloves we could find, put wicker wastepaper baskets over our heads, and blitzed the little fiends with cans of Johnson's It insecticide. The hornets weren't going down without a fight. They darted and dived at us through the toxic cloud.

'Run!' shouted Leon. 'Shut them in and wait for them to die.'

I heaved the door closed behind us and out of habit wrestled shut the huge iron padlock.

'Did you remember to bring the keys out?' said my brother.

My mother spent the weekend pulling rivets out of the corrugated iron panels with a claw hammer. She was a lot tougher than she looked. She had to be.

chapter eleven
Northern Overexposure

WHEN I WAS ten, I believed the least sufferable human settlement on earth to be the tiny hamlet of Sultan Hamud. This flyblown former trading post about 60 miles south-east of Nairobi is just visible from the main road – a shadeless clutch of tin-roofed shacks soldered onto the open roasting pan of the Athi River plains. My imagination, although lively – perhaps overly so, as I now spent most of my free time on my own in the garden of our Langata house, playing solo Swingball and talking to myself – could not conceive of a bleaker spot for people to live.

Then Leon, Lesley and I left Kenya to stay for a while with my father in Happy Valley, a small town in the Canadian province of Labrador. After that, to my mind, Sultan Hamud took on a certain down-home charm.

Happy Valley, named either as a cruel joke or for a bet, spread in a broad, untidy slew of shingled cuboids across the plain of the Churchill River. There wasn't much of anything in Happy Valley but space. Flat, drab space, tricked out in the brief summer with crab grass and mud, and snowbound throughout the long winter. It could not have contrasted more sharply with the vistas of East Africa, which even at their stillest never failed to shiver with drama. The best Happy Valley could manage was a slouch and a shrug. It was a place that appeared to exist only because it had received no instructions to the contrary.

The town was inhabited by fugitives from civilisation, alcoholic Inuit and blackfly. It was into the first category that my father and my new stepmother Joan fell after they took up posts at the hospital in Goose Bay, a large airbase adjacent to Happy Valley. When we went to join them, it was my first experience since toddlerhood of living outside Africa. By the end of it, there was not a single Third World inconvenience, danger or privation that I did not desperately miss. I would gladly have been parachuted naked into the Gobi Desert rather than spend another minute in Happy Valley.

The change in our family life was no less radical than our move from the tropics to the North Pole's suburbs. Joan was not one to suffer fools gladly – and, resolutely committed to foolish behaviour as I was, that spelled trouble for me from the off. Even at the age of ten, I realised that she must find it frustrating to have a houseful of somebody else's children in place of her own. But that arrangement had not been my choice.

In fairness, Joan worked hard at checking her temper; while I, instinctively obeying the principle of 'adapt or perish', resolved to keep my head down as best I could. Being an incorrigible wiseacre, and argumentative to boot, I didn't do a very good job of it. The further I made it up the learning curve, the longer my inevitable toboggan ride back down to base camp. It took a while to teach myself to keep my mouth shut, and when I did, so firmly did I clamp my lips together that my stepmother mistook my expression for a mocking smirk.

* * *

THE JOURNEY from Kenya to Canada marked the first time that my brother, my sister and I had travelled unsupervised. We were all three well used to the mechanics of globetrotting, but even so, this was an adventure. Air travel in the seventies was far more wayward a business than it is now. This was an era when airline magazines would print two maps at the back: one displaying your route to Toronto, the other detailing your suitcase's passage to Auckland.

Flying from Africa and connecting in Europe, severe delays were the rule rather than the exception. Hours might turn to days as you slumped across airport seating designed for aluminium service robots with concave spines, your bag straps knotted to your recumbent body for security.

Major carriers were unreliable enough, but worse yet were the Third World airlines. Until you have wasted a fortnight in Addis Ababa, waiting for Ethiopian Airways to get its plane back from the menders, you have not truly understood the meaning of despair. Nor can a mere retelling do justice to this in-flight announcement: 'The aeroplane has been commandeered by the President of Burundi, and will be making an indefinite stopover in Bujumbura at his convenience.'

I recall one Africa-bound flight from London which, putting down in Italy, was refused clearance for take-off on account of the airline's unpaid fuel bill. After several hours, the passengers took up a collection, and we went on our less than merry way.

Khartoum, Cairo, Mogadishu – preceded by the words 'stopping in' – these were names to fill the soul of the intercontinental traveller with foreboding. But worse yet was the one airport where I spent more time than any other, despite the fact that it was never once my destination. A loathsome, brain-liquefying heat-sink of a terminus from which any hope of escape seemed at first tenuous and eventually futile. Athens.

If you were unlucky, they made you wait on the runway. If you were truly blighted by misfortune, they let you disembark.

In the many years I travelled between Kenya and Europe, an unscheduled landing in Athens was mandatory for any flight with my name on the manifest. Reading down the list, the crew must have found it as depressing as I did.

FIRST OFFICER: 'Let's see: Arapkule, Bashir, Bennett. . . Bennun. Bugger.'

CAPTAIN: 'Oh well. Radio the Greeks and tell them we'll be putting down at oh-nine-hundred.'

* * *

WE BEGAN our voyage from Nairobi to Happy Valley on a creaking 707 operated by an airline from a small, backward island in the

Mediterranean Sea. Nearing Greece, the pilot informed the passengers that we had just crossed the Med on a single functioning engine, and Athens was waiting to welcome us. He sounded quite cheerful about it. I still don't believe a 707 can fly on one out of four engines, but that's what he told us. We were left to bake on the tarmac for five stifling hours before being transferred to a replacement jet chartered from British Airways' forerunner, BOAC.

This being back in the days when drinks, headsets and other such fripperies cost extra, the crew threw open the bar trolley by way of compensation. Inevitably, within 15 minutes we had guzzled the lot. Refused anything stronger than Coca-Cola, on the reasonable grounds that I was ten years old, I still managed to sink a dozen tins of the stuff.

By the time we made the approach into Heathrow, the entire cabin had long since descended into a drunken, bloated, burping bacchanalia, with fat men lurching through the aisles calling for taxis, old ladies passed out in the toilets, amorous couples slavering unsteadily at each other's faces, and nippers like me taking potshots at the lot of them with crumpled Coke cans. It was a lunatic, yawing juggernaut of a flight. Had terrorists boarded at Athens, as was then the custom, they would have swiftly concluded that this plane was already as bombed as it was going to get.

In contrast, the subsequent night flight from England to Canada was eerily empty. The three of us occupied a five-seat middle row. Empty tiers stretched fore and aft of us. The other passengers, all seven of them, were dotted around the seats at the sides of the plane.

My brother, as the eldest, had taken to giving himself the mantle of command. This didn't sit well with my sister, who was accustomed to doing the same thing with me. It didn't bother me, as I habitually ignored both of them.

'Behave yourselves,' said Leon, as the TriStar reached cruising altitude. 'Go to sleep.'

He promptly followed his own instructions, nodding off so swiftly that he didn't have time to remove his glasses.

'Who put him in charge?' grumbled Lesley.

'Mum did,' I said. 'Remember?'

'I don't have to listen to him,' she said.

'Then I don't have to listen to you.'

'Yes, you do, cos I'm older.'

'So? Leon's older than you.'

'Then he shouldn't have gone to sleep,' said Lesley, trumping my ace.

We occupied the next hour with rubber-band battles. When that palled, we lobbed ice at each other from plastic cups. Several cubes fetched up in the lap of a sleeping man in a suit, two rows back and to the right. I tiptoed over to retrieve the ice, although not before half of it had melted.

Somewhere near Nova Scotia, we flew into a thunderstorm. The plane began to buck and toss as if it were in training for a rodeo. There was a ping as the seat-belt sign illuminated.

The man in the suit woke up with a start. The colour drained from his face as the plane lurched sideways and waggled its tail like a duck. He glanced down at the damp patch that had spread across the front of his trousers. Noticing that I was watching him, he slapped a magazine onto his lap and stared fixedly ahead.

'Folks,' said the intercom, 'this is the captain. As you may have noticed, we've hit a rough patch here. There's nothing to worry about. We're just going to ride it out. Meanwhile the flight attendants will resume drinks service.'

'Would you like something?' said a stewardess at my shoulder.

'I'll have a Bloody Mary,' I said, drawing back my lips to reveal a set of plastic vampire fangs. I'd been given the fake teeth for my birthday and had since insisted on taking them everywhere.

'Ulk!' gurgled the stewardess and reared backwards. 'Ah-ha-ha,' she said. 'Very good.'

The cabin went black and I felt a sudden weightlessness pitch me upwards. At the same instant, from up the gangway, came a screech of panic and a tremendous metallic crash.

'Woah!' I said.

'Eek!' said my sister.

'Whuh?' said my brother, waking up.

'Omigod!' said the stewardess.

A moment later the plane levelled out and the cabin lights flickered back to life, revealing another stewardess leaning out of the galley. Her eyes were circular from shock, and shards of glass covered the carpet for a yard in each direction.

'Honey, are you OK?' called the first stewardess.

'I dropped my tray,' said her colleague dolefully.

'Uh, sorry about that, folks,' said the intercom. 'I think we just got struck by lightning. We dropped a few hundred feet pretty fast there. . .'

At Gander airport, we were due to pick up our flight to Goose Bay. At Gander airport, the thunderstorm had turned into a blizzard, piling up seven feet of snow. At Gander airport, we were stuck.

We sat and took stock of our resources. One cafeteria, staffed by an ill-favoured deviant who appeared to be perspiring the same grease used to blacken the burgers. One tiny souvenir shop, conceived upon the dingbat notion that anyone would prefer not to wipe the place from their memory. Twenty dollars Canadian. And a number of baggage trolleys, which I adapted for the noisy and repetitive sport of Departure Lounge Formula 53. When at last we left, 17 hours later, I had ensured that Gander airport was as glad to see the back of us as we were to see the back of Gander airport.

* * *

MY FATHER was waiting for us in the arrivals hall at Goose Bay, wearing a huge, furry Cossack hat. My sister launched herself at him as if she'd been shot from a catapult. I hung back, feeling oddly nervous. Having swiftly adapted, in the way that children do, to a new kind of life – one in which my father rarely figured – his presence now unnerved more than his absence. I must have seemed more interested in the airbase, with all its extraordinary hardware, than in seeing my father again.

During the Second World War, Goose Bay's location on the north-eastern edge of the Americas had made it a major staging post for transatlantic military flights. In 1978, when we arrived there, the base remained discreetly but unremittingly active. The landing bays were thronged with supply craft: hefty Starlifter carriers; giant Galaxies with hinged nose cones lifted to reveal the cavernous reaches of their fuselages; and dwarfing both, the Guppy, then the world's largest aeroplane, designed to carry NASA's moon rockets. Both inside and out, the grotesquely bulbous Guppy resembled its namesake less than it did Monstro, the omnivorous whale in Disney's *Pinocchio*.

Why these aircraft were here, what they were bringing, what they were taking away, and on whose behalf – these were questions you didn't ask in Happy Valley. Unless you were a bored youngster with nothing else to do but watch the aeroplanes take off and land.

'What do all those planes carry?' I would say to the folk I met.

'Eh, what planes?'

'You know, at Goose Bay. What are they carrying?'

'Eh. . . kid,' one grizzled local said to me, 'what flavour bubble gum d'ya like best?'

'Strawberry.'

'Well,' he said, 'they're carrying strawberry bubble gum.'

The nearness of the Arctic meant proximity to the Soviet Union – if not geographically, than psychologically. The military presence in Goose Bay was substantial but not much advertised, which was needlessly coy. If a ten-year-old boy from Kenya was aware of it, then there was at least a faint possibility that the Russians might be too.

With so many servicemen in the vicinity, combined with the frontier atmosphere of Canada's vast and unpopulous north, Happy Valley had the makings of a wild, good-time town. But in the months I spent there, one thing I saw precious little of was anyone having a good time. The air-force personnel seldom strayed from the base, while the few thousand residents spent their days either hankering for a return to the places whence they had come, or – in the case of those born and bred there – getting joylessly soused. Among the Inuit, as with so many American Indian tribes, alcoholism was a blight far more devastating than any of the changes which had brought it about.

Dipsomania might be seen as a fair response to life in Labrador. Winter sets in by October and grudgingly relinquishes its grip the following May. Conveniently for those with a poor grasp of arithmetic, the thermometer settles at the only point where centigrade and Fahrenheit require no conversion: minus 40 degrees. This is too cold for the senses to decipher. Objects become so painful to the touch, the air so raw on insufficiently swaddled skin, that it might as well be ragingly hot. When the wind kicks up, warmth deserts your body as if chased out by a pitchfork-waving mob.

In such savage conditions – which, mercifully, occupy on average only four or five days out of every seven – it is necessary not merely to wrap up, but to wear every piece of clothing available. The spherical figures that tottered from our front door each day, faces concealed beneath balaclavas and ski masks, could easily have been taken for a gang of obese militiamen, were it not for the fact that everyone else in town looked exactly the same.

Our house was a clapboard affair, which backed on to the river and fronted on a broad expanse of common land, across which lay the highway. Inside, thanks to a dependable furnace in the basement, it was always cosy. The basement also held a ping-pong table (I was never far from a ping-pong table) and several vats of fermenting root beer, to which my brother was very partial. The ping-pong table could be set up for a single player, by propping up one half at a right angle to the other, on a central hinge. This kept me amused for a while, until one day I bent to retrieve the ball, and in standing up knocked a heavy fire extinguisher flying from the wall, by striking its base with the top of my head.

I appeared at the top of stairs in the kitchen, blood running down my face.

'Oh my God, look at you,' said my stepmother.

'I hit the fire extinguisher with my head,' I said.

'What,' said my father, 'did you do that for?'

Joan made an ice pack for me, while my father inspected the damage.

'I'm glad to say it isn't fatal,' he pronounced.

These sudden, bloodstained manifestations of mine would carry on for years. My sister still shudders about the night I materialised in her bedroom at 2 a.m. This was at my grandmother's flat in London, where Lesley was living at the time. I had tried to open a can of spaghetti hoops in tomato sauce using a screwdriver. I was very hungry. My grandmother's kitchen drawers were a puzzle to all but my grandmother. They contained no tin opener, but half a rusty toolkit was on the loose in there. I gouged a vicious wound into my right index finger. My sister, dragged into consciousness, saw me standing before her, framed by the light from the doorway. I was ghostly pale and spattered with ketchup. Blood spurted vigorously into the air from my hand.

'Les,' I said, 'do you know where I'd find a plaster?'

'Ah' said my sister, and fainted away again.

The fire extinguisher incident persuaded me to spend more time outdoors. That, and the fact that my father had bought a snowmobile.

* * *

A SNOWMOBILE is a cross between a motorcycle and a miniature tank. It's also known as a skidoo, after the most popular make, in the way a vacuum cleaner may be generically referred to as a hoover. Our skidoo was in fact a Kawasaki.

The machine's front end rests on a pair of ski blades and is steered by handlebars. One grip controls the throttle, the other the gears. The long, open seat, which can fit two or, at a push, three, rests atop the engine, which propels a track on rotors. Even the less powerful models can get up to a fair clip once the track bites into the snow and the blades begin to fly across the frictionless surface.

If there is a more enjoyable way of getting from A to B than a snowmobile, I hope I may one day experience it. A jet pack might run it close. It was so much fun, you didn't mind at all that B was hardly worth getting to, that it looked exactly like A did, being flattish and snowbound as far as the eye could see, and that arriving back at A was no great treat either.

Snowmobiles were the favoured method of transport in the Labrador midwinter. Cars had to be fitted with electric heaters, from which a flex extended, to be plugged into the sockets supplied at most public parking spaces. Otherwise, the car wouldn't start. The skidoo was smaller, simpler, hardier, and more versatile. You fired it up and took the shortest cross-country route. The drawback was that, if it did break down, the chances of anyone finding you before you froze to death were slight. Every so often, a blue, rigid body would be uncovered in one of the huge snowfields or deep fir woods that separate the tiny settlements, much as deep space unfolds between stars, and delivered to Goose Bay hospital. Such melancholy events had been infrequent in the pre-snowmobile times of only a few years earlier. Then, sled dog teams were favoured by those locals who owned no automobile. When you lost your way, you could huddle with the huskies for warmth and, if it came to it, eat them. Snuggling up to a defunct hunk of Japanese metal was of little benefit; dining upon it, even less.

Knowing the snowmobile was berthed in the garage was an incentive to get out of bed and swathe myself in foot-thick layers of clothing. It beat the alternative of watching silent Charlie Chaplin two-reelers, which ran in a loop on the local TV channel, occasionally interrupted by the Canadian national news.

'Top stories this morning: our nation is peaceful and wealthy. Life is good. Healthcare is available to all and second to none. We enjoy American prosperity combined with a European sense of proportion. People joke about how boring we are. We don't care. A few political spats are taking place in Ottawa, but nothing serious. Some French people in Quebec want out. They must be crazy. And now, back to *The Little Tramp*.'

* * *

DRIVING THE snowmobile out into the unfenced front yard, where the snow had acquired an unsavoury grey-brown hue, I would turn left, following a path between the main road into town and the line of evergreens which ran along the river. This opened on to a patch of common land, with high snowdrifts piled along the edges, and a knoll, which during the brief summer served as a pitcher's mound in softball games. I would accelerate up to the knoll and fly over it like an Arctic Evel Knievel, albeit shorter and far less audacious. If the snowmobile rolled or threw me off when I hit the ground, it didn't matter. The snow absorbed the impact, leaving me winded at worst. The risk was no greater when I revved wall-of-death style up the snow banks. The only danger lay in getting pinned underneath the snowmobile. I spent an entire afternoon in a drift this way, and was at last retrieved at sunset when a search party was sent out to find me. Luckily for me, sunset came at four.

'Been here long?' said my brother nonchalantly.

'I'm freezing,' I moaned. 'Get this thing off me.'

I had been trying to ride down to the river, which for a boy racer on a skidoo meant miles of pure white highway. I could roar along the river, performing skids and turns, then shoot back home at full throttle, wheeling left up towards the garage a few yards before the bridge that indicated the turn. As any idiot can tell you, river ice is always thinner around the stanchions of a bridge. Any idiot, that is, but the idiot who one day decided not to make the left turn, but carry on underneath the bridge and see what lay on the other side.

The sound of crackling ice, coming from directly beneath you and 250 pounds of machinery, is hair-raising. On the plus side, it didn't last for long. Just long enough for me to twist the gearshift into reverse. Then my legs felt wet. Two seconds later, I couldn't feel my legs at all.

I dragged myself back out and crawled halfway to the bank. Then I realised I was no longer wearing my father's prized 'slave-driver' hat, the big, furry Russian job, which I'd borrowed for the ride. With the suicidal logic of the nearly dead – 'Dad'll kill me if I lose that hat' – I slithered back and fished it out of the hole.

I was now completely unable to move my joints, and icicles had formed in my nostrils – something I had thought only occurred in Saturday morning cartoon shows. I hopped double-footed and rock solid through the front door of the house.

'Oh my God,' said my stepmother. 'Look at you.' She was getting used to saying that, and she sounded concerned, but not surprised. Already she had witnessed my exhibition at an ice rink, where I travelled further, faster and in more convoluted patterns on the seat of my pants than the most expert of ice dancers could on a pair of blades, cutting a path of destruction that left few of my fellow skaters upright. She was now reconciled to the idea that the reputed attributes of the Bermuda triangle could be concentrated in a single child.

I stood for 20 minutes, fully clothed, beneath the hottest setting of the shower. If the incident hadn't taken place so near home, I would have been freezer-cabinet pigmeat. I had no business being alive. My father may have come close to sharing that sentiment when we had to winch the snowmobile out of the river and spend the next two days painstakingly chipping ice off the track wheels with a screwdriver.

'You've done a lot of dumb things. . .' said my father. I waited for him to finish the sentence, but he had decided, on reflection, that this pretty much covered it.

* * *

OVER CHRISTMAS, both my father and Joan had to work extra shifts at the hospital. We hitched up a big wooden sleigh to the snowmobile, and the whole family rode to Goose Bay that way. It amazed me that the little machine could pull us all uphill.

Lesley went off to watch my father perform a Caesarean section. Leon just went off. His self-sufficiency was remarkable. Wherever we were, he could always find something with which to interest himself. Usually, that something had feathers, but the only bird you were likely to spot in a Labrador winter weighed in at 20 pounds and needed regular basting. So Leon was probably staring at a chromatospectrograph in a hallway and working out ways it might be improved upon. Or, if there is no such thing as a chromatospectrograph, wondering why not.

As for me, I found a room with a television set.

A few other children were already watching it. They were all wearing thin, white gowns, and many of them had drips attached to their arms and suspended on wheel-mounted poles. The room was sad, bare and typically institutional. It smelled of malady and bleach. The television was a small back-and-white model, fixed high up on the wall, and there was no remote control. This was an utterly cheerless Christmas scene.

On screen, a horde of Vikings landed on a beach. It was a scruffy and unconvincing horde. Even in black-and-white, there was no mistaking the horns on their helmets for anything but plastic. The Vikings made straight for a large stone casket and the head Viking heaved off the covering slab, which evidently surprised him with its lightness.

The casket was filled with candy bars. The head Viking seized one of these, ripped open the packaging and tore off a hunk of chocolate with his teeth. Then he held what was left of it aloft and cried out, 'Wunderbar!'

'Wunderbar!' roared his Nordic rabble, nodding approval and jostling one another in manly Viking fashion.

At that moment, Santa Claus walked into the TV room.

'Ho, ho, ho, kids!' said Santa.

'Hello,' I said. The other children kept their eyes on the screen and said nothing.

Santa reached into his sack and began to hand out confectionery. He gave me something in an orange wrapper. It was a Wunderbar. It had nuts in it, but it didn't really merit seaborne pillage.

'Merry Christmas, kids!' said Santa, and left.

'Thanks,' I said. I wondered why the rest of the children ignored him. It didn't occur to me that being hospitalised over Christmas was bound to blunt their zest for the holiday.

At home, adding to the general sense of seasonal bonhomie, Poppy the cat went missing. Poppy was my stepmother's pet. Poppy wasn't quite right. She walked oddly and toppled over a lot. She never landed on her feet, because her feet were what she fell off in the first place. Poppy went out on Boxing Day, for reasons known only to Poppy – and knowing Poppy, I wouldn't assume even that much. Poppy didn't come back. By evening, a blizzard had set in.

'Poppy!' called my stepmother, standing at the open door and admitting a furious, icy gust, which snatched away her voice and covered the floor with snow.

'The cat's gone,' my father said. 'Face it, that cat can hardly stay alive inside the house. She's not coming back. And if you hold the door open much longer, the rest of us will freeze to death too.'

'Poppy!' my stepmother shouted.

'She's frozen now,' I said helpfully. 'She's a catsicle.'

'Poppy!' wailed my stepmother.

Just as in the celebrated folk song, the cat came back. The cat came back on New Year's Day. How she had survived a week in conditions extreme even for the region and the season was something only Poppy. . . Well, once again, I'm sure Poppy didn't know. Poppy didn't know which paw was which.

It was a little after midnight, and we were all in bed, when from the living room came the crash and tinkle of a breaking window. Instantly, I was awake. So, in the bed across from me, was my brother.

'Here we go,' he said. 'Three. . . two . . . wu–'

'What the hell was that?' came my father's voice from the next room.

We all stood in the corridor by the living-room door. My father pushed the door open and flicked up the light switch.

'Poppy!' said my stepmother.

'Mrrw?' said Poppy.

'*Grrrrrscrrryyyyowwwwfssssss!*' said something in the living room.

'Jesus H. Christ!' said my father and jumped backwards.

'*Krsssssss!*' snarled the thing in the living room. It was a cat, but I'd never seen a cat like it. It had one eye, one ear and was mottled with scar tissue and bare patches of skin. It stood two feet high at the shoulder, with its back arched, its mangy fur on end and its mouth drawn back to reveal a gumful of jagged and yellowing fangs.

My father slammed the door shut and retreated to the kitchen.

'Isn't that nice?' said my brother. 'Poppy's brought home her boyfriend to meet Mummy and Daddy.'

My father returned with a mop, a broom and a pink plastic softball bat. He kept the mop, and handed the broom and the bat to my brother and me, and we advanced into the living room.

'*Frrrrrrarrrrr!*' said Poppy's beau, and leapt up the curtains, which fell onto the carpet. A standing lamp toppled onto them and the bulb broke.

'Bugger off!' my father shouted, and hit the beast with the mop handle.

'Back to hell, I command thee!' intoned my brother.

'*Hssssss!*' said the cat, and clawed its way back out of the window as we closed in on it, weapons held in front of us.

'Mrrrrow!' wailed Poppy.

'Oh, shut up, Poppy,' said my stepmother.

* * *

WE COULD tell when at last spring was on the way. The thermometer edged upwards until it hovered a few degrees below freezing point. We spotted a few locals wandering around in their shirtsleeves.

With spring came the thaw. And with the thaw came blueberries and insects. Hungry swarms of tiny blackfly, and mosquitoes. I thought I had seen all the mosquitoes there were to see, hovering in clouds over tropical swamps. I hadn't seen anything.

The screens of netting over the windows and doors revealed their purpose as they turned black with humming bloodsuckers. As thoroughly as we had blanketed ourselves with clothing in winter, so we were now obliged to spray every inch of flesh with Johnson's Off, a chemical compound equally repellent to insects and to other humans. Forgetting to do so meant you would run back indoors seconds later, desiccated and overrun with livid welts. You didn't forget more than once.

Now that the snowmobiling season was gone, we spent a lot of time picking blueberries. It wasn't much of a substitute, but at least you got to eat blueberries at the end of it. We also went hiking in the woodlands, where – thanks to sinus trouble, which forced me to breathe through my mouth – I unwillingly reversed the traditional process by swallowing several ounces of mosquitoes. They tasted salty.

The walks were beautiful, if bug-ridden. Although I preferred African plains and deserts, I had to admit that Canada rivalled them for sheer scale. We tramped up the tallest hill in the vicinity, where a radar post had been blown up by the military to prevent its secrets falling into the wrong hands – like ours, presumably. We took an elegant chunk of metal, which had melted in the blast, then resolidified. It made an appealing abstract sculpture, and it still hangs on a wall in my father's home, where for years he has successfully passed it off as an early Giacometti.

When my brother, my sister and I returned to Kenya, it wouldn't be long before my father and my stepmother followed. They moved back to Nairobi a few months later. Their plane was delayed in Athens. All the luggage was unloaded onto the landing apron. A shrink-wrapped side of smoked salmon spoiled in the heat and had to be thrown away, along with everything else in the suitcase.

chapter twelve
Little Lord Me

MY SCHOOL – the Nyumba, so named after the Swahili word for 'house' – was located a couple of miles from our Langata home, down Magadi Road. Magadi Road ran alongside the edge of Nairobi National Park. A low wire fence was all that stood between the game reserve and Langata, so residents hereabouts were accustomed to having warthogs, baboons and the occasional buffalo turn up in their gardens. I found this quite thrilling, but always maintained the requisite blasé demeanour. To get excited about wildlife in your backyard marked you out as a parvenu, and was tacitly deemed poor form.

Before joining the Nyumba at the age of 11, I had briefly attended Knollpeak Primary, on the far side of Nairobi, next to the State House, which, following the death of Mzee Jomo Kenyatta, was now occupied by President Daniel Arap Moi. Parents driving their children to school were advised not to let their attention wander. One man who pulled up to the State House gates by mistake found himself surrounded by armed sentries. When he compounded his error by hastily attempting to reverse, the guards blew dozens of bullet holes in both car and driver.

Kenya's security forces were notoriously quick on the trigger. A month seldom went by without a report of twitchy-fingered coppers opening fire on a carload of wedding guests, or some other group of blameless citizens who had aroused suspicion by, understandably, looking a bit nervous. Once in a while the police even shot a few criminals. For this, one man was largely responsible.

Everything Pat Shaw did, he did largely. The head of Nairobi's CID since colonial times, Pat Shaw was a titan. His giant frame was reputed to be festooned with more gunshot scars than even he could count or recall incurring. One advantage of his size was that it greatly reduced the chances of an assailant's bullet striking a vital organ. And you didn't get two shots at Pat Shaw. He was a law enforcement officer of the old school, and the old school of Tombstone, Arizona, at that. Surprisingly nimble, and very quick on the draw, his practice was not so much to shoot first and ask questions later as to shoot first and let the questions go hang. He was Dirty Harry with diet issues, and his idea of due process involved the fitting of toe tags at the mortuary.

'The older I get,' my father once remarked, reading in the *Daily Nation* a report on Pat Shaw's latest bout of righteous carnage, 'the more sense Pat Shaw's idea of justice makes to me.' And there is no question but that Nairobi was safer with Pat Shaw than without him. He removed from its streets an awful lot of awful people: murderous, cold-blooded desperadoes, most of them. With gun-toting outlaws either dead or too frightened to show themselves, the task of endangering the public at large was valiantly shouldered by the rest of the police force.

A few years later, when I was a student at Knollpeak Secondary School, a quartet of sixth-form tearaways made off with the school signboard as a prank, and were amazed and terrified to be apprehended by Pat Shaw, who must have been having a quiet afternoon. The sign was never disturbed again. I doubt if any one of the culprits has so much as contemplated fibbing on an official questionnaire since that day.

Knollpeak Primary, where I spent a couple of terms, wasn't the kind of place Pat Shaw needed to worry about. Unlike, for example, James Gichuru School, where a traffic accident involving one of their number sent the pre-teen pupils off on an eight-hour rampage. They burned the offending vehicle, heaved rocks at any other car they could find, looted nearby shops, then upended a beer truck, drank its cargo and passed out in the street. 'They are,' said one disgusted teacher, 'like English football fans.'

* * *

MY MOTHER shifted me from Knollpeak to the Nyumba when I came back from Canada. We weren't on Knollpeak's school bus route, and the Nyumba was closer to home.

The Nyumba's headmaster, Fergus Fitzherbert, was a strapping, shiny-pated fellow, red in complexion and what remained of his hair, with the face of a particularly bellicose bulldog. My family gave him the insouciant nickname of Fergie. Fergie was at first reluctant to accept me as a pupil. He was persuaded, in the end, by my mother's persistence; she made it clear that either she or I was going to be a fixture at the school.

Fergie may also have been swayed by the prospect of a potential scholarship candidate. The Nyumba was self-assertively not primary, but preparatory, and what it aspired to prepare students for was a place at a British public school. The more names it could engrave onto the roll of academic honour, which hung in the assembly hall, the happier Fergie would be. And if my name were added to that list, my mother would be happy too. So in the end, the Nyumba took me in and began to groom me for life as a public schoolboy.

The school day ran from eight-thirty to five, including a double games period at the end of each afternoon. The uniform was a blue, short-sleeved, button-up shirt worn with khaki shorts and safari shoes (known elsewhere as desert boots), and a maroon pullover for cooler weather. A blazer and a tie were recommended, but not obligatory. I never wore either.

Most of the teachers were British expatriates, with a sprinkling of ex-colonial diehards. Any faculty has its oddballs, but some of this lot were true collectors' items. Mr Leap had a touch of the Noel Cowards about him. He favoured velvet jackets. His hair was curiously and evenly black for a man of his years. There was a roguish cast to his left eye and a twinkle to the right one, which was made of glass and tended to catch the light. Mr Leap taught art and penmanship, but not often. He was so easily diverted into storytelling, for which he possessed a marvellous gift, that it didn't take much in the way of schoolboy wiles to ensure that lessons were enjoyably frittered away. Often it took no prompting at all.

Mr Leap had been employed at private schools around Kenya for longer than any of us could guess at, and his fund of scurrilous tales about the personalities at these establishments was bottomless. He had the rare talent of making compulsive his gossip about people we hadn't heard of, didn't know and never would.

'So,' Mr Leap would say, setting down his chalk in the tacit acknowledgement that a curlicued, lower-case 'a' would be the last thing to appear on the blackboard that day, 'it seems that one of the older boys was making book – ah, that is, taking *bets* – on which master's wife might next fall pregnant, and *when* she might give birth. At the start of the new term, I heard a boy enquire of a master, *very* casually, you know, "Did you have a good holiday, sir? Oh, at the coast. . . and were there any particularly rainy days at all, sir?"

'The head said one day at assembly, "I am pleased to inform you all that Mrs Glidin"' – she was the wife of an English teacher, a *very* boring woman – '"that Mrs Gliding yesterday morning gave birth to a healthy baby girl." One chap at the back began to cheer, right there and then. Well, of course, he'd just won fifteen shillings, hadn't he? But the head was fearfully suspicious. He looked the boy up and down and said, "And just what has it got to do with *you*, I'd like to know?"'

I have terrible handwriting, but I'm not sorry.

* * *

WHEN I moved up a year, Mr Leap's place was assumed by Miss Darby. It was one of many things assumed by Miss Darby. The other things included airs and graces which, although unconvincing in themselves, became impressive en masse simply due to their profusion and variety. A youngish woman of grand manner who plainly believed her place to be on the stage, Miss Darby seemed galled by every moment she spent off it. Fate had thrust her among philistines, but she carried her head high and her nostrils higher. At school concerts she could not be dissuaded from reciting, in a robust and trilling contralto – which may, for all I know, have been technically flawless, but to us children evoked the slow passing-by of a vintage fire engine – such numbers as 'Summertime'. I can't hear that song without a vision appearing before me of Miss Darby casting her costume pearls before swine.

MISS DARBY: '*Summertiiiiiiiime, and the liiiiiving is easeeeeee. . .*'

FERGIE: 'Thank you, Miss Darby. And now, once again, Mr Jefferson will play his guitar and lead us all in singing "Lord Of The Dance".'

SEVERAL HUNDRED CHILDREN [mumbling]: '*Dance then, wherever you may be/I am the Lord of the arse, said he. . .*'

A performance at the school by a professional baritone was an excuse for Miss Darby to shoehorn herself into, firstly, an Edwardian ball gown, and secondly, a catalogue of duets, at every turn of which the visitor's conspicuous charm and humorous warmth were undermined by her own inability to project either. I can honestly say that I held these opinions about Miss Darby before she was called in to act as judge for my Cub Scout entertainment badge. She failed me as ruthlessly as if I were a tone-deaf muleteer auditioning for the title role in the New York Metropolitan Opera production of *Rigoletto*.

'Did I pass?' I asked eagerly, having proved myself to be as entertaining as any ten-year-old Cub Scout ever will be. Which is to say, not very.

'You did *not* pass,' said Miss Darby sternly, and went on to detail the extent of my inadequacy, which was abject and total. Although not exactly pleased, she sounded distinctly satisfied that, having been called upon to protect the scouting movement from children who couldn't meet the highest standards of stagecraft, she had not wavered in her duty.

* * *

THE SCOUT troop was the school's own. It met on a Thursday afternoon on a spare patch of ground between the swimming pool and the playing fields. The fields spread out to the south of the school buildings. They were bisected by a dirt road that served the neighbouring farms, and into the drainage ditch of which I was pushed every rainy season by larger boys until I myself became too large for this to be an easy task. My size fluctuated. I was never short or tall for my age, but at times I was unarguably plump – a fact brought home to me by the conjuring clown who had cornered the local market in kids' parties.

'I need a volunteer,' said Bozo. 'You, there – the heavyweight wrestler. Stand here and hold on to the end of this rope. Try not to eat it.'

When, during school games periods, we were divided into skins and shirts, I would will myself to be selected for the shirts. It never worked.

There was no apparent correlation between how much I ate (a lot), how much exercise I was made to do (a lot) and my waistline. Sometimes I was pudgy, sometimes thin. I think I was a fairly skinny Cub Scout. Why I joined the Cubs, I'm not clear on. It might have had something to do with getting out of double games on a Thursday, but I doubt I was that shrewd. I may actually have enjoyed it; like many outsiders, I craved the sense of complicity provided by a uniform. And then there was the authority.

I had been promoted to 'seconder', and although at 11 I would soon be too old for the Cubs, the way things were going I might yet taste the sweet and absolute power of commanding my own 'six'. I put the kibosh firmly on that ambition when my pack met up with Nairobi's other Cub troops for a weekend jamboree and camp-out at the scouting centre in Ngong Forest.

The obvious choice to guide the Nyumba pack would have been the school's own Reverend Frank Phillips, our divinity teacher and a man born to be a Scoutmaster. He was every bit as long-suffering and well intentioned as the Bible instructed he should be, and also as pernickety a fussbudget as ever held up his knee-socks with garters. But Reverend Phillips already shepherded a Scout troop at his church. The job of Akela thus devolved on to Mr Stanley, an affable, bearded Englishman whose temper was – as I would discover – steady, but not unshakeable.

The jamboree began amid a furious hailstorm. The assembled Cubs squatted inside a wooden hut while a Filipino Scoutmistress taught us a cheery singing round. The lyrics may have been affected by her style of speech, or perhaps they had been written that way.

Uh li-il fwog
Uh li-il fwog

Ey ah a appy cwowd
Ey av no taiwul
Ey av no taiwul
Ey showt owt ewy lowd
  Cwoak-ah   cwoak-ah   cwoak-ah   cwoak-ah   cwoak-ah   cwoak-ah
cwoak-ah
  Cwoak-ah   cwoak-ah   cwoak-ah   cwoak-ah   cwoak-ah   cwoak-ah
cwoak-ah.

Fifteen minutes in and the sing-song had begun to pall. After an hour, with the ice still drumming upon the tin roof, I had gone stir crazy. I would gladly have taken a Gatling gun to every li-il fwog in the sodden vicinity. In my mind, they had multiplied to plague proportions and, undeterred by the appropriately Old Testament hail, were advancing on all sides with the intention of overrunning the Scout hut and visiting Jahweh only knows what manner of amphibian retribution on its round-capped inhabitants.

  Cwoak-ah   cwoak-ah   cwoak-ah   cwoak-ah   cwoak-ah   cwoak-ah
cwoak-ah
  Cwoak-ah   cwoak-ah   cwoak-ah   cwoak-ah   cwoak-ah   cwoak-ah
cwoak-agggggh!

When the hail stopped, we bolted from the hut. Dozens of cubs went zig-zagging off at every point of the compass, radiating away explosively from an epicentre at which stood the Scoutmistress, shrieking, 'Noh, Scowts! Noh! Com back, Scowts!'

Those of us from Nyumba pack who were trying out for our firelighting badges went in search of kindling. There was plenty of it, and it was all waterlogged. You could have trained a flamethrower on it and it would merely have steamed at you. I had three matches.

I painstakingly constructed a miniature woodpile with the tiniest twigs at the bottom and room for the air to get in alongside them. I held the matches to the twigs, one by one, and watched them sputter out. Having watched the whole time-consuming process, Mr Stanley could take no more. He handed me a full matchbox and a copy of that morning's newspaper, then walked away whistling. Ten minutes later, I had the thing alight.

'Good work,' said Mr Stanley, reappearing. 'You've earned your badge.' This was a kind but flagrant untruth. 'Now for God's sake let's have some tea.'

Our pack turned in, with six Cubs to every tent. The tents slept five, at a pinch. The responsibilities of command demanded that myself and the sixer should bed down at the sides, with the rest of our six between us. I fell asleep straight away. When I woke up, sunlight was shining on my face and the Filipino Scoutmistress was looking down at me thoughtfully.

'Woh ah yu dung tha?' she asked. It was a reasonable question. Still in my sleeping bag, I had fetched up five feet away from the tent, resting against a tree.

I assumed that in my sleep, I had tossed and turned until I left the tent altogether. Only later did it occur to me that the sixer, exercising the qualities of leadership which had raised him to that rank, might have instructed the other cubs to drag my slumbering carcass out from beneath the tent flap and free up a bit more space inside.

After a breakfast of sausage-shaped charcoal and gristle, we went for a dip in the centre's swimming pool. Most of the pools I had swum in were sufficiently chlorinated to stun birdlife flying overhead. Not this one. At first I thought the water was green. That turned out to be the scum of algae on the surface. The water itself was yellow.

The jamboree was to close with a ceremony wherein all the Cubs gathered in a giant circle around the flagpole to celebrate the community of international Scouthood. By the time this took place, I was no longer part of that community. Mr Stanley had expelled me from the troop while I was packing my rucksack in the tent. He had told my six to hurry up. 'I shall treat that remark,' I responded, 'with the contempt it deserves.' It was meant to be a joke. I didn't know what the phrase actually meant, but my brother kept on saying it to me, and I thought it sounded pretty good.

Mr Stanley didn't. He summarily stripped me of my seconder's stripe and gave me my marching orders. Looking back, I'm surprised and grateful that he was so restrained.

My mother, turning up early in the brown Corolla to collect me, found me perched fretfully on a rock in the clearing-cum-car park, unpicking the stitches that fixed my badges to my shirt. Every other Cub Scout in Kenya was assembled by the flagpole a 100 feet away.

'Oh dear,' said my mother. 'What did you do?'

'I don't know,' I said, which, for a change, was the truth.

'You must have done something,' said my mother.

'I just said that thing Leon always says to me to Akela,' I replied, with more frankness than intelligibility.

'Oh dear God,' said my mother.

* * *

MY MOTHER'S attempts to have me reinstated in the Nyumba Cub Scout pack were eventually successful. She convinced Reverend Phillips that I was misguided but not incorrigible. His creed directed him to hate the sin but love the sinner, and he prevailed upon Mr Stanley to allow me back. I was permitted to keep my badges, but found myself busted down to the Cub equivalent of buck private.

Still, it seemed that the Nyumba was doing its job well. The cheeking Akela incident showed that I was developing into a prissy, arrogant and publicly overconfident little snot. The British public school system was going to love me, if only I could learn to keep out of trouble. I couldn't.

I was punished for attaching a dead rat by the tail to the inside of a girl's desk, so that it swung like a rotting pendulum when she lifted the lid. When I mutinied by walking out of the school gates and heading home, I was retrieved by the deputy head in his Renault 16 and sent to Fergie's office.

'I understand you're having trouble at home,' said Fergie, with a scrupulous distaste that might have seemed dainty in a less raw-boned man.

Was I? This was news to me. It turned out that he was referring to my parents' divorce.

'And that,' Fergie told me, 'is the only reason that I'm not going to administer physical punishment. Normally in this situation. . .' He thought this over. There was no 'normally' to the situation; nobody had ever been known to run or even walk away from the Nyumba. 'Otherwise in this situation, we would give you a few good hard whacks.'

Instead, I was made to write 1,000 lines. It seemed this broken home business had its uses after all. I wouldn't have dreamed of blaming my behaviour on my parents. If you ask me, I was just a recalcitrant wee sod.

Attempting to mould my inferior clay into a more worthy form, the Nyumba entered me into something called the Entwistle-Mayer History Prize, a written test in which I would compete against prep school students from across Britain. The essay paper turned out to be full of subjects on which I was worse than clueless; what little I knew about them was gleaned from half-remembered and laughably unreliable sources. My specialist topic, the Civil War, did not feature at all. Oh, there were questions on the Civil War, all right. Problematically, they were all concerned with the American Civil War, about which I knew one thing and one thing only: it had featured few, if any, Roundheads and almost certainly no Cavaliers.

I wound up improvising on the assassination of Abraham Lincoln. Not so much improvising, in truth, as vamping. I did things to history that Count Basie would have balked at trying on a piano keyboard. It's quite conceivable that I wrote Count Basie into the murder plot, unless I was saving him for the question on the Magna Carta. Aided by a few shady factoids I had encountered in cheap, cut-and-paste books of weird trivia with titles like *Believe It or Die!*, I put poor Abe through an ordeal even more strange and grisly than the one which brought about his end. I had the doctors failing for the best part of a day to turn him over and find the fatal bullet wound – 'or they might have saved him!'

When Fergie summoned me to his study some weeks later, I'd forgotten about the history prize. I took it that my free pass had been revoked, that he had reconsidered the 'disrupted home life' excuse, which I had never found very convincing myself, and that I was finally about to receive the thrashing I most probably deserved. I wasn't sure what my crime was on this occasion, but no doubt Fergie would know.

'You finished highly commended in the Entwistle-Mayer History Prize,' said Fergie. 'Well done. You will receive your certificate in assembly tomorrow morning.' It looked as if I hadn't finished riding my luck just yet.

That I did quite well was not a matter of pride for me. I knew that most of what I wrote was drivel. It simply meant that the majority of pupils at British prep schools were even more ill-informed than I was – an alarming indictment of private education. As for Fergie's favour, it was almost as frightening as his displeasure. I would have preferred to keep out of his trajectory entirely.

* * *

BY THIS time my father and stepmother had moved into a house not far from where we children lived with my mother. Their airy bungalow stood on an acre of ground, with a broad lawn that sloped downhill in terraces to the vegetable patch and chicken run.

When my father asked me if I wanted to live there, I said yes without thinking. I don't know why. The trouble was that I had developed a habit of automatically agreeing to things without regard to scale or consequence – one which I have found it hard to shake off. I had no reason to be unhappy with my mother, who herself had every reason to be upset and aggrieved by this latest development. If she was, she had the customary grace not to show it.

The households divided up on gender lines. My brother and I moved up the road to my father's new home, and stayed at my mother's house once or twice a week. My sister remained with my mother. Her own school, Korongo, was situated nearby. The Korongo uniform was a green, stiff A-line dress. Leon and I referred to it as 'the pup tent'. This never failed to leave Lesley incensed – which, of course, is why we kept on doing it.

My sister's days at Korongo came to an end when my mother attended a parents' meeting about sex education. One of the older pupils had asked a question about reproduction in biology class. The teacher referred the matter to the principal, who invited the parents to express their views.

Had they witnessed the convocation of lipless, hatchet-faced bluenoses gathered at Korongo that evening, the Puritans of Salem would have hung their heads in mortification, and damned themselves by comparison as a vice-ridden rag-bag of libertine rowdies. A heavy pall of repression stirred in with hysteria choked the atmosphere, as one Pharisaical throwback after another stood up to denounce the school, its staff, their families and their pets and their families' pets. How dared the school introduce the issue of introducing their issue to the unspeakable act that had led to their existence?

'The less our children know about that sort of thing the better,' fulminated one puce-hued matron, whose teenage daughter would not so very much later turn up at my father's surgery with what he described as 'a slight touch of pregnancy'.

After an hour of this overwrought assembly, combining as it did the least agreeable attributes of a Stalinist show trial with those of the torch-bearing rabble which brought *Frankenstein* to a climax, my mother tentatively raised herself from her plastic stackable chair, waited for a suitable gap to emerge between the clouds of sulphur, and said, mildly but pointedly:

'I think it's a good idea.'

To duplicate the effect, which was instantaneous, you need only place a drop of detergent in a petri dish of oil. The other parents shrank away from my mother at all sides, as if she were infected. She stood alone at the centre of a circle defined by a circumference of silent, seething horror and opprobrium. She opened her mouth once more, looked at the faces around her, and thought better of it. Soon afterwards, Lesley joined my brother at Knollpeak Secondary.

Meanwhile, as my schoolmates prepared for the common entrance examination, I and two other boys were readying ourselves for scholarship tests. My mother was convinced that I should go on to a British public school. My father was just as resolute that I shouldn't.

'If he's going to grow up with anyone's neuroses,' he told my mother, during one of their many set-tos on the subject, 'I want them to be mine, not some housemaster's.'

My father was in a position to veto both myself and my mother on the matter, for the simple reason that boarding schools are expensive, and Kenya implemented austere foreign currency controls. He would be the one who had to find and stump up the necessary sterling if I failed to obtain a full waiver of fees. I think he was relieved when I managed to win only half a scholarship, and he could put his foot down and insist I attend Knollpeak.

I was disappointed at missing out on public school, but worse, I now carried with me an air of insufferable superiority, an ingrained notion that I was meant for better things. Fergie had done his job well – and, of course, whether I took up the scholarship or not, he had another name to add to the roll of honour. Off to Knollpeak I went. It's a wonder they didn't lynch me within a week.

chapter thirteen

Kenya Cowboys

To qualify as a Kenya Cowboy, you required the following:

- Family in the safari tour operator business: one (1)
- Failing that, family in the farming business: one (1)
- Pick-up truck or four-wheel-drive vehicle, use of: one (1)
- All-over tan, toddlerhood, acquired in: one (1)
- Cloth hat, floppy-brimmed: one (1)
- Khaki shorts, pairs of: two (2)
- Shirts, short-sleeved, button-up: two (2)
- Bottles of White Cap lager (*baridi sana**) to be sunk over 12-hour period without noticeable effect: eight (8)
- Bottles of White Cap lager (*baridi sana*) to be sunk thereafter with highly noticeable effect: five (5)
- Terms (three per annum) spent at Knollpeak Secondary School, education, for the ostensible purpose of: eighteen (18)

**baridi sana* = very cold

Not all pupils at Knollpeak Secondary were Kenya Cowboys. But all Kenya Cowboys were or had been pupils at Knollpeak Secondary. What the Ivy League is to preppies and Roedean is to unbalanced posh girls, Knollpeak was to KCs, as they were universally referred to, even by themselves.

It was conceivable – just – that by way of an alternative, a KC might attend Saint Mary's School ('Saints', it was called colloquially, pointing up an unwitting assumption that of the numerous Kenyan schools named after a saint no other was worthy of mention). A fierce and long-standing rivalry, bordering on enmity, was said to exist between Knollpeak and Saints. In my time at Knollpeak, I never saw the least evidence for it. It may have been similar, in a microcosmic way, to the supposed antagonism between citizens of Australia and New Zealand, which seems to obsess the latter and concern the former not one bit. Knollpeak students felt they had nothing to prove, a view which was reflected in the academic performance of many.

A Kenya Cowboy could be described as part squire, part redneck and all-round party animal. A more amiable and less essential group of people may not exist anywhere. Kenya Cowboys possessed the easy confidence that comes with unquestioned privilege, minus the usual accompanying toffee-nosed objectionability. A KC might be a bigot, a clod or a yahoo; but stuck-up, never.

Arriving at Knollpeak Secondary, fresh from the Nyumba, I was 13 years old and snooty enough to cancel out a dozen KCs before breakfast. I swiftly learned to lose the attitude. Knollpeak may not have offered a language laboratory, compulsory service in a military cadet force and a fast-track to Oxbridge – all benefits, or at least attributes, of the British public school I might have attended – but it did rescue me from becoming the most unbearable human being in the Commonwealth. I can say this with some certainty, having since met several people who took the path that once beckoned to me. Whatever my defects (and there are plenty), stood next to that lot, I am suddenly imbued with the savoir faire of Cary Grant tempered by the down-to-earth affability of Jimmy Stewart. This is not to overstate my allure. Stood next to that lot, the same might be said of Hermann Goering, or a wall-eyed Glaswegian tramp. My point is that I had a lucky escape.

Going to Knollpeak instead of a UK boarding school had another advantage. It allowed me to put off dealing with the fact that I would one day have to leave Kenya. Most KCs were Kenyan citizens. I was not. My passport was of the navy blue British variety. When, in less than five years' time, I turned 18, I would lose my automatic right of residence as a dependant. By then, undoubtedly, the break would be that much harder to make. But five years was an impossibly long way into the future. I couldn't know that I had just reached that point in life when time ceases to be a slow upward trundle to the top of the helter-skelter, and abruptly switches into an ever-accelerating plunge down the chute.

* * *

WHERE THERE were Kenya Cowboys, there had to be Kenya Cowgirls. A Kenya Cowgirl's career generally involved a stint at Knollpeak, followed by a course at Victoria Road Secretarial College, where she acquired the skills she would promptly cast off in order to marry a Kenya Cowboy, move 'up country' and produce Kenya Cowbabies.

Knollpeak didn't have only Kenya Cowgirls in its classes. It had every variety of girl imaginable. Approaching my fourteenth birthday, I found myself surrounded by girls of every shape and cast and hue: Kenyan girls, English girls, Scots girls, Italian girls, Dutch girls, Swedish girls, Israeli girls and one girl from the Ivory Coast. I had not the first notion of how to talk to any of them, and they all frightened the hell out of me equally.

GIRL: 'Hi.'

ME: '. . .'

The Knollpeak school uniform was a practical one. For girls, a blue skirt or trousers (the trousers were seldom preferred) and a matching sleeveless jacket worn with a plain top and sensible shoes. The bolder girls were constantly engaged in skirmishes at the frontier of the dress code, customising this demure ensemble with skirt slits approaching the hipbone, and adding their own weight in make-up and earrings – until, inevitably, and much to the disappointment of all but the most militantly proper pupils, new edicts were handed down barring these refinements.

For boys, the uniform comprised a khaki safari suit with short or long trousers and, again, a sleeveless jacket, combined with a button-up shirt and safari shoes. The shorts option was taken up almost exclusively by Kenya Cowboys, who were never happier than when flourishing their knees at the world. Free at last from short pants, I chose long trousers. As with most of my clothes, my uniform was handed down by my brother, who had just departed Knollpeak two years ahead of schedule, with a grab-bag of top-grade A-levels, bound for Cambridge by way of various scientific research projects in the East African bush. This left me with two problems. First, a level of expectation among the staff as to my scholastic aptitude which I could not possibly live up to. And second, the most preposterous pair of strides ever to constitute the lower half of a safari suit.

By 1982, no one in the West had worn flared trousers for half a decade. In Kenya, no one had worn them ever. Except for Leon. Somehow my brother had obtained the only pair of beige bell-bottoms in sub-Saharan Africa – and quite feasibly the only pair anywhere at that time. Now I was compelled to wear them.

It hadn't been so bad for Leon, who had probably chosen the trousers at random. He wouldn't have noticed or cared if they had featured paisley-embroidered hems, polka-dotted pockets and a humorous walrus motif around the zipper. He had an enviable and in many ways admirable disregard for what other people thought of him, which carried over into every aspect of his life, sartorial or not. During my first weeks at Knollpeak, several sixth-formers asked me, 'Are you the kid brother of that guy who talks to trees?' Apparently, I was.

Straight away marked as Weirdo, Junior, I had the shmutter to match. Lacking my brother's boffinish insensibility to outside opinion, I found it disheartening when I looked down and couldn't see my own feet. My all-encompassing trouser cuffs fell so low as to meet the ground, collecting enough soil, grass and unidentified organic matter to furnish a small market garden, and lending my movements the uncanny levitational quality of a hovercraft. At the other end, the waistband rose to a point well north of my diaphragm. To the casual observer I might – like the statue of Ozymandias – have consisted entirely of two vast and trunkless legs. Only the abrupt onset of gigantism would have enabled me to grow into these trousers, let alone grow out of them and demand a replacement; preferably one which would not have been the first choice of a Louisiana sideshow freak.

Worse still, the khaki dye in these fatuous pantaloons and their matching waistcoat registered several shades darker than the usual type, and assumed a yellowish, ureic tinge fraught with deeply unpleasant associations. Had you set out to visit upon an already awkward teenage boy every discomfort and humiliation associated with puberty, and a surplus bushel-load of self-invented miseries besides, you could not have devised any means more effective than that safari suit. The onset of acne, which diverted attention away from my trousers, came as a relief.

* * *

THE KENYA COWBOYS regarded me with a tolerant amusement. 'Geek' and 'nerd' were not part of Knollpeak's particular vocabulary, which mixed old-fashioned English schoolboy vernacular with local patois and a smattering of Americanisms. If you saw someone you knew, you greeted them with 'Yo!'. Your parents were 'muhthay' and 'fahthay'. Should they refuse a request, that meant they had 'jammed'. When you arrived at a specific location, you had 'rocked up'. If you were driving there – as many underage KCs did, using illegally procured licences – you took the 'gari'. If you were involved in a smash – as many underage KCs with illegally procured licences were – you had 'pranged' your vehicle.

Thus a snippet of conversation might run: 'Yo, fahthay jammed me from using the gari 'cos I pranged it when I rocked up at the Sailing Club.' I overheard that exact sentence once or twice a week.

Knollpeak parlance would have classified me as a 'swot', but my unswot-like propensity for getting into trouble soon had the KCs confused. It had me confused, too. It wasn't as if I were a rebel; I suffered from a craven fear of authority that has dogged me to this day. Unfortunately, as one of my father's American friends once observed, 'That kid of yours has one hell of a mouth on him.' I was a lippy bugger, afflicted with an inability to control my outbursts, which bordered on Tourette's syndrome. My knack for saying exactly the wrong thing at the wrong time to the wrong people had developed synchronously with my power of speech, and now both were flourishing in tandem. The things I said left me just as shocked and startled as the people I said them to. Probably more so, as I knew who would have to bear the consequences.

I swore in the presence of my stern and pious physics teacher. I made disparaging remarks about Knollpeak's founder and former headmaster – an upright septuagenarian named Walter Finlay who remained very much involved in school life – in conversation with his family, when they had considerately offered me a lift home one day. I heralded the arrival of Mr Petrie, the burly, bristling Welshman charged with knocking mathematics into our recalcitrant skulls, with a ditty sung to the tune of the Hall and Oates' hit, 'Man Eater':

Woah-oh, here he comes
Watch out, boy, he'll teach you maths
Woah-oh, here he comes
He's a maths teacher

Mr Sibi-Okumu, a Kenyan actor and broadcaster of conspicuous talent and cultivation whom circumstance had obliged to become French master to wealthy brats, showed remarkable patience where I was concerned, but even he had his limits.

'Mr Bennun,' he would say, frowning, 'the French language contains no such phrase as *merde du boeuf*.'

My English teacher, a twitchy, thin-skinned Scots lass, was made of frailer stuff. Miss McCahill became convinced that I was the ringleader in a class plot against her. The idea that I might have held any sway over the bunch of reprobates in question was laughable; I was hateful towards her on my own initiative, and so were they. Between us, we drove her to the brink of nervous collapse.

Miss McCahill was devoted to horses, and finally snapped when I rhapsodised about the flavour and delicacy of finely sliced smoked Dutch horsemeat. Thereafter, she opened each lesson with the same words: 'Good morning, class. David, get out.'

So far removed was I from genuine delinquency that I spent my weekly exile working on set texts in the library, where I managed to aggravate the librarian into a running feud, which culminated in his confiscating my Sony Walkman. I wasn't bad, just obnoxious – and that was bad enough. My thoroughgoing charmlessness towards the faculty was reflected in the nickname conferred upon me by my biology teacher: 'Gollum'.

The Kenya Cowboys found this all very funny, but I didn't do it for their benefit. God knows why I did it. Most of the time I wished I could stop myself. I wanted to shut up and be good. Still, the fact that I entertained the KCs delivered me from my fated rank of egghead pariah.

My behaviour must have been an embarrassment to my mother, who in order to obtain reduced fees for my education had taken a job in a junior school run by the same company which operated Knollpeak. The headmaster, Mr Hendry, might have said more to her about me had he not had problems of his own.

Mr Hendry's daughter, Aralia, was a pert little baggage whose notable mammary endowment made her an object of lust among many of the younger male staff. Although trouble (like many of the younger male staff) followed Aralia around, it never quite caught up with her. The same couldn't be said of Mr Hendry's son, Tarquin. He was either more fractious or less canny than his sister. Either way, wherever he went, trouble had usually got there first. Hot water was Tarquin's natural element. He was a born scallywag, with a streak of devilment running through him like the stripes in a stick of rock. This made it very hard on poor Mr Hendry, whose attempts to enforce discipline were bound to be undermined by his own son's status as the most unruly child in the school. I suspect he saw more of Tarquin in his office, where the boy was dispatched on a daily and sometimes hourly basis by a succession of despairing teachers, than he did at home.

* * *

KNOLLPEAK SECONDARY is indelibly associated in my mind with school plays. I had persisted in volunteering for these at one school after another, but at Knollpeak, I really overdid it. I may have decided that I had a feeling for drama. I didn't. I must have believed that I was good at it. I wasn't. I was a show-off, which isn't the same thing.

By the time I finished my A-levels, I had participated in two *Macbeths*, *A Midsummer Night's Dream*, *Oh! What A Lovely War*, several works by thwarted dramatists among the teaching staff, and a musical about Admiral Nelson titled, if I remember rightly, *Horatio!*. I perished in the ranks of prepubescent armies. I danced with improbable clumsiness in a mass waltz, partnered – thanks to a benevolent director – by a remarkably pretty girl, whom I managed in my alarm to insult and alienate in short order. I joined choirs in which I was barred from singing, but allowed by kindly music teachers to stand and mime. I was the eternal extra and bit-part player, always auditioning for the lead role, never coming close to landing it – and never getting the message. I had no business trying to be a performer. I could not set the stage alight, although on one occasion I did burn a good-sized hole in my Pierrot costume by standing too close to a candle.

To understand why I kept on doing this, I can only go back a decade to St Michael's Kindergarten, where my earliest encounter with school drama instilled in me a love for the theatre which was to stay with me for at least seven or eight minutes. It was all very thrilling at first. I was five, and I sat with two dozen of my classmates as it was revealed to us that we were to stage a nativity play.

The way Mrs Flint told it, the world could wait no longer for St Michael's to replicate the glory of our Redeemer's birth. Mrs Flint was the head teacher. Her Dickensian sobriquet was certainly apt; she was a hard-tempered old crow. At the time, my literary grounding being on the meagre side, I thought of her more as a character from the Brothers Grimm – the kind whose liking for children expresses itself solely in terms of recipes.

Mrs Flint made an exception for the baby Jesus. Him, she was very fond of. The pupils at St Michael's belonged to many faiths. In addition to Christians, we had Hindus, Muslims, Sikhs, one or two Bahá'is, and my own family was Jewish. Some teachers, including my mother, made occasional and furtive efforts to tell their classes about Eid or Diwali. But Mrs Flint was not running a multi-denominational establishment here. The stance at most private schools in Kenya, was essentially this: if you wished to follow some risible and probably heathen creed, for no better reason than that your ancestors had done so for centuries, that was your look-out. Easter and Christmas, those were the festivals celebrated by St Michael's. Participation was obligatory. Maybe a bit of the Gospels would rub off on you and do you some good.

Another Nairobi head teacher had suspended from his junior school several Hindu pupils whose parents kept them at home during Diwali. The resulting row proved, in every sense, unholy. Eventually the government was obliged to intervene and explain to the principal that his actions were prohibited by law; at which point he backed down with an ill grace that could hardly be described as Christian.

At St Michael's I had already created a minor scandal among my peers a few days earlier, while we were decorating the classroom for Christmas, by announcing that I didn't believe in Jesus. Not because I was Jewish, but because I was as yet unaware that I was supposed to believe in anything.

'You'll go to hell if you don't believe in Jesus!' said one little girl, on the brink of tears. That struck me as unlikely. But she was so upset, I told her I hadn't really meant it. She accepted this as readily as she had accepted Christ and eternal damnation. She was a very trusting child. She's probably in a cult now.

Once Mrs Flint had instructed us to venerate Jesus via the magic of theatre, there were plum roles to be filled. 'David,' said my class teacher, Miss Woodrow, in the tone of one dispensing a munificent boon, 'how would you like to be Joseph?'

Mistaking this for a genuine question, I thought about it. I was familiar with the story of the nativity. Joseph featured in it a lot. Being Joseph would probably be difficult. 'Not very much,' I said.

'You won't be anything if you don't keep your mouth shut!' snapped Mrs Flint. I kept my mouth shut. The risk of hellfire may not have scared me, but Mrs Flint did.

Instead of Joseph, I became a Roman guard. So did my friend Mihir Chandaria. It was an object lesson in typecasting. For the next four years, at St Michael's Kindergarten and then at St Michael's Junior School, we would play Roman legionaries every Christmas. We stood at either post of the gate of Bethlehem – a structure conjured into solidity by our soldierly presence alone – then walked from side to side three times, like leisurely cricketers passing en route to the crease, and exchanged our two lines.

1ST SOLDIER: ''Tis a cold night.'

2ND SOLDIER: 'Yes.'

When we were eight, and Mihir had his leg in a plaster cast, we were still made to act as sentries. The scene took on an even odder, almost Beckett-like aspect when the holy family failed to show up on cue, leaving the two desperate sentinels whistling 'God Rest Ye Merry Gentlemen' in an ever-shifting blend of keys, as urgent whispers and vague bumping noises filtered out from the wings. I had never regretted so strongly turning down the part of Joseph.

* * *

WHEN, AT THE AGE OF 13, I reached Knollpeak Secondary, I was fed up with the entire business. So what was it that kept me in the cast of one production after another for the next five years? I think I relished the sense of conspiracy that surrounds even the most amateurish of theatre; the feeling that everyone involved is plotting some manner of trickery to which the rest of the world is not privy. It was a satisfying reversal of my more usual suspicion – that the rest of the world was up to something and I hadn't been told.

At 15, I took part in a production of *Macbeth,* which, on every night of its mercifully brief run, sank with all hands in a typhoon of mirth.

On the terraced slope that served as an outdoor stage, swords held in belts would jam point-first into the earth and crumple. Actors slipped on the grass, slick with rain or evening dew, and sledged on their tights towards the astonished and gleeful audience, who by now required either oxygen or hosing down. The cruel slaying by Macbeth of Macduff's family was met with an uproar bordering on hysteria, as was the murderer's own bloody demise and subsequent reappearance as a papier-mâché head.

I had been cast as Malcolm, or 'the fairy prince', as I disdainfully characterised the role. Bringing news to Macduff (played with a broad Cheshire accent by a boy from Macclesfield) of his family's demise, it was hard to keep a straight face when the front two rows were occupied by a party of cackling children bussed in from a nearby primary school for a bit of cultural improvement.

MACDUFF: 'What, all me pretty chickens and their dam
          At one fell swoop?'

ME (shrilly): 'Dispute it like a man!'

MACDUFF: 'Aye, I s'll do so – but first I moost feel it like a man.'

KIDS: 'Yahahahahahahahaha!'

ME (thinking): 'With the spotlight behind it, his nose looks really hairy. I wonder if he has to shave his nose?'

KIDS: 'Yeeheeheeyahaheeha!'

ME (thinking): 'Jesus, I hope I didn't say that out loud.'

For the roles of two noblemen who propel the narrative, our director, Mr Spencer, had settled upon inspired choices. The school's fattest boy, a hefty Kikuyu lad who resembled a roving solar eclipse, was cast opposite the thinnest, a sharp-cornered English fellow constructed from razor wire and pipe cleaners. Watching their scene from the wings, I could not stop myself from softly whistling the Laurel and Hardy theme tune, causing two witches to miss their cues and one more to collapse wheezing halfway through her entrance. I was not what you would call a born trouper.

On the last night, as Birnam Wood came to Dunsinane, the debacle rumbled to a halt and the lights, following the rest of the production, went down. In the brief silence before the applause, a clarion female voice in the front row declared, 'I'm not clapping that.' This, presumably, was the mother of one of the cast.

We took a little consolation in the *Macbeth* staged that same year by the Archeoptryx Players, who boasted of being the only professional theatre group in East Africa. In their interpretation, Banquo's ghost manifested itself at the banquet via a two-way mirror, while the three witches were evoked by a trio of light fittings salvaged from the cocktail lounge of a scrapped Greek cruise liner and lowered on strings from the flies. Our *Macbeth* wasn't quite that awful, but awful it assuredly was.

After a power failure at a crucial and climactic moment, our leading man escaped actual decapitation by milliseconds. Our director blamed the fiasco on the cast's disregard for the old superstition, that *Macbeth* should be referred to as 'the Scottish play'. But in truth, every one of our attempts at Shakespeare seemed cursed, and risible to boot. In *Romeo and Juliet*, Romeo's enemy, Paris, neglected to bring his sword to their fatal quarrel, obliging the pair to grapple like drunken stevedores until Romeo necessarily but rather unsportingly skewered his defenceless foe. Less heroic still was Romeo's stunt on the last night. Unnoticed, he contrived to smuggle a cantaloupe onstage – evidence of a singular talent for prestidigitation, if not for romantic tragedy – and dropped it on Juliet as he bent over her coffin. His own death scene was marred by a faint but persistent snuffling from the tomb behind him.

'Why did you drop a cantaloupe on her?' I asked him afterwards.

'I couldn't find a watermelon in time,' he replied, enigmatically.

I lost count of the unscripted appearances made by Winston, a mooching, lugubrious bassett hound who had identified Knollpeak Secondary as a more reliable source of foodstuffs than his own nearby home. Winston had a knack for shuffling into the action at precisely the wrong moment. There was no such thing as the right moment, admittedly, but he still timed his entrances for maximum bathos. Mid-hanging in *The Caucasian Chalk Circle*, he cocked a leg against the gallows – a touch Bertolt Brecht might have appreciated, but the director assuredly did not. He nonchalantly and inexplicably navigated the swirling waters of *The Tempest* in the middle of a shipwreck. His supreme moment in the spotlight took place during the anguished renunciation of Desdemona by Othello – a powerful scene which Winston nonetheless dominated with his forceful and unambiguous display of a hitherto closeted homosexual passion for our chemistry teacher's Jack Russell terrier, Hobart. Although little known, it stands as arguably the most sensational and unquestionably the most public outing in the history of the theatre.

* * *

IF ONLY I had said yes to the part of Joseph, I might have spared myself all of this. I might not have spent the remainder of my schooldays trying to make up for a stage debut as the second spear bearer. Failing that, having said no to Joseph, I should have said no to the rest of it, and concentrated on some more fulfilling pursuit. And almost any pursuit – a worm farm, or collecting beer mats – would have been more fulfilling. It was typical of me to exhibit sounder judgement at the age of five than at any time during the subsequent 12 years.

My adolescent off-hours would have been better filled the Kenya Cowboy way: getting pickled at the KC night spot of choice, the Sailing Club, on Nairobi Ddam. I did manage a fair bit of that, to the point of winding up in the back of somebody's pick-up with a Scandinavian diplomat's daughter, which makes me wish I had managed a whole lot more. I was too drunk to do anything sufficiently stupid to scare the girl off. I was, I thought, too drunk to do anything at all, although she later assured me I did.

You never, so the cliché runs, forget your first time. I forgot it while it was going on. I wouldn't have known it had happened if David Hewson hadn't told me about it the following Monday.

David Hewson stood five-foot-nothing in his sports socks (the only socks he ever wore) and, had you weighed him directly after lunch, might have topped the nine-stone mark. He was the toughest kid I have ever met. A natural-born rugby fly-half, he scored tries simply through never grasping where or when to stop. The only thing he grasped was the ball, and that he held on to as if it were stapled to his fingers. Disappearing beneath a mound of huge opposing forwards, who had dived upon him in the formation known as 'the Mongolian clusterfuck', he would emerge wriggling between the knees of some colossus, his eyes sealed shut with bruises and blood, greenstick fractures protruding from his limbs, and claw his way towards the posts, the ball still clutched to his remaining ribs.

Away from the playing field, David did not let up. He was the Napoleon Complex incarnate, a short man whose fuse was shorter still. This is not to say he was indiscriminately aggressive. He was amiable as you like towards me. To be well thought of by David Hewson could only enhance your standing in the Knollpeak hierarchy, so I was pleased when he ambled up to congratulate me on an evening well spent.

'You had a good time of it on Friday,' he said.

'Did I?' I said. 'I mean, yeah, I did.'

'Good thing I rocked up when I did,' said David. 'Those guys were about to give you a hammering.'

'What guys?'

'The ones who thought you were me.'

It was coming back to me now. Waiting at the Sailing Club's bar the previous Friday evening, I found myself surrounded by a gang of very angry-looking hardnuts. They had heard tell that some KC called David reckoned himself a scrapper. They intended to prove David wrong. I was ready to prove it myself, by running like a spooked spring hare, when the authentic David appeared and ushered them out of the club and into the car park, where he settled the matter to his satisfaction, if not theirs. That accounted for the splendid shiner he was flaunting this Monday morning.

'So I'm on my way back inside,' Hewson went on, leaning against my locker, 'to get some ice for the eye, and I spot you tuning that blondie by Huff's pick-up.'

Tuning, by the by, was a deliciously apt piece of slang for what the British call 'chatting up'.

'And then I'm on my way back out again, and you're in the pick-up with her and it's all going off.'

I had no idea what David Hewson was talking about. I remembered the girl, but not the event. I decided he too must have confused me with somebody else. Obviously, I didn't want to say so. My stock had shot up since Friday. I was no longer a pimply and peculiar virgin. Now I was just pimply and peculiar.

'Tell Huff thanks from me for using his pick-up,' I said, which seemed both non-committal and suitably rakish.

I spent many fruitless hours trying to coax that memory out of whichever ganglion conceals it. It seemed only fair that the key moments in my life should have been ones I was aware of. I've since realised that the reality must have been tawdry and disenchanting compared to the many ways I've imagined it. In 40 years' time, if I live that long, the choicest of those fantasies will have ingrained itself as memory. Even if I can't look back on it, it's something to look forward to.

chapter fourteen

The Coup

EARLY ONE Sunday in 1982, I was woken up by my stepmother pulling back the curtains in my bedroom to let the sunshine spill through the window. 'Good morning,' she trilled cheerily. 'It's eight o'clock, there's a coup going on, and there are scones for breakfast.'

My family liked to put light classical music on the stereo of a weekend morning. I was accustomed to padding into the lounge to the accompaniment of Vivaldi or Haydn or the cheerier bits of Beethoven. Today, a small shortwave radio was plugged in. 'Buffalo Soldier' by Bob Marley and the Wailers crackled through the single speaker. 'Buffalo Soldier' was one of four records owned by the radio arm of the VoK (Voice Of Kenya). On some days it might be broadcast a dozen times. The other three records were the Kenyan national anthem, *The Carpenters' Greatest Hits* and a children's song, which I assumed was titled 'Hymie the Laughing Hyaena'.

As the corporation's sole long player, the Carpenters album came in particularly handy. The DJ could drop the needle on it and vacate the studio to do whatever was more important than his job. Which, to a government employee, was anything at all. Only two things stopped Kenya's civil servants from being the most corrupt in Africa: the fierce competition for that title, and their almost superhuman lethargy. Graft probably sounded too much like hard work. To see a bureaucrat sitting behind his desk without his feet up on it made a story worth repeating at dinner.

Sometimes the DJ would give himself enough time to nip back and turn the record over, but often as not the hypnotic rhythm of the stylus bumping in the playout groove would be all that stood between the VoK and half an hour of dead air. In later years the DJ might have been able to pass this off as purist Chicago house music, but not in 1982. In 1982 it just went *bump-hssssh-bump-hssssh-bump*. Then, after a while, the national anthem would come on.

At frequent but irregular intervals, 'Hymie the Laughing Hyaena' put in an appearance. I took it from Hymie's voice that he was a failed cartoon character, now remembered only thanks to his theme tune's unlikely revival on an African radio station. Why the monopolistic VoK found it fitting to impose a singing hyaena on its captive audience was a mystery.

'Hymie' began with an overture of jaunty strings. Then a nasal strain with more than a hint of Woody Woodpecker piped up:

Ah'm Hahmie the Lahfing Hah-yeena
Ah'm lahfing all day lawng
Beecawse when ah take all mah troubles awah
Ah go singin' this ha-happy sawng

At this point a female trio reminiscent of the Andrews Sisters chimed in:

He's happy no matter what happens
He's singing his happy song
So when you get up in the mo-o-orning
Don't ever be whiny
But make life so shiny

HYMIE: *Lahk Hahmie the Lahfing Hah-yeena*
    Ah lahf and ah lahf and ah lahf some more

SISTERS: *He laughs and he laughs and he laughs, ha! ha!*

The song now dissolved into an disturbing finale of *ha-ha-haa*s more suggestive of Bedlam than of anything you might encounter on the Serengeti plains.

Since the days of my earliest recollection, this record had been on the airwaves, becoming scratchier and fuzzier with each passing year –

*Chhahm   Chhhhaahmhhhheee   chhhuuh   chhhlafhhhinhhh
chhahhchhyeeenhhhuuuh*

– until finally the words were gone altogether, although they were
chiselled into my memory as though by a master stonemason. I often
wondered what the pen-and-ink Hymie looked like. Many years later I
caught what might have been a fleeting glimpse of him on a cable TV
channel in the middle of the night. The cartoon ended the second I
switched it on. So perish all our efforts to recapture our childhoods.

The VoK was an odd institution. Its television arm screened such
titbits as British seventies sitcom *Mind Your Language*, chock-full of
imbecilic racial stereotypes, in what passed for its prime time schedule.
The only way to make sense of the VoK was to presume that every
decision there was taken instantly and at random. Even the
advertisements were confused, with jingles that mixed up English and
Swahili into a cheerful hybrid:

Sanyo eko juu (juu!)
Sanyo eko top
Sanyo have the one for you
Sanyo – top of the pop!

'Buffalo Soldier' was a relatively recent acquisition by the VoK.
Whether it took years of planning and rubber-stamping to procure a
fourth record, or whether somebody left it in the studio by mistake, I
can only guess. But on this Sunday morning, it was the music of choice
for the rebels. The national anthem was inappropriate under the
circumstances, and no doubt the Carpenters and Hymie were dismissed
as insufficiently stirring. Although had anyone asked me, I think I could
have made a case for the hyaena.

'Buffalo Soldier' had a nice martial tone to it, as befitted the members
of Kenya's air force who had staged the putsch and even now were
sitting in the radio station a little way down the road from our house,
playing it over and over again. Had it not been for announcements

between every broadcast, to the effect that the government had fallen, it would have been hard to tell that anything was amiss.

Until, that is, the machine-gun fire started up. We ate our scones in the sunshine on the patio and listened to what we would later discover was the army retaking the radio station. 'If it gets any closer,' said my father, 'get inside and duck.' It didn't, so we played cards and tuned in to the World Service. A contact in the fortified basement of Nairobi's US embassy – the same building which Muslim zealots would bomb in 1998, killing hundreds whose nearby workplaces were not so solidly defended – had telephoned the BBC in London. In this roundabout way, we kept track of what was going on. The VoK wasn't much help, even though the loyalist troops had by now recaptured it. 'Do not panic,' said a stern voice, making no mention of what it was we should refrain from panicking over. 'Do not,' it added forcefully, 'go running from here to there.'

This last bit of advice was being wantonly disregarded. On the Ngong road, a few hundred yards away across the fields and in plain sight of our verandah, a bewildered throng, shrugging and mumbling en masse, surged in the direction of the radio station and disappeared from view. More machine-gun fire stuttered from near the station. The crowd surged back again, much more quickly, but apparently unharmed.

* * *

FURTHER DOWN the road lived close friends of ours, whose house abutted the radio station itself.

Hans Glass was, and remains, an exceptional individual – a one-time schoolteacher and now a self-made millionaire businessman. A hard-bitten native of Namibia, he is the only white man I know or know of who speaks the dialect of the Kalahari bushmen. Or so he maintains – after all, he could be emitting a meaningless series of haphazard clicks. But the fact that he possesses proven fluency in every other language he has ever encountered makes his claim ring true.

During the late seventies, Hans ran a vast and prosperous ranching operation in northern Tanzania; so prosperous that a covetous member of the then socialist government appropriated it and had Hans detained without trial for the best part of a year. His wife eventually negotiated his release, on condition he leave Tanzania and abandon any claim to the business he had built – which, administered under those sound egalitarian principles which had transformed Tanzania from a land of bounteous natural wealth into an economic basket case, promptly went bust. It never for a minute occurred to the state-backed bandit that the secret to the farm's success lay not in its own existence, but in that of Hans.

Hans was undeterred. Reunited with his family, he celebrated by buying an entire mountain range in the south of Kenya. His ability to conduct the deal in immaculate Maasai helped smooth its path.

Hans's outstanding skill as a linguist stands in stark contrast to my own bumbling monoglotism. It is a source of shame to me that, out of laziness, I never bothered to acquire more than a smattering of Swahili. Language scholars have observed that, in English, words for foodstuffs – beef, pork, veal – can be traced back to French origins, while those for animals – cow, pig – find their etymological roots in Anglo-Saxon. This, it is thought, is because, following the Norman Conquest in the eleventh century, it was Anglo-Saxon serfs who raised the livestock, and their French masters who ate it.

The modern equivalent would be those anglophone Americans in strongly Hispanic areas, whose knowledge of Spanish is limited to Mexican menus. Or, for that matter, the likes of me – perfectly able to order a beer in Swahili, but incapable of carrying out a conversation.

My attitude was all too prevalent. Our local MP, a Kikuyu man, had died suddenly in the run-up to recent parliamentary elections. His widow, an Englishwoman, put herself forward in his place. The Kenyan electoral system, although by and large a closed shop, was in some ways a little too open. The idea of a secret ballot, for example, was decried as a colonial imposition. Instead, supporters lined up behind the nominees, all of whom had to claim membership of the same and indeed the only political party, Kanu. The candidate with the longest line was declared the winner.

Mrs MP's campaign was well under way before a rival candidate pointed out that electoral rules required proficiency in both of Kenya's national languages, English and Swahili. Mrs MP could barely instruct her servants to bring her a cup of tea. Upon being struck from the ballot, she tearfully appealed to President Daniel Arap Moi to exempt her from this condition. He, quite rightly, declined to do so. Mrs MP could not explain, even in English, why she deserved this advantage. Nor could she spell out what her potential constituents might gain by returning her to parliament. Perhaps she felt that her late husband's seat belonged in the family, like silverware or a carriage clock.

In Kenya, nepotism was an accepted fact of life. Wealth and privilege were rare and fiercely guarded. The gulf between the affluent and the poor in Africa was unignorable, even when, like me, you had a talent for ignorance. Our own employees were, by any Western standard, firmly in the category of have-nots. Yet simply by virtue of being employees, they were immeasurably better off than the destitute population of Nairobi's slums.

If, arriving from town at the Karen Roundabout, beside the *dukas*, you turned onto Dagoretti Road, and instead of making a right onto the street which led to our home, carried straight on to the north-west, within half a mile, you reached Dagoretti township itself. Nairobi had more than its share of pitiful, God-forsaken shanty towns, but Dagoretti was the most dismal of them all – a scattering of filthy hovels and lean-tos, through which trickled a putrid stream which served as both water supply and open sewer. The smell would have been insupportable had it not been blotted out by the reek from the slaughterhouse, where half a ton of animal skulls rotted against the outside wall in a flimsy wooden cage. No people could be more deprived than the denizens of Dagoretti and live, which was not something anyone in Dagoretti was likely to do for very long.

Our *shamba* man Robert was appalled by Dagoretti. My father had once taken both Robert and myself along while test-driving one of the motorised wrecks he was forever fixing up. The engine cut out in the middle of Dagoretti. There could not have been a worse place for this. There could not have been a worse place, period. To pass through Dagoretti was enough to fill anyone with horror and pity. To get stuck in it was more than enough to fill Robert with dread. He became twitchier with every sluggish turn of the starter motor.

My father tried to reassure him. '*Pole pole* [take it easy], Robert,' he said. 'I told Lesley to come and fetch us if we weren't back in twenty minutes. We just have to stay in the car. We've got no money, no watches, nothing to steal.'

'You do not understand,' muttered Robert. 'In Dagoretti, if you have nothing, they take your head.'

In the event, the car restarted and we drove away. No sooner did you follow the bend which hid Dagoretti from sight behind a line of trees than you were back on a dappled, gracious avenue, with horses trotting by the roadside and estate cars trundling by, their back seats filled with groceries from the *dukas*. It was easy to forget the fetid desperation that lay such a short distance away. So I did.

Hans Glass, however, did not. He knew how dangerous people can be when they have nothing to lose. He believed firmly that his family's home was its castle, and this almost literally became the case. He surrounded the compound with high fences, backed by thorny hedges, and staffed the grounds with Maasai warrior *askaris* from his private mountain range, fiercely loyal watchmen armed with bows and arrows. Their instructions were to shoot first and ask questions later, with a bounty of five pounds per skewered intruder.

But not on the Sunday of the coup. On this particular Sunday the *askaris* were, very sensibly, indoors. Along with the rest of the household, they were crouching below the window sills, when a crew of barflies who had drunk the night away in an adjacent watering hole vaulted the fence in pursuit of sanctuary, a triumph of adrenalin over alcohol.

Hans was away on business that weekend, but he had instilled in his sons with his own watchful philosophy. The eldest boy present, Karl, a spirited fellow of 16, leapt to his feet and marched into the garden.

'Hey, you!' he bellowed, above the crack and whine of stray bullets. 'You can't come in here.' Karl was a strapping lad, and you wouldn't want to argue with him. Some of the drunks were scrabbling back up the spiky hedge when a fresh flurry of concentrated gunfire rattled out from the radio station a few yards away. Karl's mother raced out, gripped his earlobe and dragged him back into the house, Karl still issuing thunderous threats. The lushes, acting on the horizontal impulse of boozers everywhere, hit the deck.

* * *

COME MID-AFTERNOON, the World Service informed us that the government were gaining the upper hand. So, in its singular way, did the VoK: 'Everything is within control. Do not go running from here to there.' Then it played 'Buffalo Soldier' again – although a more calming choice such as 'Goodbye To Love' might have been welcome – followed by the national anthem.

The Kenyan national anthem has a tune of nursery rhyme simplicity. It puts one in mind of 'Three Blind Mice' as arranged for a military funeral and introduced by a drum roll at which, by habit become instinct, we always stood to attention. This was required by law. All public performances – plays, films and so forth – were preceded by the national anthem. Failing to show suitable respect and awe caused far more trouble than it was worth. Anyway, it was an appropriate response to a melody of such Stalinist severity.

The gunfire was more intermittent now. We put away the cards and unfolded the ping-pong table, our game interrupted only by our Pavlovian habit of stiffening, frozen, every few minutes as the national anthem struck up yet again and the ball bounced unheeded into the flowerbeds.

'Forces loyal to President Daniel Arap Moi have thwarted an attempt by air-force officers based in Nanyuki to overthrow the government of Kenya,' announced the World Service. So that was that. It was good news for us. The status quo suited us: a new, military government would bring uncertainty and the prospect of violence.

Moi was at that time not long in office; the successor to Mzee Jomo Kenyatta, father of the nation, he was only the country's second president since independence in 1963. Leader of the single legal party, and unopposed at every election, he represented the stability and economic equilibrium that Kenya alone enjoyed in East Africa. Twenty years after the coup attempt, his rule was at last forced to an end. The stability and economic equilibrium were long gone. He seemed, in 1982, something of a benevolent despot. There is, of course no such thing.

In hospitals on the other side of town lay the bodies of Asian children no older than I was. They had been battered to death by mobs which smashed down the doors of their homes, and looted their families' shops. Students who had supported and perhaps even fomented the failed takeover rioted. Dozens of them died.

When the late afternoon cool began to spread across the ground, we packed up the ping- pong table. Everything was quiet, apart from the distant sound of radios alternating 'Buffalo Soldier' with the national anthem. Lesley and I walked along the hedge driveway, and picked the tart fruit for my stepmother to make into jelly. The process took about a week, straining the boiled pulp through a pair of old tights stretched across a metal pan, then pouring it into jars and leaving it to set. It went very well with pork.

chapter fifteen

The Mighty Leopards and Joe the Dentist

AFTER I went to live with my father and stepmother, my mother moved to a handsome two-storey house not far from Lavington Green, a shopping centre that uncannily evoked the Arcadian village England of a Powell and Pressburger film. It would have been much more comfortable for her if she had gone straight from the house in Langata to this pleasant new home. But in between, she had taken up residence in a gloomy and rather weird little bungalow, which she shared for a time with a gloomy and rather weird little Russian woman.

Nataliya turned up on my mother's doorstep one morning with a suitcase and a Soviet-issue washing machine – a Zilch or Kaput, or some such brand. How Nataliya had found my mother is something my mother was always vague about. The two were strangers until that day. Having lost her own digs, and being understandably reluctant to return to her motherland, Nataliya had come to the right place. My mother's generosity was already presumed upon by everyone she knew. Now people she'd never heard of were getting in on the act.

Nataliya turned out to be quite entertaining, in a mordant way. Like many of her countryfolk, she relied on humour as the final bastion against despair. She was full of stories about the impossibility of life in the USSR. Some of these were liable to cause offence, a fact of which she remained altogether insensible. Nataliya was thick-skinned. You could have run her through her own primitive Dregz or Slopp laundry drum and she would have emerged uncrumpled and ready to drip-dry. If, that is, you could find a socket adaptor to fit the thing. The plug alone weighed two pounds and featured prongs recycled from a rusty pitchfork.

'So a bunch of Jews got on Aeroflot flight from Moscow to Kiev,' Nataliya would recount, unaware or unconcerned that her audience also comprised a bunch of Jews. 'It is their plan to hijack plane to Israel. But security officer at airport is suspect. He calls his chief, saying, "Do you know everyone on this flight is a Jew?" "So what?" says the chief. "Who else can afford to fly to Kiev?". . .' And so on, late into the night.

Nataliya stayed and stayed and stayed. She was eventually dislodged only when my mother moved house. She may have been the reason my mother moved house. My mother very likely found it easier to pack up and leave than to ask Nataliya to do the same. She was compelled to do something entirely alien to her. She lied. She told Nataliya that she was going to a much smaller home.

'It's only a maisonette,' said my mother.

'In Russia,' said Nataliya, in her now familiar tone, which contrived to be both expectant and glum, 'whole family lives in maisonette. If they are lucky.'

'Not here,' said my mother, with uncommon resolve.

Once she realised that she would not be a component of my mother's next household, Nataliya stoically refilled her suitcase and offered my mother fulsome and no doubt genuine thanks and protestations of eternal fellowship. Then, as a token of her gratitude, Nataliya presented my mother with the absurd and worthless washing machine – the Satanik or Krankk, or whatever it was called.

'I don't know what to say,' my mother told Nataliya. It's not every day you receive half a ton of scrap iron where a bunch of flowers might have sufficed.

* * *

MY MOTHER'S new house stood two minutes' drive from Lavington, along a street lined with jacaranda and frangipani trees. When the rains came, the branches would blossom with purple and succulent white flowers, which soon covered the ground, turning the roadside into a kaleidoscopic mélange of petals, perfume and mud.

The house was narrow and tall, looking on to a half-acre garden at the back. A patio led on to a small, rectangular goldfish pool, and beyond that lay the lawn and a few flowerbeds. These were the domain of an unnamed tortoise and a woman known only as Mama, who came by two afternoons a week to tend the plot. Mama determined that the garden wasn't big enough for both herself and the tortoise, to which she bore an odd likeness. Mama might have been 40, or she might have been 80. She was four foot high, and roughly the same length from nose to stern. Her head jutted forward and slightly down from her disfigured shoulders and back, hunched into a parabola from years spent lugging bundles of firewood.

Because Mama so strongly took after a storybook crone, my benevolent mother automatically concluded that her character belied her appearance. It did not. Mama was a conniving old hag, who took full advantage of my mother's kind heart.

Mama's misconduct began with the tortoise. This blameless reptile slept most of the time, emerging from its shell only to munch upon the occasional bit of greenery. On the days Mama was in attendance, the tortoise would often be discovered outside the gate – having, if Mama was to be believed, made a dash for it while her back was turned. Each time, we had to retrieve the tortoise from further and further away. That tortoise would have required the legendary sprinting prowess of Harold Abrahams, 1924 Olympic gold medallist and subject of the film *Chariots of Fire*, to have legged it, unaided, so far so fast. What puzzled me was, if the tortoise could self-evidently not move so swiftly, how did Mama manage it? In terms of athleticism, there wasn't much between them.

'You know,' I said to my mother, 'it's either going to be Mama or the tortoise. I know you feel sorry for her, but I think you're better off with the tortoise.'

'She's just frightened of it,' said my mother. I doubted that. Mama wasn't too frightened of the tortoise to carry it away and dump it in the street every time she came by. Mama was frightened of nothing. Fear would have been frightened of Mama.

Exactly what Mama was doing with her time apart from tortoise abduction – Lord knows what happened to the creature in the end, but Mama got rid of it somehow – it was hard to work out. Mama always looked busy. Yet the uncut grass grew ragged. The weeds usurped the flowerbeds. The small vegetable patch near the scullery door went emphatically to seed. My mother began to do her own gardening, at weekends.

'Then why are you keeping Mama on?' asked my brother.

'She needs the money,' said my mother, struggling to uproot a gargantuan, baleful and particularly tenacious weed which, unchecked, all but irreversibly entangled itself around her rose bushes. At night, you would swear you could hear this affront to botany snickering to itself in the herbaceous border.

'Mama's had a hard life,' my mother said.

'And now it's your turn,' said my brother.

Early one evening I knocked a ball into the garden's furthest corner and went to retrieve it. There I discovered what had been occupying Mama's working hours. Behind a clutter of overgrown shrubbery were laid out three neat rows of greenery. Long, pointed leaves fanned out symmetrically from the stalks. Mama had turned my mother's backyard into her own little dope plantation. You couldn't fault her for enterprise.

This was too much even for my mother's forgiving nature. She dismissed Mama, who protested that she had never before seen the *bhangi*, and that it must have sprouted from accidentally discarded seeds. My mother, being my mother, might have given her the benefit of the doubt had the bushes not been so immaculately arranged and tended. Mama had to go.

We now faced the problem of what to do with the marijuana. We had to get rid of it fast. I worried that Mama would exact vengeance by heading straight to the nearest police station and pinning her own crime on my mother. She had shown herself to be no less ruthless with the tortoise, which I guessed had been nibbling at her harvest. That would have explained both Mama's animosity towards the creature, and the fact that it was markedly somnolent, slow and partial to its lettuce – attributes which, in a tortoise, have to be strongly pronounced before they become striking.

When the authorities uncovered a *bhangi* farm, the plants would be uprooted and heaped into a pile seven or eight feet high. Then, as senior policemen, district commissioners, MPs and any other dignitaries who fancied a photo opportunity stood solemnly around it, the marijuana would be set alight. The assembled panjandrums remained fixed in place, swaying slightly, until they were satisfied that the entire mound had burned itself out. By this time they were less solemn. Generally, they were giggling and pushing each other over. But these were not the images which appeared the following day in the ruling party mouthpiece, the *Kenya Times* – if for no other reason than that the photographer could no longer recall which button operated the shutter. Afterwards, everybody wandered off for a snack.

Burning the plants was not an option for us. A column of smoke rising from the garden and blanketing the entire neighbourhood in a haze of odorous and soporific goodwill would have been sure to attract attention, in addition to grounding all the local birdlife.

'You could always sell it,' said my brother, unhelpfully. 'Just take it down to Kariabangi.'

Kariabangi was the district where Kenya Cowboys went to buy large bags of pot at knock-down prices. The ready-rolled spliffs touted on city centre streets were scornfully regarded as tourist fodder. Without question Kariabangi was where Mama's produce had been bound. A popular joke at my school ran:

'Knock-knock.'

'Who's there?'

'Kariabangi.

'Kariabangi who?'

'Kariabangi with caution or you might get arrested.'

Plenty of Knollpeak Secondary students had tried marijuana, and many were regular smokers. Our headmaster, Mr Hendry, had issued grim warnings in assembly about the drug acting as a gateway to stronger stuff, which nobody took very seriously. For a start, it was hard to imagine that there *was* any stronger stuff than the powerful Kariabangi weed, which mimicked the sensation of being pinned to the ground with croquet hoops while determined gnomes pushed an entire duck-feather duvet into your brainpan one inch at a time.

We dug up the marijuana bushes and buried them where they had grown. That patch of ground may even now be home to Africa's hungriest and idlest earthworms.

* * *

THE CHILDREN of divorced parents are said to find it confusing and traumatic to switch constantly between households. Maybe because I had the emotional depth and sensitivity of a potted cactus, I was perfectly content at either place. I was happy anywhere that I could sit and read or listen to music undisturbed. That neither of my parents were in town for two successive birthdays – my fourteenth and fifteenth – should, supposedly have me sobbing on a therapist's couch today. In fact, I stayed over at a friend's house, had a fine time, and forgot about the birthday business altogether. The only damaging consequence has been an inability to remember birthdays. Any birthdays. Mine, for instance. And worse – much worse – my girlfriend's.

Many teenagers feel that their life is a battle, that they are being hounded and persecuted. So did I. I happened to be right. The danger to my psyche did not lie in parental neglect or indifference, of which my mother and father were never guilty. It lay in my schoolmates, and even then it could not be considered nearly as grave as the danger to my person.

I looked forward to staying with my mother, but I dreaded the ordeal of taking the school bus to her house. The first problem was finding the right bus. There were three, but the drivers alternated the routes between themselves, and delighted in feeding me misinformation. None of the regulars appeared to have this problem, so one solution was to hang back and see who boarded which bus. But I preferred to get on early and bag a seat near the front. The further back I sat, the less likely it was that I would make it off the bus at all. Almost everybody else rode the bus past Lavington and on to Westlands, where their parents would collect them. But because the route went directly past my mother's house, I got off at the nearest junction – a crossroads controlled by a stop sign.

It became a sport among my fellow travellers to prevent me from leaving the bus. I had an interval of about 12 seconds in which to bolt from my seat to the front door. I could have got up earlier, but standing at the front of the bus made me the ideal stationary target for a posse of rubber-band marksmen. These sadists could shoot wadded paper ammunition with the unerring accuracy and reload capacity of SWAT team snipers ranged out across a tenement roof. They fired at me anyway, as I ran along the aisle, but my movement reduced their hit-rate to a mere 60 or 70 per cent; the rest of their ammunition pinged against the windows or rebounded off the heads and napes of other hapless passengers.

As I lunged for the door, feet would appear from every row of seats attempting to trip me or kick me in the shins. Behind me, hands seized my collar and the straps of my satchel. Ahead of me, voices urged the driver not to tarry, but to keep going straight across the junction. I resembled an ill-designed character from a video game, lashing out wildly at attackers while hurdling obstacles and yelling at the driver to wait, goddammit. There was not a kid on that bus who didn't want to see me forced to make the hilly two-mile walk home from Westlands. I was equally determined that this should not happen, even if it meant dragging my assailants off the bus with me, clinging to my rucksack, in a hail of pellets and abuse.

My mother wondered why I invariably stumbled, panting, bruised and dishevelled, through the door, collapsed in a chair and, wincing, spent the next ten minutes massaging my ankles and my upper arms.

'Is there a problem?' she would ask.

'Ah no, no problem,' I would say, maintaining the code of the schoolyard.

The other kids didn't pick on me because they hated me. Most of them had no feelings of any description towards me. They picked on me because I was there. If they'd known how much it upset me, they would have behaved differently. They'd have sought me out in school hours and made my life hell then too.

Instinctively, I knew not to react any more than was physically necessary to get off the bus. This may have been a misjudgement, as I found out, by accident.

One boy, hanging on to my backpack as I fought my way past his seat, broke the strap. The next day I went up to him and told him that he should pay to replace it.

'I'm not going to pay for it,' he said.

'Why not?' I said. 'You're the one who broke it.'

'It's only ten or fifteen bob.'

'So what? You broke it, you can pay for it.'

'Hey,' he grinned, 'you're a real Jew, aren't you?'

I pushed him against his locker. 'I don't fight with people,' I told him, which was true. I particularly didn't fight with people like him: wiry bruisers who would have kicked my cowardly keister from one end of the school to the other. 'But if you say that to me again, I'll knock your fucking head off.'

'Whoah, OK, all right,' he said. Whatever it was that he saw on my face had unnerved him. 'Take it easy. What's his problem?' he appealed to his friends, who were looking on. 'I only said he was a real Jew.' They shook their heads, unable to account for my fury.

* * *

CURIOUSLY, that brief bout of nonchalant anti-Semitism did me a favour. From then on, I was left alone. Word got around that Bennun was some kind of psycho. He didn't respond to ordinary taunts and torments, but then some harmless, chance remark – such as calling him a 'real Jew' – would set him off. Go figure. Still, nobody wanted to take the risk.

It was a useful reputation to have, because unless incensed to the point of blind rage, even the most basic self-defence was beyond my mastery. I had gone to a judo class when I was ten, but it consisted of rolling around on mats, so I never went back. Any difficulties I had with bullies were unlikely to be settled by my producing a mat and performing a somersault on it. Running away, on the other hand, worked nine times out of ten, and required no special training. I already knew how to run away. I was very good at it.

My father encouraged me to play rugby. Or rather, as rugby was compulsory, refused to help me get out of it.

'It builds character,' he said. This was true. Specifically, it built character in other boys who learned how to trample over feeble and defenceless opponents like me. I was always stationed at fullback, as this reduced my participation in the game to a minimum, something that suited myself, my PE teacher and my team more or less equally. It also meant that I constituted the last line of defence. When an opposing winger broke free and sprinted up the field, he would pass by me as if I were a waxwork mounted on a slowly rotating pedestal.

'Why didn't you do anything?' my team-mates would angrily demand.

'I don't know,' I would lie. I couldn't give the honest answer: 'It might hurt.'

Weary of the insults and contempt directed at me every time my side conceded a try, I developed a new technique. I pursued my adversary with loping strides, making a great show of straining to catch him, then launched myself into a lunging tackle in which my clutching arms closed on the air inches behind his boots. I would judge my landing so that I sprawled upon the softest and greenest patch of ground available, then watch my quarry place the ball between the goalposts, my features carefully set into an expression of exhausted but virtuous disappointment.

Mr Llewellyn, the PE teacher, was delighted with this improvement. 'Look at Bennun,' he would tell the other pupils. 'He's not the best rugby player in the world, but at least he really tries.'

I certainly did. It took a fair bit of effort to run that slowly while appearing to give it all I had. I was a decent mover, having developed both speed and endurance in my long experience of running away from things.

After rugby term would come cricket term. I was dreadful at cricket too. This might well have been down to ineptitude, but I never became interested enough to find out. You couldn't hope to invent a duller sport than cricket. Not without nodding off halfway through. Of course, you wouldn't have to invent one, as golf already exists. But well equipped as my schools were, none of them had a golf course. On the only occasion I attempted golf, at a hotel near Nanyuki where my mother was attending a Scottish country-dancing weekend, I brained a playmate on my back swing, dropping him like a bag of fertiliser slung from a tractor. Flat on his back, he howled in agony and indignation. His mother came over to see what the matter was.

'I'm sorry,' I said, miserably, as children do when they find themselves in trouble. And as with most children, the person I was sorry for was me.

'Oh, it's his fault,' she said, and briskly rubbed at her keening progeny's forehead, where a plump goose egg had already begun to sprout. 'He shouldn't have been standing so close. He does things like this all the time.'

Fielding at cricket, I was dispatched to the boundary, where I lay down and went to sleep. For this I was given detention, and a job as scorer. My debut effort, recording a First XI match against a boarding-school team that had travelled 100 miles for the event, plumbed new lows of legibility. I was summoned to the deputy head's office and told that my slapdash scrawl was quite possibly the least decipherable form of human communication since the discovery of the Rosetta Stone unravelled the mystery of Egyptian hieroglyphics. Amazingly, I was not sacked. Faced with the alternative of actually having to play the game, I became a punctilious cricket scorer. It was boring, but the likelihood of being hit by the ball was almost nil.

* * *

CRICKET TERM gave way to hockey term. Hockey was fun, for a while. The pleasure I took in hockey was doomed, but at first I seemed to be on to a winner.

'My God,' said Mr Llewellyn. 'You're actually good at this.'

I was. I could run, dribble, win tackles, even score the occasional goal – although that was the easy bit. Invariably, the goalkeeper was a milquetoast who (just as I was positioned at fullback in rugby) had been put there to keep him as far away from the action as possible. By the time you scrapped your way past the defenders, the goalie would be cowering with his stick held in front of his face, while trying to shield his entire body behind pads intended to reach no higher than his knees. When you sent the ball in one direction, he emitted a terrified squeak and dived in the other.

Hockey was a satisfying game. The crack of the curved stick against the ball gave me the same tingle that leather on willow reportedly does for a cricket buff. Hockey looked dangerous, but if you played it well, you were unlikely to get hurt. Unless – as I found to my cost – you played it against girls. Just when I felt I had found ways to survive my bus rides, playground affrays and sports lessons, the girls' First XI all but did me in.

The girls' team had a difficult match scheduled against Loreto Convent, so the second-string boys were drafted in to give them a practice game. If the convent girls were regarded as a tough side, I can only be grateful that I didn't have to play them instead.

'Go easy on them,' said Mr Llewellyn. He was talking to the wrong team. From the instant the whistle sounded, the girls took the game to us. They didn't bother with such trivialities as outplaying us, tackling us or passing the ball. They scarcely touched the ball at all, except as an afterthought. They simply hit us with their sticks until we fell over. Then they took the ball away. When confronted in possession, they let the ball roll to a halt, waited until they could see the whites of your eyes, then resumed the hitting-with-sticks tactic. If one of the boys scooped the ball away while this was going on, another girl would be poised to hit him with a stick too, until he thought better of it. They knew all about teamwork.

All but the bravest or most stupid of the boys quickly sized up the situation. If we played the ball, we would be hit with sticks. If we left the ball alone, we would still be hit with sticks, but not quite so much, so hard or so often. As for the bravest and most stupid – or maybe those affected by a hitherto unsuspected case of analgesia – the girls had another manoeuvre for dealing with them. They hit the ball directly at the face of any boy reckless enough to maintain a challenge on them.

By half-time, I was filled with nostalgic longing for those amicable, gentlemanly rugby matches I had so recently shuddered at. Even the despised 'British Bulldogs' was a Mardi Gras by comparison. British Bulldogs began with a solitary boy facing down the rest of his male classmates as they stampeded across the playing field. The object was to tackle the runners, who then had to join the tacklers on the next run, and so on. Guess who was chosen to be the initial tackler seven times out of ten.

I would have taken a term's worth of British Bulldogs in exchange for being excused the second half of that hockey match. Mr Llewellyn, as referee, had until now been too embarrassed to punish the girls for their blatant fouling. When our centre-forward went down to a stick in the face from the girls' inside-left, even Mr Llewellyn could not ignore it. He blew his whistle and called play back to the spot.

'Come on!' he hissed at us boys. 'Stand up for yourselves.' He blew for the restart and turned in the direction of play, missing the sight of the girls' inside-left stepping up to our free ball and belting it. The ball flew up like a rifle shot and thumped him in the small of the back. Grimacing with pain, he was forced to substitute himself. The girls' PE teacher, Mrs Gordon, took over. 'Play on!' she sang out merrily at every hack, gouge and shunt. 'Oh, get up, David. It's only your knee.'

The girls scored nine goals against us. We nicked one: the ball trickled between the posts while their fullback was busy fouling our winger. It was a rout, a massacre, a pounding. I felt dreadful. It wasn't the humiliation of being defeated by girls that smarted. It was my legs. And my left elbow. My collarbone, my ribs and my coccyx. And most of all, my groin, which seconds before the final and blessed whistle had absorbed the full force of a point-blank slug launched with pitiless accuracy by the opposing centre-half.

* * *

MOST OF THE THINGS I liked about playing hockey – until that painful afternoon – are the things I now like about watching football: the combination of excitement, pace, precision, reading the ball, split-second timing and ever-unfurling complexity. A great field sport is chaos theory in action; each event brings about a multitude of other possible events, only one of which will come to pass. The hockey game against the girls was chaos in action, with no theoretical aspects whatsoever – unless you categorise as a theory the belief that repeatedly and ferociously knocking about the competition will result in their submission and your victory.

I wish I had played football. During my days at the Nyumba, it was tacitly implied that football was for oiks. There was no team, no coaching, no acknowledgement of the game's existence. When the school day was over, I might have a kickabout with friends near the car park while we waited to be collected. That was as far as it went. I don't wish to suggest that football was robbed of a nascent talent. I would have been a God awful footballer. My not playing football deprived nobody but me, and me of nothing more than the joy of the game.

Knollpeak Secondary had little of the Nyumba's toffee-nosed attitude, but still football was off the curriculum. Instead I pursued the more genteel sport of tennis, which I became reasonably good at, and which, to my relief, kept me away from the rugby pitch most afternoons. I was as inefficient a percentage player as the tennis court has known, always going for the killer ball. It was my father who taught me that patience and consistency would not only win me more matches, but also allow me to set up more of the spectacular shots I so enjoyed.

'Play with *chochmas*,' he repeated, invoking the Yiddish word for wisdom. Like most things, it sounded better in Yiddish. I played with *chochmas* and my game improved enormously. We often played on the school courts at weekends. My father offered me 100 shillings if I beat him. I never did.

At tennis, I could give a decent account of myself against my peers. It was a new and enjoyable feeling. Here was something I could do, and do well, and even win at, without being beaten up by girls. The only player I had no hope of defeating was a boy called Paul Wekesa, already well on his way to becoming an international pro. His languid style of play looked downright insolent whenever he took me down love-and-love. Sometimes he would put his hand into his pocket to retrieve a tennis ball, and leave it there for the rest of the match, removing it only to toss up for service. 'Bennun,' he would say when it was over, 'you are a withered flower.' He said it to everybody. It was his favourite insult. I don't know where he got it from, but I had to admit, it was a good one.

I once took three games off Paul in a single set. I didn't win them. He agreed to adjust the scoreline afterwards in exchange for half of my lunchtime apple.

At Knollpeak, I became fitter than I have ever been before or since. The boys underwent double training sessions at least twice a week. 'It really works,' said my sister, who seemed to have been paying close attention. 'After a few weeks, you can see the muscles developing in their backs.'

I couldn't play football, but I could still watch it. The first team I supported was Manchester United – although 'supported' may be too strong a word. Back in Wamagata Road, when I was seven my English friend Alan Forrest had owned a table football game. He always insisted that the little red men on spindles should be his to rotate against the little blue men, 'Because they're Manchester United, the greatest team in the world.' I had never heard of Manchester, let alone United, but impressionable as always, I agreed, and vowed they would be my favourites too. United are widely mocked for the southern origins of their fan base. By skewing the curve some 4,000 miles south of Old Trafford, I can hardly have helped.

For a team I could follow at slightly closer range, I adopted Abaluhya FC. Kenyan football sides were drawn up on lines either tribal or occupational. Kenya Breweries, for instance, had a squad in the first division. They didn't win much, although that may have had something to do with the half-time refreshments.

The league was dominated by Abaluhya and, to a lesser extent, Gor Mahia; one or the other could be guaranteed to hold off Feisal, Maragoli, Kisumu Hotstars and Liverpool. Adopting illustrious foreign names was a Kenyan practice so routine that after a while it ceased to be noticeable. In Nairobi, one could shop at Tesco, Woolworths or Marks & Spencer (the last being a grimy haberdasher's parlour in a litter-strewn side street), and stop in for a burger at McDonald's afterwards. As for Likoni's Hilton Hotel, I'm almost certain it did not bear Conrad's imprimatur. It was a six-foot square grogshop, topped off with corrugated iron, which catered to foot passengers on the nearby ferry route and bore its name in proud red letters slathered with more boldness than symmetry onto its clapboard wall. In fairness, I never went inside. The interior may have been much plusher.

Abaluhya were a wonderful team. They had spirit. They had commitment. I – in 1979, the year they first won the East and Central Africa Club Cup, the roster of bones broken in tackles included the left- back's leg and the goalkeeper's arm. And they had flair, embodied in their star centre forward, Joe 'JJ' Masiga, the footballing dentist. Masiga it was Masiga who in that same year scored the winning goal against Ghana's Black Stars, the African national champions, in a club-versus-country triumph.

The next year, in keeping with a sports council directive that team names with tribal associations were no longer acceptable, Abaluyha became AFC Leopards. With Masiga at their helm, the mighty Leopards kept on winning. From 1982 they took the East African Cup for three years running, pausing only to defeat the English visitors of Norwich City 1–0. Joe Masiga, DDS, slotted in that goal as well. Whether it was a cavity or the back of the net, the man never missed.

AFC Leopards were as thrilling a side as ever took to the pitch, and they dominated East African football in the eighties. That Kenyan players were an excitable bunch was attested to in one memorable Leopards match, with the opposing goalkeeper being handcuffed and dragged away to jail by police. And the players had nothing on the fans. To them, a good game was incomplete until it was capped with an exuberant bit of rioting.

Moi International Sports Centre, with a capacity of 60,000, might have been designed specifically to promote public disorder – which is odd, as it was built by the Chinese government, who know a thing or two about crowd control. The arena's over-generous tally of entrances made it impossible to regulate the flow of spectators. The pitch too was furnished with so many points of access that attempting to defend it from invasion was pointless. Referees were regularly stretchered off it when supporters begged to differ over a decision. Or when somebody scored. Or when somebody didn't.

My mother barred me from going to matches at Moi, and with good reason. I went anyway, throughout my mid-teens, until the Cup Final day when I found myself in the thick of a ticketless rabble baying for admission. The crowd surged at an opening manned only by one nervous young policeman. He retreated until his shoulders touched the gate, then ineffectually swept his truncheon back and forth in an arc before him. 'Please stand back,' he quavered. 'The doors are not yet open. Tickets are still available for purchase at . . .'

A ten-year-old boy darted out of the crowd, leapt up and stole his hat. 'Ayayayay!' yelped the indignant copper, and lashed out at the grinning prankster with the truncheon. He was instantly engulfed by the mob. I last saw him, stripped to his underwear, boots and a few ragged strips of uniform, gibbering with rage and fear as he was carried above the heads of the throng sweeping inexorably through the gate. He was lucky. If they hadn't picked him up, he would have been trampled to pudding.

I was lucky, too. I managed to wriggle away from the swarming supporters and flee. It had been a while since my aptitude for running away was put to the test. I was pleased to discover that it was as keen as ever. Some things you never lose. Like gutlessness.

chapter sixteen

Twinkletoes the Rat

IN 1983, WHEN I was 15, my father bought a house in Karen, an affluent, sylvan quarter on the edge of Nairobi. For the first time, Leon, Lesley and I would be able to sleep under the same roof without anyone having to share a room. It's hard to say who was most relieved about this, but I'm guessing it would have been my father. One less excuse for bickering meant money well spent.

I never found moving house to be a wrench, emotionally. But I did think it was hard work, to which I had a strong aversion. My stepmother had to visit my room and glower at me repeatedly before I got my packing done. As the hour of the move approached, she delegated this task to my father.

'Aren't you packed yet?' he growled.

'Huh?' I said, unplugging a headphone from my ear. 'Almost done.'

My cupboards and drawers appeared to have come under the type of concerted grenade attack once favoured by the Vietcong. Very little of what had been blown out of them had landed in the waiting boxes.

'You've got thirty minutes,' said my father. 'Whatever's left, we're leaving behind.'

I weighed up the options – half an hour's labour versus losing most of my possessions – and unwillingly settled upon the first.

Karen takes its name from its celebrated former resident, Karen Blixen. Blixen, who in 1937 wrote *Out of Africa*, is now thought of as the exemplar of the Kenyan colonial. This wasn't the case in her own time. Born Isak Dinesen in Denmark, she was looked upon by her

English neighbours as a Bohemian fruitcake of dubious virtue. They weren't necessarily wrong, but this was rich coming from a social caste that included the notorious 'Happy Valley' clique of murderous, bed-hopping wastrels.

Blixen's lover, the bushwhacker-cum-playboy Denys Finch Hatton, may be considered the original Kenya Cowboy, both in his life and in the manner of his leaving it. It was difficult to attain lethal speeds in the automobiles of 1931, so Finch Hatton was obliged to finish himself off in a biplane. Those who have seen Sidney Pollack's film of *Out of Africa* will recall Finch Hatton as a charmingly rugged roué, flaxen of hair, square of jaw, crinkled of smile and twinkling of eye. That's because they're thinking of Robert Redford. Blixen's real-life boyfriend was a gangling and spear-bald gadabout.

The shoot for *Out of Africa* took place on a plot of fallow land directly across the road from Knollpeak Secondary School. Once filming was over, Knollpeak's students were invited to tour the set. I was the only one out of my year who hadn't already seen it. My classmates had spent much of the previous term playing truant to appear as extras. Thanks to the school's safari-suit uniform, the boys didn't even have to change their clothes. Despite the lucrative and glamorous nature of the work, I had refused to get involved. We had exams on the way, but that wasn't the reason. I just didn't want to get my hair cut.

The headmaster, Mr Hendry, eventually got wind of this mass bunk-off. It demanded little in the way of artful detection, what with khaki-clad figures sneaking out of the school gate at a rate to rival Albanian asylum seekers making a dash for the Chunnel. He made justifiably indignant announcement at the next school assembly, barring his charges from any extra-curricular cinematic escapades. The stern, no-nonsense line he took was somewhat undermined upon the film's eventual release. There he was, on-screen, during the denouement, his eyes jelled by camera fright into that glassy stare observed in case studies of the pioneering Dr Mesmer.

When my family arrived in Karen, Blixen and her paramour were long gone, but the type of haughty colonial who had so disdained them was still prevalent. Many residents were of a suitable vintage to have snubbed the pair personally. Karen was the horsiest neighbourhood south of the Shires. As with all horsey people, even when deigning to use their own legs for propulsion, Karenites had the knack of looking down upon you from a height of nine feet.

One toad-like dowager, deaf as teak and invariably gin-happy by brunch, made a habit of sideswiping parked cars at the local shops and driving off, oblivious. My stepmother numbered among the wronged parties. It was no use complaining: this superior crone believed that guilt was quite beneath her, and denied what little she would admit to hearing.

AGGRIEVED OWNER: 'You scraped off the paint all along one side of my car at the Karen *dukas*.'

MRS TOAD: 'Young woman, I've never met you before.'

AGGRIEVED OWNER: 'What's that got to do with it?'

MRS TOAD: 'That's right, I had nothing to do with it.'

AGGRIEVED OWNER (pointing): 'I can see my paint on your fender – right here.'

MRS TOAD: 'I bought that car in 1965.'

And so on until the exasperated victim either gave up or put the matter in the hands of lawyers. That didn't help. The old termagant collected solicitors' letters the way some people keep Christmas cards. On such backbones was the empire founded, and by such brass was it maintained.

Zoning laws forbade the partition of Karen plots into less than five acres. This gave it a feel that was rustic, almost agrarian in places. The land around our new house was divided into two, ostensibly by a low wire fence, but in practice by geology. The house stood upon – and, it turned out, was slowly sliding down – a slope of rich Kikuyu earth. Where the land levelled out, the topsoil became black cotton. The fertile incline around the house functioned as a lawn and garden. The flat terrain below, sprouting thinner grass and lined with the shallow-rooted gum trees common to Nairobi, recommended itself only for pasture. Refusing to learn from previous disasters in husbandry – the colossal eggless chickens, sheep ripped to little woolly pieces by our neighbour's German shepherds, a goat which served as Satan's emissary to the animal kingdom – my father decided to buy cows.

* * *

OUR FIRST cow was a Jersey to which Joan gave the name Elsie, after the cartoon mascot of the Borden milk company, a fixture of her Canadian childhood. This Elsie was no less an icon of happy cowhood. Instruct the most able of commercial artists to draw, in super-naturalistic detail, down to the gloss of the hide and the sheen on the eyeballs, the epitome of cowness, and the result would be the very image of Elsie.

Tended to by Robert, our *shamba* man, Elsie followed a life of quiet pleasures. Grass, cud, water trough and milking stool – these were the markers of Elsie's days.

On his way to work, my father spotted, on the corner of a residential road, a bathtub discarded during a refit of a nearby house. By the end of the week, it hadn't moved. Come Saturday, he mustered Obisa, Robert and me. We climbed into our blue Mitsubishi pick-up and went to retrieve the bathtub. It was a monster – a huge, old-fangled, cast-iron, claw-footed thing, which the four of us had difficulty lifting off the ground. As we teetered and shuffled, inching the freakish tub towards the flatbed, a neighbourhood loiterer peeled himself from a stone ditchguard where he had been squatting and slouched over to us.

'Hey,' he shouted. 'You can't take that! That's mine.'

'Then why did you throw it out?' said my father.

'I did not throw it out. It comes from this house here.'

'So it's not yours.'

'But I was going to take it.'

'And now I'm taking it.'

'But that's stealing,' said the outraged loafer.

'Not if the owner doesn't want it.'

'But *I* want it. You're stealing it from me.'

'You mean you wanted to steal it first? Then you should have taken it. It's been here all week.'

'I was going to.'

'But you didn't.'

The argument was resolved by the deep and emphatic clang – as if a cathedral bell had been struck by a girder – of the tub landing upon the bed of the truck. Obisa and I climbed into the back to hold it in place, and my father quickly drove away, the laggard dwindling into a furiously gesticulating speck.

'If this thing moves,' I said to Obisa, as we sat wedged between the tub and the tailgate, 'we won't be able to stop it. It'll crush us.'

We deduced that the only place we would be safe from the bathtub was inside the bathtub. We got in, one at each end, treating passers-by to the apparent spectacle of a man and a teenage boy sharing a dip in the back of a speeding pick-up. Still, the boy was white, and that explained everything. Everybody knew the *wazungu* were crazy. From my position, perched in a high-velocity bathtub, it would have been difficult to argue the point.

If my father had braked suddenly, the tailgate would have had no more chance of halting that tub than a Japanese paper screen might have of repelling a bazooka round. We would have shot out of the back and down the road, skittling anything in our path. It was a rare Nairobi car journey that did not demand sudden braking. This was one. Which explains why I am not at this moment languishing in a Kenyan jail with a faucet-shaped hole through my midriff.

* * *

WE STATIONED the bathtub by a standpipe in the pasture, where it functioned as Elsie's drinking trough in those first halcyon months following her arrival. There was a certain thrill to be had, glimpsing Elsie through the living-room window as she placidly masticated in the field below, the embodiment of all that is serenely bucolic. Marie Antoinette must have felt this way during her moments of greatest felicity, perching daintily amid her beribboned flock. My father took to referring to himself – with irony, but also with some satisfaction – as a 'gentleman farmer'.

Elsie was, in her stolid, unknowing way, a precious source of calm. With Leon out in the bush, and Lesley based at my mother's, most evenings now found just three of us at home. And at least one of us wasn't too happy.

My stepmother, when the mood took her, could open her mouth and melt the paint from the walls. And the mood took her more and more often. My own reaction was one I had learned from school; that is, no reaction at all. Perhaps as a result, she concentrated her fire on my father, who saw no reason to mimic my detachment. Tongue-lashings and recriminations followed one upon the other. I loathed these confrontations. Having endured one household break-up, I had no desire to be involved in another. I came to value those moments of peace when my father and Joan would stand, hand in hand, out on the patio at sunset, watching Robert lead Elsie from bathtub to stable.

Then, abruptly, Elsie went nuts.

First, she began to low – regularly, repeatedly, incessantly, desperately. Fixed to one spot every 30 seconds she gave out a call which seemed to resonate, if not from the farther reaches of her bovine soul, then at least from the third of her four stomachs. Eventually she broke this off to charge about the pasture, after which she would again take up her foursquare stance, and the lowing would resume.

If we had known the first thing about cows, we would have realised what this meant. Instead Robert, who knew everything about cows, explained it to us in his usual succinct way.

'What the hell is wrong with that cow?' said my father.

'She is calling for the bull,' said Robert.

Elsie's call was answered by a mammoth Friesian belonging to our neighbour, a very senior government minister. The bull smashed its way through our adjoining fence to get at Elsie, and was thwarted with seconds to spare by a team of farmhands who courageously hauled the sex-crazed beast back to its quarters. Joan had something different, and less romantic, in mind for Elsie: a breeding scheme sponsored by the Ministry of Agriculture for the benefit of dairy and beef farmers in the region.

'It's wonderful,' said my stepmother. 'You just call them, and they come round to you.'

The next day, a spanking new white pick-up truck packed with shiny chrome cylinders pulled up in the driveway. The driver emerged carrying a large binder, and guided Joan through its contents with the expertise and panache of a sommelier assisting a nervous diner with an elaborate wine list. He would henceforth be known as the AI. Man – AI. standing for 'artificial insemination'.

'Your cow is a Jersey,' he noted. 'Would you prefer to use the same breed?'

'Oh, I think so,' said Joan.

'I would certainly advise it. The Jersey is a small cow, and a half-breed calf may be too large for it to deliver. Let me see,' said the AI Man, thumbing to the section headed 'Jersey'. 'Bull Number 627 is very good this year.'

As 627 was also my father's number, my stepmother very nearly choked on her cold coffee. It was her habit to leave cups of coffee all around the house and sip at whichever one came to hand throughout the day. Obisa, and everybody else, had learned the hard way never to clear away any of these cups.

'Six-two-seven will be fine,' she sputtered.

So Bull Number 627 became the sperm *ordinaire* of our barnyard.

The efficiency of the AI Service was too good to last. *Magendo* – a Swahili word that describes not only an individual act of crookedness but also Kenya's all-encompassing culture of corruption – put paid to it. The money to sustain the scheme's delivery was funnelled into somebody's back pocket. The white pick-up drove to somebody else's *shamba* and never came back. Now, when the cry went up from the pasture for Bull Number 627, my stepmother climbed into our own pick-up, drove out towards Ngong, and sat, as she put it, 'with all the other farmers' wives', knitting and waiting her turn to drive home with the AI Man, his metal tank, his rubber hose and his thin, elongated spout.

Thanks to AI Man and Bull Number 627, Elsie begat Binnie, and Binnie begat Ellie, which alarmed a friend of ours of the same name, until Joan reassured her that this was a coincidence. If we wanted to insult someone, we named a goose after them, a tradition which began with a woman married to an associate of my father's. Blanche was so evidently a fowl-shaped package of rubber-necked antagonism and honking stupidity that it would have been remiss of us not to commemorate her with a similarly bird-brained namesake.

The birth of Ellie did not go smoothly. It was, to quote Edward Bulwer-Lytton – author of *Paul Clifford*, a volume remembered chiefly for its opening words, 'It was a dark and stormy night' – a dark and stormy night. Not just dark, but utterly black, a claustrophobic black which swallowed everything further than half an inch from your face. Electric lines were down all over Karen. The outdoor security lights which, when working, picked out every blade of grass on the lawn with unnerving clarity, were out of commission. Lying in bed at the other end of the house, it took took several minutes before I picked out from the elemental frenzy the sound of soft tapping from the kitchen's split Dutch door. I walked to it, carrying a candle, and swung open the top half. The candlelight dimly revealed Robert, from the waist up, like a sodden Mr Punch. Robert never knocked. I think he would have considered it too demonstrative.

'The cow has trouble,' said Robert.

As an obstetrician, my father was all too used to rising in the small hours and setting off to conduct a delivery. Tonight, he was less enthusiastic than ever. 'I normally draw the line at twelve pounds,' he grumbled.

We dragged on clothes and gumboots, and lumbered down to the pasture, where an insistent bellowing could now be heard. With every few steps, a convulsion of sheet lightning imprinted a dazzlingly illuminated and photographically flattened world upon the retina. The rain pelted down so hard it stung.

I held the cow steady with one hand and shone a torch with the other while my father and Robert combined to ease out the calf.

'I can see the head!' I shouted.

'Damned if I can,' said my father.

'That is not the head,' said Robert.

'Oh, Christ,' said my father. 'It's a breech presentation.'

The calf was coming out backwards.

'Don't tell me I have to do a Caesarean on my own cow,' said my father.

'I can change it,' said Robert. He slowly began to push the calf back into Binnie's uterus, clutching one of its back hooves with hidden fingers. With painstaking care, and not the slightest haste or impatience, he began to turn the calf around within the uterus, using the hoof as a handle, like a conjuror operating with his hands beneath a cloak.

'For God's sake, Davie, keep that torch steady,' said my father. Shivering, with sore arm muscles, and with my sense of wonder at nature's greatest miracle ebbing fast, I had let the beam dip.

The rain was still battering on the roof when Robert eased the hind legs out into the air and used them to hold up the calf so that the mucus could drain from its lungs. When he was sure it had begun to breathe, he gently placed it down beside Binnie.

No sooner had her offspring touched the floor than the usually sedate Binnie, seized by maternal instinct, gave forth a furious snort, lunged at me and batted me backwards against the side of the barn. The torch fell from my hands and broke on the concrete floor, extinguishing the only source of light within three miles. At the same moment I was pinned to the wall by 900 pounds of invisible Jersey beef, doing its damnedest to stove in my ribs.

'SNRRF! FRRR! BRBRBRBRBRFR!' grunted Binnie.

'Ow! Uf! Christ! Urf! Urk!' I said.

'For God's sake, Davie,' said my father, 'what did you do with the torch?'

It took a few days before Binnie reverted to her former docile self, and until then we all approached her with trepidation. When my stepmother wandered down to the field and stepped under the fence wire, Binnie wheeled around and lumbered along the pasture perimeter towards her. My stepmother emitted a piercing shriek and began to sprint along the inside of the enclosure. She had a good 30 yards on Binnie. Had they both kept going, she would have lapped the cow inside of a minute.

'Climb through the fence, dear,' called my father unhurriedly from the garden.

Joan let out another shriek and, still running, ducked under the wire in a single, seamless limbo step. Binnie cantered to a halt and resumed her grazing.

* * *

I COULD sympathise with my stepmother. I spent much of my youth being chased by animals. I have no idea why the animals were so keen to catch me. They were wild animals, so perhaps they were simply wild at me.

I was often in a car when I was being chased by animals, which is a good thing. The car was usually driven by my father, which was not always such a good thing. I think he liked being chased by animals. He certainly didn't try to discourage them – by going away, for example, when it became clear the animals were about to chase us.

It was elephants more often than not. You could always tell when an elephant was about to chase you. You would need to have been a lump of sod not to tell when an elephant was about to chase you. It would fan its ears, sway its head, make gouging motions with its tusks, stamp its feet and trumpet like the massed buglers of the apocalypse. A Toyota Land Cruiser-load of children would then begin to give off signals of its own, by bouncing up and down on the seats and shrieking, 'Let's go, Dad! Dad! Dad! Let's go! Dad! Dad! Dad!'

But my father would not be hurried by anything except the elephant. When it finally charged, he would slam the car into gear and reverse down the track. He was very adept at it. He had to be. Elephants chased us backwards through forests, over hills, across plains, down a semi-vertical mud bath flanked by a cliff on one side and a chasm on the other.

On one especially memorable occasion, an entire herd of elephants chased a three-car convoy several miles through a thick wood in the Aberdare Mountains. At the head of the convoy was my father. He knew exactly how fast elephants could run, and delighted in driving at the same speed until they'd had enough. Behind us were two cars occupied by family friends. They didn't know exactly how fast elephants could run. They couldn't overtake. I don't know if they ever forgave him.

Forest elephants are littler than their plains-dwelling cousins, but not nearly little enough. If they were, say, two or three feet high, that would be just fine. But forest elephants remain by definition elephantine – and denser, in every sense, than plains elephants. They pack the same amount of elephant into a slightly more compact form. They also cram into that bulk levels of belligerence and obstinacy more commonly, and mistakenly, attributed to that maligned creature, the gorilla. A forest elephant likes to start fights, and it never picks on anything its own size. There isn't anything its own size within 200 miles.

Over time, Joan developed a relaxed approach towards being pursued by elephants. She simply kept on knitting. Joan's knitting basket accompanied her to every corner of Kenya, earning her the nickname 'Madame Defarge', from Dickens's *A Tale of Two Cities*. Just as Madame Defarge knitted through The Terror, so my stepmother coolly knitted through every moment of peril, crisis or panic that beset us on safari.

'Let's go, Dad!' the kiddie chorus would pipe up. 'Let's go, Dad! Dad! Dad!'

'Would you shut up?' my father would snap. 'I'm *trying* to go! Leon! Get your head down. I can't see the road behind.'

'*BLAAAAAAAAAART!*' This from the elephant, 20 feet and closing.

'Oh, phooey,' Joan would say. 'I dropped a stitch.'

The only thing more belligerent and obstinate than a forest elephant is a rhinoceros. Rhinos wouldn't hesitate to chase you, if they could see you. Rhinos don't see a great deal. They are hostile but myopic. If the rhino came at you from the side, you were fairly safe. It took a bearing on you and ran, but by the time it reached you, you'd moved. It would go thundering past and run off into the distance. If it charged you from the front or back, however, you had a problem. Rhinos are as bloody-minded as they are short-sighted. They will chase you all day, unless you can fool them with a sudden, sharp turn and disappear off their map.

RHINO: 'Kill. Kill. Kill. Kill. Kill. Huh?'

Buffalo left you alone if you were in a car. They knew their limits.

Walkers are frequently tossed and gored by buffalo. It helps not to surprise them. Clapping your hands slowly and loudly as you walk is as good a plan as any. I should have been doing just that the day I stepped around a bush in the Aberdares and met a buffalo face to face. We were both quite surprised, and took off in different directions. The odds on that, I'm told, are around 50-50, not factoring in the solely hypothetical possibility that I might have chased the buffalo.

When a buffalo travels through the undergrowth, it does so in the fashion of a highly localised earthquake. I could hear things splintering far into the distance, and I remain deeply grateful that none of them were me.

Hippos are the same, only more so. They don't so much attack as simply occupy the same space as other objects. A full-grown hippo dwarfs a small jeep, as many the occupant of a small jeep has discovered – usually while crossing the path between a browsing hippopotamus and the nearest stretch of water. Hippos do not take kindly to being cut off from water. They head back swiftly, just to be on the safe side. I have no idea what might stop a fully motivated hippo in its tracks, but I doubt that there are wheels on it.

When we camped in the Masai Mara game reserve, our tents enclosed by a bend in the river, hippos would forage through the site in the darkness, grunting and honking and snapping the guy ropes. The only way to get rid of them was to shine a powerful spotlight in their direction. A dozen tiny red dots would stare out of the murk. Then came an indescribable tumult as umpteen tons of hippo flesh thundered straight off the edge of a 20-foot embankment and crashed into the river below. The indignant hippos would honk and grunt all night in protest, but they never chased us, which was a mercy.

Baboons would chase you, given half a chance. They could be hair-raising – whole packs of them, baring sharp, curved, canine teeth at you. The best way to deal with baboons was to chase them back. You had to charge at them whooping like a Sioux warrior and waving a big stick above your head. They usually ran away, but sometimes they just sat there and stared at you with all the contempt you suddenly and foolishly felt you deserved. Then you had to back off and wait for them to leave.

One troop, having been seen off with the whooping-and-big-stick treatment, returned in the still of night, climbed a nearby tree and crapped en masse on our tent. *Wheee-thwack, wheee-thud, wheee-squelch.* Until I heard this rain of excreta, I never considered animals to be capable of acting with malice afterthought.

Once, when I was still attending the Nyumba and staying at my mother's house, I got mugged by baboons on the way home from school. School was cancelled because a couple of lions had turned up in the driveway. That was the trouble with living next door to Nairobi National Park. Lions would jump the fence and eat your dog. Park rangers turned up and shot the lions with drugged darts, but no parents (except for mine, who weren't bothered) allowed their children to stay. So I walked home and en route was ambushed by baboons. I threw them my sandwiches and escaped. I never did like baboons. Baboons are bastards.

Lions would chase you, and with good reason. They were hungry. Fortunately, I never met a hungry lion while on foot or that would have been that. Also, the lions were provoked. By me, mainly. I used to bait them. I had read in the Willard Price kiddie pulp novel *Lion Adventure* that aftershave functioned as lion catnip. My father had been given a bottle of evil cologne with a Greek-sounding name by a supposedly grateful patient. I suggested we douse some foam rubber with the stuff and see if it drove the lions mad.

On a plain in the Masai Mara, we located a pair of big male lions, superb specimens, one black-maned and one golden. Standing half out of the Land Cruiser's open roof hatch, I lowered the foam rubber on a rope and we drove back and forth past the lions.

Lions, it must be stressed, are the world's laziest life form. The typical indolent housecat is a whirlwind of energy compared to a lion. A sloth is a dynamo. Lions hunt and mate, and that aside, they restrict their activity to an occasional flick of the tail and ears to see off flies. Only these movements mark them out in the long grass. Once you've watched them do nothing for long enough you conclude that lions are, in truth, boring. It was largely from a wish to see lions do something that I conceived the idea of lion-baiting in the first place. Unfortunately, it worked.

'How's it going out there?' shouted my father.

'Pretty good,' I yelled back. 'One of them almost woke up.'

It took a few passes, but at last, perhaps aroused by the aftershave, the lions perked up. Black Mane paced behind the foam rubber for a while. Then he grabbed it between his jaws and sat down. Only now did it dawn on me that I hadn't fixed the other end of the rope to anything. The car was driving away from the lion, the rope was tightening in my hands, and I suddenly understood that if I didn't let go, in one quarter of a second I would be plucked like a cork from the back of the Toyota and find it necessary to settle the matter *mano a mano*, or rather, *mano a leo*. I let go of the rope.

Golden Mane seized his opportunity. Specifically, he seized the end of the rope, and made a run for it. Black Mane immediately set off at a tangent, foam rubber still clenched between his fangs. The rope snaked up from the ground and, for a miraculous instant, snapped taut, freezing the giant rivals at mirrored angles to the ground with a whiplash judder, like vibrating bookends. Then it broke. Golden Mane galloped over the horizon, trailing the rope behind him. Black Mane watched him go forlornly, mouth full of foam rubber. He methodically shredded the rubber, lay down and went back to sleep. We had to go back later to clear up the evidence.

I subsequently improved on this method by tying a plastic water *debe* to the car's rear bumper. The lions loved this. One lioness was happy to be dragged all over the landscape, *debe* clamped in her teeth and all four feet jammed straight out in front of her to act as brakes. It was very much like playing with outsize kittens, and instilled in me a continuing belief that your cat would eat you if it could. This is why I now live in a country where you are unlikely to encounter any predator larger than a stoat.

* * *

THERE ARE those who would argue that Kenya's wildlife was entitled to try to eat me. After all, I had eaten plenty of Kenya's wildlife.

On a bare hillside overlooking Wilson Airport, a group of Nairobi entrepreneurs constructed what remains, even after two decades of dedicated gourmanderie, my most fondly remembered restaurant. I have supped with the high estate and in the low halls of Paris; dined upon the finest that London, New York and San Francisco have to offer; savoured the unsullied flavours of Lisbon and Andalucia; gladly subsisted upon the authentic fare of Italy, China and Sindh; relished the cuisines of Peru, Nepal, Morocco, Lithuania, Vietnam and Ethiopa. I have also eaten in Columbus, Missouri, and in the unlikely event you ever go there, I recommend you take your own food. But that's by the by. The point is, I have never discovered anything to surpass the joys of the glorified chophouse that was (and still is) the Carnivore.

Here was a restaurant that could have been made for us, a family of militant meat-eaters. Here, the local fauna lay, for a change, at my mercy.

In a country where people ate all the meat they could afford (usually not much), whenever they could afford it (generally not often), vegetarianism wasn't just odd, it was perverse. An average Kenyan would have found the notion completely unfathomable, and even if he had been able to bend his mind around it, would very likely have dismissed it as yet another aberrant indulgence of the privileged *wazungu*. If you ask me, the average Kenyan would have been bang on the money.

On my sixteenth birthday, my father took Joan, Leon, Lesley and me to the Carnivore as a surprise. It worked. I wasn't just surprised. I was staggered. My first glimpse of the place, as we walked from the car park, revealed an exterior comically cod-African in appearance, built of stone and wood, and mimicking an open *banda*, with wide spaces between a low perimeter wall and a high roof supported on posts, giving the effect of an anthropologically vague tribal hut swollen far beyond the point of absurdity.

The interior made the outside look understated. I was faced upon entry with a gigantic circular fire pit, over which roasted haunches and sides of flesh skewered on Maasai swords. Combining a Brazilian-style grill with the Kenyan love for *nyama choma* (roast meat), the Carnivore had a simple policy: if it moves, shoot it and cook it on a spit. In addition to the traditional butcher's window, it served up giraffe, eland, impala, crocodile (it was rich and slightly rubbery) and kudu (greater and lesser), along with anything else that might have strayed across the gunsight that week.

The tables were entire varnished cross-sections of enormous tree trunks; the plates heavy, black-iron skillets, hot as the coals they had just been pulled from, onto which the waiters whacked the sword-skewers point-down as they carved off chunks of meat.

'What do you think?' said my father.

'Jesus,' I said. 'It's amazing. I've never seen anything like it.'

To truly appreciate the degree to which the Carnivore stood as an overblown, kitsch burlesque of its own homeland, you would have to imagine a Graumann's Chinese Theatre in Nanking, or a Disneyland located in Narnia. Its owners intuitively grasped that for the tourist trade they sought to capture, the experience of being in the real Africa would never be real enough. They provided their customers with a hyper-real Africa, an Africa of Rider Haggard and Edgar Rice Burroughs, an Africa fit for Las Vegas, concentrating every myth and fiction of the continent into a few hundred square yards of hinterland, where all about it stretched unseen the actual Africa, in its magnificence and its mundanity. At the Carnivore, you could sink into the fantasy of Africa while gnawing upon the very bones of its corporeality.

It was quite brilliant.

It took a while for me to realise that the Carnivore was more than just a demented theme restaurant. It was a marker of change in Kenya, a definitive moment in the passing of former colonial ways. Before the Carnivore, Kenya's most celebrated tourist draw was Treetops Hotel, the lodge on stilts in the Aberdare Mountains where – you were never allowed to forget – the visiting Princess Elizabeth had become Queen upon the death of her father.

Treetops, with its enforced hush, its austere air of history and its white hunter escorts, was now a very British anachronism. The Carnivore, with its frenzy of hot flesh, its embrace of all things loud and brash, European and American, and its nightclub annexe, where every evening was a lurid bacchanalia. . . the Carnivore was the future. And for all that I relished the Carnivore, I had to wonder if I didn't belong to the fading Kenya of Treetops, low key, reserved and with its feet nowhere near the ground. This future was looking more and more like one that had no use for me.

* * *

MY FAMILY went back to the Carnivore as often as possible. Not only was the food splendid, but it was reassuring to know that all the animals inside were no longer alive.

Our previous restaurant of choice had been a Chinese place which we'll call the Emperor. One night at the Emperor, my sister noticed a woman seated across the room staring at our table.

'Well, stare back at her, then,' said my father.

Lesley and I fixed the woman with expressions of such hostile petulance that she swiftly looked away. Within a minute she was at it again, and so was her husband. We returned their stares once more. They hurriedly paid and left.

Two days later, my stepmother was carrying her groceries to the car at the Hurlingham shopping centre, close by my father's surgery, when she was approached by a female stranger.

'Excuse me,' said this person. 'You don't know me. But you may have thought I was staring at you the other night at the Emperor.'

'Oh, yes?' said Joan, guardedly.

'The truth is, I wasn't looking at you. I was watching a very big rat which walked out of the kitchen and stopped next to your table. It was cleaning its paws. I hope you didn't think I was being rude.'

Whatever the Emperor's little mascot was licking off its feet, we didn't fancy sharing it again. We had enough trouble with rats at home. They nested in the loft. Their feet drummed and scuffled rhythmically on the ceiling, as if they were staging a vermin revue, tap-dancing across the plasterboard in tiny cummerbunds and top hats. They became, to our way of thinking, a single silver-heeled rodent, which we nicknamed Twinkletoes.

Twinkletoes the Rat was a bloody nuisance, and insouciant to boot. He went where he pleased, bedding down in the laundry hamper, or sauntering across my father and stepmother's duvet late at night.

'Jesus Christ,' said my father, 'what the hell was that?'

'I think it was Twinkletoes,' said my stepmother, as the rat scuttled off into the corridor.

'Right, that's it!' fumed my father, leaping out of bed and grabbing from his wardrobe a box containing his gas pistol.

Other families owned air rifles. Several boys I knew had a weekend hobby of shooting each other across open fields with the oddly shaped pellets, which over 100 yards or so didn't break the skin, but left multicoloured bruises to be proudly displayed at school on Monday morning. Air rifles were self-powering, but the gas pistol required shiny chrome bulbs of compressed carbon dioxide, much like the ones used to charge up soda siphons. We had one of those too.

The gas pistol was a stocky, angular item, cast in heavy black metal. Had it been even half as dangerous as it looked, I could have used the thing to down low-flying aircraft. It fired miniature ball bearings, one at a time, so slowly that if you squinted you could see them travel. It was slightly less accurate than a kumquat struck skywards with a frying pan, but about as deadly. I had once succeeded in shooting a pigeon with it. The bird was briefly and mildly bothered, to the extent of switching branches.

Nonetheless, this was my father's weapon of choice in the onslaught upon Twinkletoes, who had Gone Too Far. My father burst out of the bedroom doorway, stark naked and waving an eight-pound gun, roaring, 'Where are you, you sonofabitch?' At the other end of the hall, Twinkletoes stopped polishing his whiskers and froze, startled, as well he might have been. My father drew a bead on Twinkletoes and fired. The house reverberated to the sound you might hear if you stuck a drawing pin into an outsize party balloon, accompanied by the thud of my father hitting the floor as the shot, missing the rat by a good two feet, ricocheted off the walls.

'I'll let the dogs in,' said Joan, opening the adjacent garden door and whistling. 'They'll catch him.' Within half a second, she had four overexcited mutts leaping and foaming around her, drunk with the joy of being called inside by their mistress. Twinkletoes darted through the tangle of legs and swinging tails and flitted into the night.

Where the gas pistol had faltered, rat poison prevailed – although not before I had lost my footing on the rafters while putting down the pellets in the loft. Fragments of plaster and hardboard flew from the ceiling as a disembodied right leg appeared and kicked frantically to and fro.

'Oh, for Christ's sake,' said my father.

'Well, you always send me up here,' I protested. 'And if I'm always the one to go up, then I'm going to be the one to fall through.'

'Oh, for Christ's sake,' said my father again, more quietly.

The poison was slow to act, but effective. Various manifestations of the Twinkletoes collective crawled off to die in corners, cupboards and vents. My brother opened the cutlery drawer in the kitchen one morning, in search of a teaspoon, and discovered a nine-inch rat, stiff as plywood, lying on its back among the butter knives, its teeth bared in a rigor-induced snarl and its legs clenched up across its underside.

'Really, Joan,' said Leon, poker-faced, 'you ought to be more careful what you keep in here.'

It was all over for Twinkletoes the Rat. He had tripped the light fantastic for the last time. He burned briefly but brightly, on a small fire which Robert built for that purpose at the far end of the pasture.

chapter seventeen

The Day We Hit the Cow

WE WERE a few miles south of Nyeri – my father, Joan, Lesley, Leon and I – driving back down to Nairobi in our Toyota Land Cruiser, when we hit the cow. It's due to exactly this kind of occurrence that so many four-wheel-drive vehicles are fitted with cow-catchers or bull-bars. Ours was not.

Nyeri sits a short way below the equator. It is an attractive and industrious little burg, home to a soft-drink bottling plant and a huddle of small factories, as energetic and bustling as most Kenyan towns are drowsy and lackadaisical. This may have something to do with its location in the Kikuyu highlands, for the Kikuyu are not only Kenya's single most numerous tribe, they are also regarded as its most enterprising. Among other tribes, the Kikuyu are often disdained as prosperous money-grubbers, a derogatory stereotype which – in so agriculturally minded a nation – may well have its origins in the highlands themselves.

The Kikuyu land is rich and well watered. Entire carefully terraced hillsides are occupied by big farms and co-operatives; others are carved up into individual *shambas*. A profusion of varying greens – maize stalks, banana fronds, leaf vegetables – quilts the landscape in every direction, dotted with glimpses of the reddish-brown loam beneath. Near swathes of the close, compact bushes which bore them, bright red coffee beans are spread out to dry in the sunshine on broad wooden pallets. The only thing more colourful than the scenery is the taste in clothing displayed by the farm folk. The women's traditional wrap-around *kangas* are vivid, but more resplendent still are the thick knitted jumpers and hats worn by both sexes on even the warmest days. The impression is one of an ubiquitously attended clearance sale at an equatorial outlet of Primark.

It is a world of dense fecundity. In every corner something sprouts. Everywhere you look, you see children – cocooned on the backs of their mothers, running down pathways, waving from the roadside. In fact, everyone waves, or at least raises a hand in greeting. People here are friendly. There are, inevitably, exceptions. Such as the vicious ten-year-old wretch who deliberately drove his cattle into the road that day in 1985, and near as dammit killed the lot of us.

* * *

WE WERE returning from a trip to Kitich, in the Matthews mountain range, near the Northern Frontier District. This was a place so remote and secluded it featured on no tourist itinerary. We had heard about it from a safari operator friend, who knew of it only because he remembered a failed attempt to set up a luxury camp there. The qualities that made Kitich so alluring – it was an untouched beauty spot, blessed with stillness and solitude – resulted from its almost complete inaccessibility. We had to crawl and grind our way across a wide expanse of stony desert, creep through wadis and dongas and inch up shelves of rock, hour after hour.

To keep a permanent camp supplied by road is difficult when you have no road. The only other option for the camp's owners would have been a small-scale, tropical version of the Berlin airlift. Logistics and economics prevailed over the entrepreneurial dream, and gave rise to a new twist on the old philosophical conundrum: if a business topples over in the back of beyond, does it make a sound?

Once we climbed into the mountains and found our own campsite, it was more than worth the trek. It was wild, and quiet, and well shaded handsome trees. Nearby, a freshwater swimming hole offered the only clue that this site had ever before been seen by outsiders: an old radial tyre hung on a rope from a branch above the water. Kitich was close to paradise, and we had it all to ourselves.

But not for long. Soon we were visited by the locals, herders from the Samburu tribe, northern cousins of the Maasai. We greeted each other politely, a process that involved nods, gestures and vague but cordial noises. We offered the men water from our cooler. They accepted, and drank with shocked expressions and one or two exclamations. They hadn't encountered anything so cold before.

Although the Samburu spoke no Swahili, they had a little English. Two words, to be exact: 'Hundred shilling.' They had come to offer us goods, and this was the only unit of exchange they were prepared to deal in. Whatever the wares might be – an exquisite, double-edged traditional knife in a sheath of deep red leather, of a craftsmanship unobtainable in Nairobi, where inferior blades sold for much greater sums; a small, grim pouch which one would hesitate to handle with tweezers – and however their apparent value might vary, there was one price and and one price only: 'Hundred shilling.'

'This is worth forty.' [Hand gestures to match]

'Hundred shilling.'

'Fifty?'

'Hundred shilling.'

'Fifty for this' [pointing] 'but two hundred' [fingers held up for illustration] 'for that.'

'Hundred shilling.'

The Samburu weren't greedy. They wouldn't take less, and they wouldn't take more. It was 'hundred shilling' per transaction. We bought the knife, a fine *rungu* – a thin, sleek club with a large and bulbous head – and a small, hollow branch filled with honey, still in the comb. So strong and sweet was the honey that you were best advised to sit down before eating it: it made the head spin. The comb was redolent of the smoke used to clear the hive, and with every second bite a dead bee crunched between your teeth. I have not tasted anything like it since.

Joan wanted something the Samburu hadn't brought with them: a cowbell to put on the back door at home. She made a bold attempt to explain this to the tribesmen. '*Mimi n'taka*,' she said, 'a ding-dong *ya ngombe*.' ('I want a ding-dong of the cow.') Even if they had understood

Swahili, this would very likely have flummoxed the Samburu.

'Ding-dong!' said my stepmother. 'Ding-dong?' She craned her head forward and tilted it from side to side. The Samburu leaned in, fascinated. 'Mooo!' my stepmother said. 'Moooo!' She described an undulating motion with her neck, and clapped her hands together below her chin. 'Ding-dong!' she repeated. The Samburu straightened up again. To a man, they looked deeply perturbed. Raising their hands in farewell, they turned and hurried away.

'Nice try, dear,' said my father.

'Maybe I should just have said, "Cuckoo! Cuckoo!",' Joan sighed. 'I don't think it would have made any difference.'

The next morning, as I slept, a regular, repetitive noise drummed its way into my unconscious mind with gathering volume, until my frontal lobes sulkily acknowledged that I wasn't dreaming and stirred into wakefulness. The first, frail light of dawn was picking out shapes in the tent, and above the sound of birdsong – in itself so familiar as to usually pass unnoticed – I heard, louder with every beat, a dull, wooden clatter:

'*D'clonk-d'clonk-d'clonk-d'clonk. . .*'

And approaching from another direction, a metallic pulse:

'*Tang-tang-tang-tang-tang!*'

And from yet another quarter, softer but clearer than either, a well-tempered chime:

'*Ching-ching-ching-ching-ching.*'

And then, zeroing in on the campsite from every point of the compass, more clanks and clangs and thunks and dings than the ear could track or the brain register. There were enough cowbells in our campsite that morning to supply a medium-sized Swiss canton through the remainder of the century. Joan chose the one she liked best, and the rest were returned by the Samburu, without comment or rancour, to their original bovine bearers. The price, of course, was 'hundred shilling'.

* * *

THE WOULD-BE managers of the Kitich camp which never came to pass had sold on the land for a song. When we sought out the new owners to arrange our stay there, we discovered that they were neighbours. The Mahmoud family lived at the other end of our road, where three brothers ran a car repair business at the back of their house.

'We're having a barbecue Friday,' said one of the brothers, Habib. 'Bring the family over. You like Middle Eastern food?'

'That's lamb, right?' said my father, who seldom eats anything else.

'You bet,' said Habib.

Originally from the Arabian peninsula, the Mahmoud brothers were a hardy, genial crew. Over shish kebabs and ginger beer – Tanga Wizi brand, a thrillingly aggressive soft drink made with fresh, fierce ginger, which fought its way down the gullet as if determined not to sell its life cheaply – Habib told us about his own latest safari.

'Took the wife and kids for a weekend down in Amboseli,' he said. Amboseli, now a national park, was then a game reserve, located where the otherwise unswerving Kenya-Tanzania border nudges upwards to circumnavigate Mount Kilimanjaro. Legend has it that Africa's highest peak was once part of British East Africa, and would today belong to Kenya, if Queen Victoria had not given it to her grandson, Kaiser Wilhelm II of Germany, as a birthday present. While there is no documented proof of this, it would be no sillier an explanation for the imperial frontiers than those for which evidence is plentiful.

'We were staying in the *bandas* near Kili,' Habib told us. A *banda* is a fixed dwelling, generally on the basic side – it might be a wooden hut or cabin.

'Second night,' Habib went on, 'some Maasai guys thought they'd try their luck. Broke the door in with their *rungus.*' Habib always spoke as if he were reading out a telegram. 'Well, I told these guys to bugger off out of it. Wouldn't listen. Guy at the front kept waving his *rungu*, shouting "*Kabidhi pesa! Kabidhi pesa!*" [Hand over the money]. So I said to him, "*Hakuna pesa, la hasha*" [No money, no way]. He didn't like that. Hit me over the head with his *rungu.* Pretty bloody hard. Broke his *rungu* in half. That really annoyed me, so I got up from where I was sitting and punched him out cold. Then the other guys ran away.'

Habib, as my stepmother accurately observed, was one tough cookie.

We had often stayed in the Amboseli *bandas* ourselves. They were relatively well appointed, with running water, little kitchens, and after sundown, electric light from a petrol-driven generator. At the front of each *banda*, a small garden of bougainvillea and dry-weather succulents was marked out with white-painted stones, giving it a pleasant cottage aspect. The *bandas* stood in two rows, the frontmost directly on to Kilimanjaro. It was a scene which, trite as it may sound, demanded the description 'majestic'; in the morning, when the broad, snow-covered peak rose unconcealed by clouds, the sheer hugeness of the mountain towering over the plain turned the eye back to it again and again. Whenever we booked, we were sure to specify that we preferred a *banda* in the sightline of Kilimanjaro. We didn't want to find ourselves in the position of the German woman we once heard complaining loudly and bitterly to the manager from the *banda* behind ours.

'I must haff zer hull phew!' she snarled. 'You hear? Zer hull phew!' She did not, to my recollection, preface these remarks with the phrase '*Achtung!*' or conclude them with '*Schweinhund*', but her inflection as she excoriated the poor chap, who was gamely trying to be as obliging as possible, rendered them redundant.

* * *

THE ROUTE to Amboseli had been my favourite of all our journeys since I was very young. Instead of following the road the long way around to the gate, we cut across a perfectly flat and barren stretch of desert, which had once been a lake bed, in the primeval days when the Amboseli plain was the Amboseli forest. Here, even as an eight-year-old, I was allowed to take the wheel: there was nothing I could do to endanger my family. I could twist wildly one way or another, or let go of the wheel entirely while pressing the accelerator with the stretched-out tip of my shoe. There was nothing to hit, and no chance of rolling the vehicle in the soft, thick dust. Every so often I would pilot the car into one of the dust devils – whirlwind columns playing across the desert – which formed the only visual interruption to the red-golden surface stretching in every direction to the horizon.

As a nipper, it was the Range Rover I pointed at the Amboseli plain. As a teenager, I steered a Toyota Land Cruiser, without question the best safari vehicle then available. Its nearest rival, the old-fashioned Land Rover, had its devotees. The Land Rover was the motoring icon of the *bundu*. It was robust, simple, reliable, and easy to repair when something did go wrong. But it was also underpowered and devilishly uncomfortable; its stiff suspension amplified every bump. This may have accounted for its one major structural shortcoming. There were campsites all across Kenya where the undergrowth had spread over broken and discarded Land Rover half-shafts.

If your fan belt broke, as it had done more than once on our Land Cruiser, you could substitute a strip of inner tube or canvas, which might just see you home. Nor was your journey necessarily at an end if your accelerator cable snapped. My father once picked me up from school in the Land Cruiser and handed me the frayed end of wire that he had fed from under the bonnet into the cab through the passenger window.

'When I tell you,' he instructed, 'pull that. Now.'

I tugged on it, the throttle opened, and we drove away.

My father, who loves working on cars, had customised our Land Cruiser estate into a machine that could go just about anywhere and make it pleasant to be there when you did. At the front, he fitted a power winch with a long spool of inch-thick cable. Unlike the relatively feeble electric winches, which drained car batteries and left you doubly marooned, the power winch connected directly to the engine. Given something sufficiently solid to pull against – a tree or a rock formation – there was nothing it could not drag us out of. Even black cotton mud, notoriously slippery and sticky, allowing our tyres not the smallest purchase, on a savagely angled uphill climb in the Aberdare Mountains nicknamed 'the vertical bog', could not hold us back.

We once had a little trouble high on the slopes of Mount Kenya. Our wheels spun and settled in the black cotton. We confidently reeled out the winch cable, only to find there was nothing to attach it to but bamboo stems, which it simply plucked from the sodden earth with the eagerness of a famished panda. We looped the wire around ever larger clumps, until finally we hauled ourselves from the mire. As the treads bit into firmer ground at the top of the slope, we heard below us a tinny whine rising to a thin crescendo. Looking down, we saw another car, a compact hatchback, as it rounded the furthest visible corner, slithered crabwise across a mud slick and sunk to the top of its wheel-arches. The engine, which would have had difficulty propelling a rider mower, coughed and expired.

The driver's door slowly opened, pushing out a solid wave of mud ahead of it, and a gaunt, forlorn figure uncurled itself from the tiny seat and surveyed the situation. It didn't need much surveying. The driver had taken up a near-impassable road a car which had no more business being there than a pedalo in pack ice. That he had made it this far was cause for amazement. There was nothing else for it. We tramped our way back down the slope with the winch cable.

'The name's Chad,' said the driver, an Englishman in late middle age who inclined with the habitual stoop of the very tall. 'My wife,' he said, indicating a woman dressed from the knees upwards for a Women's Institute garden party. What she was wearing below the knee is impossible to say, as it was concealed by the muck in which her legs were planted.

'Whatever is going on, Chaddy?' came a voice from inside the car. 'Why have we stopped?' A face peered through the rear window.

'My mother,' said Chad (or as he always would be known to us thereafter, Chaddy Baby), as if imparting news of a bereavement. Chaddy Baby's mother was 90 if she was a day. You could only conclude that Chaddy Baby really hadn't thought this excursion through.

As we were slowly winching Chaddy Baby's Isuzu uphill, a large yellow Jeep Wagoneer slalomed around the bend and roared past us, spattering us all with mud. A smug, ruddy face leaned through the driver's seat window.

'Any messages for the top?' chortled the face, in an accent that confirmed its owner as another Englishman.

Ten minutes later, and halfway up, we pulled the hatchback past the Jeep, which was thoroughly bogged down at a dramatic tilt in the roadside gulley.

'Sorry, did you say something?' my brother asked the driver. 'I didn't quite catch it.'

* * *

IN ADDITION to the winch, our Land Cruiser was kitted out with fore-mounted gunmetal jerry cans of fuel; a rear roof hatch for game viewing, the inside edges of which were padded to prevent bruising to the ribs on bumpy tracks; and a brace behind the back seat for our portable electric refrigerator, a robust Lilliputian marvel which allowed us to enjoy White Cap or Coke *baridi sana* while ogling cheetah or bat-eared foxes.

Although we seldom needed both, we carried two spare wheels, one in the back and another conveniently slung on a metal harness fixed to the undercarriage.

It seemed my father had all eventualities covered, but this arrangement nearly proved our undoing on a ride down to the escarpment at Ngurumani. Like Kitich, this required a trek through some very rough country before you headed up to a green, shady spot by a freshwater stream. Unlike Kitich, if you left early in the morning, it was possible to make a day trip of it. We would take a picnic and spend the afternoon in the stream, building a makeshift stone dam to create a swimming pool. In slow-moving water there was a risk of infection by bilharzia, a thoroughly vile disease caused by a parasite which infests the urine of water snails. The brook at Ngurumani was brisk enough to be safe and warm enough to bathe in.

On our first visit, thunderstorms in the mountains had set off flash floods across our return route. We stopped at a dip in the road, bone-dry when we had crossed it that morning. White water was raging through it.

'David,' said my father, 'go and see how deep it is, will you?'

I hopped out of the car.

'But don't go in above your waist,' he added considerately.

I waded in to the deepest point, which reached my upper thighs, and struggled back.

'Stand next to the front wheel,' said my father. He quickly compared my water line to that of the car. 'That'll be no problem,' he said. I climbed back in and he nosed the Land Cruiser across the ford.

'My legs are cold,' I said.

Between that visit and the latest one, we had travelled to every arid corner of the country. The route to Ngurumani ran south through the centre of the Rift Valley, past soda-encrusted Lake Magadi, deep into

Maasai country. As far as Magadi, where the heavy industry of soda extraction dominated the landscape, the road was tarmacked smooth. When the front right tyre went flat a few miles short of the lake, we felt it almost straight away.

The first spare, in the back, was covered by bags and baskets. We lowered the second spare from the undercarriage, jacked up the car, and heaved it into place. The dust was almost an inch thick on the rim, but as we tightened the nuts, it seemed to reduce to nothing. We resumed our journey, and were just gliding into sight of Magadi when we saw our wheel describing a graceful arc into the roadway ahead of us. It bounced jauntily into the distance, easily outpacing the car – thus either confirming or disproving one of Galileo's theorems; I'm still not clear which – and vanished into the scrub. The car continued to coast evenly.

'Jesus Christ,' said my father, and took his foot off the accelerator. The Land Cruiser slowed but maintained its balance. Then he gave the brake the lightest of taps. Instantly, the car lurched forward and to the right, and a fearful screech flew up from the road beneath us. We stopped in three seconds flat. The wheel hub had carved a blackened, smoking trench into the tarmac.

'Right,' said my father. 'We're going to split into two search parties. Leon and I will look for the wheel. Joan, David and Lesley will find the nuts.'

He was wrong. We didn't find a single one of them. Working loose against the compressed dust, they had shot out into the Rift Valley with such force that they may have bounced off the sides. Having retrieved the wheel, we had no choice but to cannibalise a nut from each of the remaining hubs, dig out the second spare, and trundle tentatively into Magadi.

'We'll find some nuts here,' said my father confidently.

About that, he happened to be right. Nuts, wackjobs, layabouts, ne'er-do-wells – the streets were full of them.

Magadi was a factory town, spread around the parched fringes of the lake and baking in a brackish haze. Where the soda crust was thickest, the water was sufficiently alkaline to skeletonise any body part its owner was foolish enough to immerse. Where the crust was thinner, a layer of algae coloured pink both the lake and the flamingos, which dipped elegantly into its shallows. Together, the soda plant and the lake created a weird fusion of natural spectacle and mechanical brutalism.

Why anybody who was not required to work here would elect to spend their days by the scorched roadside, anticipating the day wayfarers might happen by in search of wheel nuts, is beyond me. But there they were, and it seemed this was the moment they had been waiting for. Brandishing every spanner and wrench in our toolbox, they fanned out around Magadi.

We waited. My brother wandered off to the nearby hot springs, to catch a species of cichlid adapted to temperatures that would have left any other fish nicely poached. Soon, our army of nut-mongers swarmed back to base. They had unfastened nuts from every vehicle in Magadi, and not one of them fitted the Land Cruiser threads. Magadi was a Land Rover town.

'Don't you know of anyone around here who owns a Land Cruiser?' said my father.

Somebody thought that maybe a senior engineer of the soda plant did. Off we went in search of the senior engineer.

'He is at home today,' said the man in the front office.

The senior engineer's house was a blank, shadeless villa which looked as if it hadn't been built from the ground up, but lowered in its entirety and soldered onto the cracked earth.

'He is in the bar,' said the senior engineer's wife, directing us back the way we had come.

The bar was the only dark corner for 50 miles, a sanctuary from the acrid glare of Magadi. We located the senior engineer deep within the murk, nursing a pot-bellied bottle of White Cap export. He was less than pleased to be disturbed, but when we explained that we would pay for the wheel nuts from his Land Cruiser, he perked up at the thought of a subsidised day's drinking and accompanied us back to his house.

There, in what would have been the senior engineer's back garden, had anything other than carcinomas been able to grow in it, lay the dismantled hulk of a Land Cruiser just like ours. The thing was in a thousand pieces, six of which were promisingly wheel-nut-shaped. We paid the senior engineer and bought several rounds of beers for the idlers who had snapped out of their lethargy to assist us. Then we carried on to Ngurumani, over the tarmac causeway which ran gleaming across the soda to the southern shore of Lake Magadi, attended on either side by great flocks of flamingos.

* * *

ON OUR return journey, my father stopped off and bought the rest of the Land Cruiser from the senior engineer for 5,000 shillings. Weight for weight, this may make it the cheapest car purchase ever conducted in East Africa. He had the chassis towed back to Nairobi, piled with boxes holding what had once been its working parts, and much to my stepmother's displeasure, set it up on blocks in our front drive.

'We already have a Land Cruiser,' said my stepmother.

'Well,' said my father, in his best Afrikaaner accent, 'we've got two now, eh?'

It took my father months to reassemble a Land Cruiser from those fragments, but he did it. My stepmother didn't feel her efforts as a gardener were much improved by a newly salvaged wreck heaped up amid the flowerbeds.

Once the second Land Cruiser was fully up and running, my father and his friend Keith Hills, the editor of Kenya's only motoring magazine (I once won an odd, quasi-modernist rocking chair in its caption competition), teamed up to buy a beautiful but dilapidated early 1960s Mercedes-Benz. This revealed itself to be so thoroughly rusted that weeds sprouted up through the holes in the undercarriage.

Undiscouraged, he brought home a Lancia Delta coupé, which was an even flimsier rustbucket, and broke down more often than it ran. It featured electric windows, which when they worked were fun, until they nearly choked one of our dogs to death. Dismissing the Lancia as 'a steaming heap of spaghetti', my father replaced it with a Mark VIII, the largest Jaguar ever built. When I opened the front door and caught my first glimpse of the boot protruding into the open-air carport, I mistook it for the front half of a VW Beetle. Stepping outside, I could hardly take in the whole car at once. It was a leviathan, an Amazonian automobile, massively and magnificently curved. The dashboard incorporated half an acre of walnut, and featured a starter button, a speedometer and very little else. The Jaguar handled like a steamship, and demanded a similar turning circle. It was one of the most beautiful things I have ever laid eyes on. By the time my father had finished restoring it, adding red leather seats and a baby-blue paint job, he was fending off bids for it on a weekly basis. Eventually an American collector made him an offer he couldn't refuse, and the Jaguar was shipped off to the States.

Next, my father bought another Mercedes. The vendor was an Indian businessman who had customised it to his taste, fitting to the top of the dashboard yellow and red carpeting with matching four-inch tassels, which swayed back and forth across the instrument panel when cornering. He had also furnished the car with a musical horn and a selection of tunes including 'Colonel Bogey', 'The Battle Hymn of the Republic' and other martial favourites.

This Mercedes was mobile, if only briefly. It gave my father, my stepmother and I a scare when we drove it to the barren expanse of Bushwhackers camp, some 50 miles off the main road to Mombasa, for the weekend. When the time came to go home, the battery was so flat the clock had stopped.

The camp was deserted save for an ancient and wizened *askari* (watchman), who volunteered the information that there was a farm some six miles away. He shuffled away, and four hours later returned with the farmer, atop the farmer's tractor.

'Great,' said my father to the farmer. 'Where's your battery?'

'Battery?' the farmer said.

'You don't have a battery in this thing?'

'Oh no. No battery.'

'Then how did you start it?'

'The usual way. I put it in gear and rolled it down the ant hill.'

We hitched up the Mercedes to the tractor and drove in circles around Bushwhackers until sunset, but the electronic ignition on the car could not fire without a spark. Another battery was essential.

My father was due in the operating theatre at eight the next morning. We agreed, dejectedly, to set out at dawn, walk the 50 miles to the main road, and hitch a ride from there.

Then, so faint it might have been an auditory mirage brought on by desperation, a distant rumble floated into earshot on the torpid twilight breeze. Cheetah-like, which is not a description often applied to me, I stiffened, then bolted off harum-scarum across the scrubland, hurdling bushes and ditches as I went. I hadn't gone more than 100 yards when my father shot past me as if I were jogging on the spot. I had 29 years on him and stood lighter by at least twice that number of pounds, but still he matched me by three steps to my every two. Kenya has dominated middle-distance running events in international athletics for two decades, but neither Henry Rono at the Commonwealth Games in Edmonton, 1978, nor Peter Koech in Stockholm 11 years later, put in so decisive a performance against such heavy odds as my father did in covering the three miles which brought him, heaving and panting, to the junction where he intercepted the lorry.

The lorry driver was happy to help out. Using two pieces of wire, which we subsequently reaffixed to the Bushwhackers fence poles, we improvised a pair of jump leads, started up the Mercedes and off we went.

'I think, dear,' said my stepmother to my father as we pulled up to our front door, 'you can take your foot off the gas pedal now.'

Three weeks later, we all piled into the same Mercedes for a drive down to the coast. A mile outside the waystation at Voi, close to Tsavo National Park, a noise from the engine suggested it was grinding itself into thin metal shavings, which it was. The previous owner had driven the car without oil, fatally disabling the motor, then temporarily concealed the damage with an infusion of grease. We coasted powerless into the garage at Voi, where every head turned wincing at the shrieks and clatters emanating from our transport. We abandoned it there and had it towed back to Nairobi a week later.

An entire reconditioned engine had to be smuggled in from Germany, masquerading as industrial supplies for a friend's farm. Contraband was something of an art form in Kenya, one at which our family excelled. In the course of a decade, we brought back from our trips abroad wing mirrors, windscreen wipers, all sorts of foodstuffs, hogsheads of malt whisky, a side panel for an MGB GT coupé and a complete colour darkroom, most of it in our hand luggage. I think the MG side panel was passed off as a novel form of fold-up perambulator.

My father, again to the chagrin of my stepmother, retrieved the camshaft from the wrecked Mercedes engine and polished it up to a superb sheen. It now stands upright on their coffee table, beneath the melted mock-Giacometti from the exploded Canadian radar post, where it has undertaken a long and successful impersonation of a collectable artefact from the Bauhaus.

* * *

TO A TEENAGE boy, there was an obvious advantage to having a father who collected cars. When, on my seventh attempt, I secured a driving licence, I straight away had something to drive. The MG became mine by default – nobody else in the family had any conceivable use for it.

To drive a sports car is a teenage dream, but I wished I had a larger vehicle. Not because I was spoilt and picky – a motorised vegetable stall would have been good enough – but because it was difficult to navigate the little car around potholes which could have swallowed it up and left room for a couple of milk floats. Also, the roads were full of things, like the Kenyan Army's terrifying trucks, which threatened to crush my MG to flypaper.

All the same, I had my own car. I had never before been trusted with any machine more complicated or valuable than an egg whisk. To let me loose on the streets of Nairobi took a leap of faith on the part of my parents. And not just because of my own tendency towards carelessness. Kenya's roads are appallingly dangerous.

Kenyan drivers comprise perhaps the most demented and hell-bent demographic west of Kabul. In Nairobi, fatal accidents are less frequent than in the countryside, not through any greater application of common sense, but thanks to a lack of opportunity. Space is tighter and speeds slower. Smashes occur all the time, but fewer people are actually killed. Even so, climbing into the driver's seat gave one a sense of 'Right-oh, chaps, I'm going in – see you back in the mess later, what.' Climbing out again was never to be taken for granted.

Car crashes were the biggest killer by far among my peers. Several acquaintances of mine died in this way, including a close school friend named John Hemsworth, killed in a single-vehicle accident on the road to Mombasa. Irony could not make this loss any sadder: John's father worked as an auto insurance broker, and numbered my family among his clients. A little while after John's death, I was despatched on an errand, delivering paperwork to Mr Hemsworth's office. I said nothing about John to his father – no words of sympathy, not even an affirmation that I had been glad to know him. It was a failure both of nerve and of compassion which troubles me to this day.

Who lived through such mishaps, and who did not, was a matter of luck. I came within inches of death half a dozen times on Kenya's roads, and never closer than on a drive down to the coast with my mother and sister in my mother's Honda Civic, along the same Mombasa Road which claimed my friend's life and many more.

Statistics rank Mombasa Road among the most hazardous stretches of highway on earth. This is particularly alarming when you consider that it is Kenya's main artery, running 300 miles south-east from Nairobi in an almost entirely straight line. Its surface is poor – holed, rutted and chipped at the edges. But that alone does not explain why it claims so many lives. The undeviating course of the road produces an hypnotic effect on drivers accustomed to hilly twists and turns. It's easy to drift, and when you do, it takes only one ill-placed bump or pothole to send your car into a spin or send it lethally rolling top over teakettle.

We were taking the long drive in shifts. Lesley was behind the wheel. Somewhere near Makindu, the car abruptly fishtailed off the road, hurtled backwards into the scrub, described a figure of eight, righted itself and rocketed forward directly at the only large tree this side of the horizon. It's said that time slows down at such moments. Not exactly. The incident happened with astonishing speed, but my brain moved even faster.

'So. . . you're going to die now,' my brain mused impassively. 'This is what it's like.' By then we had missed the tree and settled to a standstill amid a maelstrom of red dust.

A minute or so passed in silence, until we could once again see through the windows.

'Shall I drive for a while?' said my mother.

* * *

WHEN MY father came across a crash scene before the emergency services had arrived, he felt impelled, as a doctor, and out of common decency, to stop and help. When travelling with his family, he was faced with a dilemma: should he assist, and risk exposing us to horrors he could do little to alleviate, or should he drive on?

On the roads outside Nairobi, bad overtaking on hills and corners caused the majority of disasters. Often, the culprits would be the owners of *matatus*, a cheap, popular and unlicensed form of mass transit, with the emphasis on 'mass'. A *matatu* is just a minibus, but its conductor will, with a sunny optimism unblemished by cruel experience, stuff it with enough human cargo to sink an ocean-going freighter. When his *matatu* roars across the brow of a hill on the wrong side of the road, and collides head-on with a truck coming the other way, these poor souls haven't a chance in hell.

A police pound by the road to the Ngong hills housed in open view the wrecks retrieved from such tragedies. It was a morbid exhibition. In my younger days, I would try to imagine the forces which had transformed ordinary vehicles into these crushed and blackened lumps, and the fate of those inside when it happened. As time went on, I no longer had to imagine it. I saw it for myself all too often.

One afternoon, on the main drag near Nanyuki, we arrived only seconds after the police and ambulancemen at a *matatu* crash. It was not the first time I had encountered death, but it was unquestionably the most dreadful. Death leered from this atrocity. Death had stamped itself with hideous finality across a welter of human flesh. The victims were packed so tightly in the van that even the force of the impact could not shake them loose, but instead left their corpses dangling from the metalwork, their faces obliterated as if a giant thumb had smudged them out.

'Oh dear God,' murmured Joan. 'We should stop.'

'We can't do anything for these people,' said my father, and eased the car around the crash site as quickly as he could.

If we children had not been in the car, I know he would have got out to help, even if the chances that anyone might be saved were as remote as they appeared. As a surgeon, he had seen worse. He had been on call at Kenyatta National Hospital in November 1974, when a Lufthansa jet crashed on take-off just outside the airport. A few days later, we drove out to look at the wreckage. I climbed up on the fuselage, and played in the ravaged cabin. I had been six years old then, and the twisted metal held no meaning for me. I felt differently about it now.

* * *

ON THE DAY we hit the cow, my father and stepmother were riding in the front seat, my brother, my sister and I in the back. We had passed through the familiar sights of Nyeri. The bottling plant. The plaque marking the clinic of local physician Joseph Wamburu, M.Med (failed). The quiet churchyard enclosing the grave of Lord Baden-Powell, hero of the siege of Mafeking and founder of the scouting movement to which I had been such a discredit. The sole epitaph on Baden-Powell's plain tombstone, movingly enough, takes the form of a circled dot – the tracker's sign for 'I have gone home'.

We were barrelling downhill on the approach to Gichira when we saw, 200 feet ahead and gathered by the left-hand side of the road, a dozen Boran cattle; hefty brutes with fat humps above their shoulders and loose folds of hide dangling from their chests and bellies. We saw the young cowherd holding his stick by his side as he waited for the road to clear. We saw him as he saw our car. We saw his features set into an candid exhibition of malicious cupidity as he spotted the white faces inside the car. We saw him raise his stick and flail the hindmost Borans about the quarters until the reluctant creatures loped into the roadway. We saw, looming in our windscreen, the beast singled out by chance for destruction. Its head was in profile and its right eye fixed on our car. I can only guess if the terror I read in that eye was real, or my own panic reflected back at me. It was so close that it seemed we might drive straight through the black pupil and into oblivion. Then there was an almighty thump, felt as much as heard. The windscreen was full of blurred colours. Next we were stationary, on the opposite verge.

'Everybody OK?' said my father quickly. We were. He pulled away immediately. In the rear-view mirror, a crowd was gathering out of nowhere, as Kenyan crowds are apt to.

What did the cowherd have in mind? Money, one way or another.

Perhaps, to give him the benefit of the doubt, he was thinking of blackmail. Mob justice is a feature of Kenyan life. Unless rescued by the police, a thief – or an innocent taken for one – may be well be beaten to death. Accidents were not much different. If we had stayed, compensation would have been demanded, and the price of the defunct animal would have risen instantly and conveniently to everything we had on us. We would have been lucky to keep the car.

It could be that the cowherd had intended only to shake us down. It's also possible that he knew there was every chance that the entire carload would be maimed or killed. It is a curious fact about fatal road accidents in rural Kenya that no money, jewellery or possessions of any kind are ever recovered from the victims' cars. If the cow had rolled up the bonnet and through the windscreen, that would have been the end of our family, and a bonanza for the homicidal tyke.

Luckily, my father wasn't new to such hazards. He had removed his foot from the accelerator as soon as he noticed the cattle. He had resisted the impulse to transfer it to the brake, which would have caused him to lose control of the car. At the very last moment, he had swerved to the right and struck the animal with the corner of the Land Cruiser, knocking it away from our direction of travel. It was our good fortune that no vehicles were coming the other way as we lurched across the road.

A few miles further on, we stopped to inspect the damage. We had a broken headlight, a dent in the fender, and a twisted jerry-can rack. We had got off very lightly indeed.

'We'll have to report this,' said my father. 'Keep an eye out for the next police station.'

At Ngunguru, we followed a sign down a dirt track and arrived at a small concrete building staffed by a bored, portly officer tinkering with his Lee Enfield rifle. This ex-British Army ordnance was standard issue among the lower ranks of the Kenyan police. CID and other special units carried the sinister and osseous Sten gun.

'You have fled the scene of the accident,' said the sergeant. 'This is a serious crime.'

'Not if I report it at the first available opportunity,' replied my father, who knew the law.

The sergeant grimaced. We had him there. He put down his gun and listlessly rifled through a drawer for the appropriate form. Failing to locate it, he tore a partly used sheet of lined paper in half and grudgingly began to take down the details.

'Where did the accident take place?'

'About five miles up the road, near Gichira.'

The policeman's surly expression brightened. He saw a way out of this.

'Then you must return to the police station at Gichira and report it there,' he said, with great satisfaction.

'I'm reporting it here,' said my father. 'And you will give me a written acknowledgement, or I will go to the police headquarters in Nairobi to report *you*.'

This would have been about as much use as inscribing the sergeant's name on blotting paper with invisible ink and posting it to Santa Claus, but the sergeant didn't know that. Obstreperous *wazungu* might be a pest; coming to the attention of a superior in Nairobi would be a hundred times worse. Oozing disgruntlement, he filled out a report, added the obligatory rubber stamp and sent us on our way.

A month later, an official letter arrived to notify my father that he would be charged with abandoning the scene of an accident. He threw it away. It was the last we ever heard of it.

chapter eighteen

Dauntless Achilles

WHETHER OR not we named him Achilles before he revealed his talent for carnage, I can't remember. What I do remember is that shortly after he arrived – he would have been six weeks old or so – he ran out of the front gate to launch an assault upon a passing Irish wolfhound. The wolfhound was a creature of easy temperament and, even by canine standards, low intelligence. It had never caused any affront to our household, aside from one long-gone Christmas, when it made off with my stepmother's ham roast. Now vengeance had materialised in the unlikely form of a Jack Russell puppy dangling by his teeth from the robber's neck. Momentarily taken aback by this ambush, the wolfhound swatted at Achilles with a giant paw, finally dislodging him. Then – more in sorrow than in anger, I believe – the wolfhound bit Achilles very nearly in two.

That was how Achilles came to pay the first of many visits to the vet. Dr Sercombe, inevitably referred to by my father as Dr Cision, stitched him back together and he pulled through.

As a teenager, I grew up alongside Achilles. Both of us were misfits. I knew it, and he didn't. I envied him that. Where I was self-conscious, he was self-confident. Where I was timid and hesitant, he was bold and decisive. While I planned to survive at least into my twenties, which was as far ahead as I could imagine, Achilles was suicidally indifferent as to his own preservation. In short, I was a boy and he was a dog, and with an adolescent's quintessential self-pity, I often suspected he had got the better deal.

Achilles developed into an odd-looking terrier, with a sprinter's compact ribcage, legs twice the usual length in the breed, and ears that hung down close to his skull instead of pointing skywards. This didn't prevent him from hearing the bark of another dog at distances unscannable by satellite tracking devices. The elongated shanks and runner's build enabled him to cover these distances in remarkably short order and, unannounced, plunge his fangs into the hide of the startled quarry. Achilles always arrived unannounced. Like a stealth missile, he streaked silently towards his target with deadly intent. His purpose in life, his only joy, was to fight other dogs. No Dog Too Large Or Small; if dogs had mottos, that would have been Achilles's motto.

We became very attached to Achilles, which was foolish, in the way that falling for a kamikaze pilot would be foolish. That he survived into adulthood was remarkable. That he survived as much of his adulthood as he did was miraculous. He was not a very old dog before he was semi-toothless, having left a selection of gnashers lodged in the pelts of his helpless foes. Often, unfortunately for Achilles, the foes would prove far from helpless, and Achilles would drag himself home punctured, shredded, blood-soaked and wheezing piteously. He would then be rushed to Dr Cision's office in my stepmother's VW Golf, which should have had its own flashing blue light on the roof.

Dr Cision eventually proposed a course far more radical than that suggested by his nickname. 'It seems that the only way to stop him fighting,' my stepmother announced briskly, bringing Achilles home from surgery, 'is to cut his goolies off.'

My father had often grumbled that thanks to Achilles, he was putting Dr Cision's children through college instead of his own. All the same, he vetoed the idea without hesitation.

'That's not going to happen,' he ruled.

'Then he'll keep on getting in fights,' said my stepmother.

She was right, of course. And it was only a matter of weeks before she again found herself in the vet's waiting room, surrounded by prune-faced *memsahibs*. Dr Cision put his head round the door. His eyes lighted upon her. 'Mrs Bennun!' he boomed. 'Given any more thought to castration?'

'Yes, I have,' said my stepmother. 'But my husband won't hear of it.'

* * *

TAKING WALKS on the nearby Ngong hills, we would bring with us an assortment of dogs, who foamed and lolloped in the rear of our car and slobbered down the backs of the seats. Achilles needed to be physically restrained from repeating an earlier coup. He had flung himself out of the window, at speed, in pursuit of a dog glimpsed subliminally in passing. Then, dizzy and disoriented, he padded around the middle of the road as dozens of vehicles hurtled around and in one instance over him. How the wheels failed to find him was as puzzling as the way he lived through everything else he did.

Once we reached the hills, the dogs would be free to gambol, Achilles excepted. He had to be walked on a lead in case he met an unfamiliar dog. Even this was not always enough to keep him out of trouble. If he saw the dog before you did – if it was the kind of low-slung dog that travelled close to the ground, below cover of radar – he would lure it closer with the wagging of his stumpy tail and the prospect of mutual sniffing activities. Then he would do his considerable best to kill it.

One of the enduring images of my childhood is a long-haired dachshund describing a wild orbit in the air, while Achilles acted as a radial connection to my father, in the centre, swinging him by his hind legs in a vain effort to make him release the other dog's craw. They attained a momentum worthy of an Olympic hammer thrower. At that moment, it seemed that if Achilles were to let go, the dachshund would fall to earth in Langata, some three miles away. Achilles didn't let go. Achilles never let go. Not until his jaws were prised open with a stick. The dachshund's owners calmed down eventually, but their dog looked as traumatised as a dog can do.

Achilles was, frankly, a liability, but at least he was not an idiot. Rufus was an idiot. He was also idiotically handsome, a strawberry blond cross between a collie and a German shepherd, with the looks of both and the IQ of soup. A human version of Rufus would have taken up surfing. This was not an option for Rufus, but he still found himself a hobby. He took up barking.

It would be a further ten years before I encountered another dog that actually produced the noise, 'Woof'. That animal I suspected of being a man in a dog suit; a sort of giant poodle get-up in which he would hunker on his Brighton balcony and shout 'Woof!' a lot. He sounded just like Rufus.

Rufus favoured the middle of the night to practise his vocation. He didn't bark at anything in particular. He wasn't frenzied, or in any way agitated. He just liked barking. Rufus poured as much subtlety, shade and volume into his craft as any meistersinger.

'Woof!' he would offer, by way of prelude. 'Woof! Woof-woof!'

Now he was into his stride. 'Woof woof woof woof woof! Woof. Woof, woof, woof.'

A well-measured pause for effect. Then, 'Woofwoofwoof! WOOF! WOOF! (Woof.)'

By now I would usually have slung open my window to scream at him: 'Shut up, Rufus, you moron!' He would turn and gaze at me with a look of loving gormlessness, slavering in appreciation of my apparent praise for a job well done.

While Rufus's barking was generally a solo turn, my attempts to silence him would invariably rouse every dog in the neighbourhood to a response. What had begun as an aria swelled into a chorale. Far and wide, labradors, rottweillers, spaniels and mongrels joyously gave tongue, while their owners bellowed at them to knock it off, my family loudly berated me for my role in the pandemonium, and Achilles, driven mad by the possibilities, tried to bolt in a dozen directions at once.

* * *

DOGS WERE everywhere, always. At my mother's house lived Vicky, a Rhodesian ridgeback-German shepherd cross. My mother, ever a soft touch where waifs and strays were concerned, had adopted Vicky from the pound at the Kenya Society for Prevention of Cruelty to Animals. Vicky had two bad habits: she was flatulent, and she was racist. Most owners would have seen this as ample cause to get rid of a dog. Not my mother.

'It's not her fault,' my mother would say, as Vicky crouched by the gate, hackles up, frenziedly sounding off at either end, to the dismay of some innocent passer-by. And of course, it wasn't. Vicky's previous owners had evidently been of the odious type who trained their dogs to bark at or attack anybody with black skin – which in Kenya was almost everybody. My mother now had to keep the gate closed even in the daytime, and could not drive in or out without first making sure that Vicky was shut up indoors. And when Vicky was shut up indoors, you immediately wanted to be outdoors.

'My God, that dog stinks,' I said.

'Yes,' said my mother. 'Poor thing.'

'It's us you should feel sorry for,' said my sister.

At the house in Karen where I lived with my father and stepmother, the bigger dogs were barred from the house. When we had chops for supper, each bone, when stripped of meat, was thrown out of the dining-room window into the darkness. The small 'thud' was followed by a brief tumult of galloping, yapping and snarling which stopped abruptly as soon as the dispute was concluded. There was something enliveningly medieval about it.

The small dogs made their home in the kitchen, which looking back strikes me as both peculiar and unhygienic.

Unlike Achilles, Frodo followed the standard Jack Russell design model of a barrel mounted on toothpicks. He was no great warrior: his conquests were of a very limited nature. One sunny December afternoon, my brother was strolling in the garden with his miniature Zeiss binoculars, a twitcher's godsend. As he scanned the herbage at 50x magnification, in search of Yentl's Menorah and the Startled Shrike, he flicked past something unexpected and swivelled back to take another look. This was a highly unusual bird sighting. For one thing, it was upside down. For another, it was hovering just above the other side of the hedgerow. For a third, it was a dead chicken.

Leon put down his binoculars and confirmed his spot with the naked eye. 'Dead chicken' was not on his wish list of rarities, but all the same he approached for a closer look. The chicken had a bedraggled appearance. An upraised hand of unseen provenance was clutching its legs, and its neck swung limply from side to side.

From behind the hedge came a mournful voice: 'Your dog has had a fight with my chicken. Now I will have no Christmas.'

The voice and the lifeless poultry belonged to next door's house servant, thereafter dubbed the Christmas Chicken Man, while Frodo was accorded the sarcastic title of Chickenslayer. The Christmas Chicken Man's assessment of events flattered both Frodo and the chicken. It hadn't been much of a contest. We reimbursed the Christmas Chicken Man and banished Frodo to his basket. This bothered Frodo not at all. Frodo's favoured pastime was to lie on his dog bed with his nose near his uneaten dinner and growl at any living thing that came near him. I could understand why he didn't eat his dinner. It smelled foul. I just didn't see why he was so keen to guard it. He was a wholly ill-tempered creature. We should have got him a manger. He would have been the perfect dog for it.

The names of the dogs, in case you're wondering, were chosen by a committee consisting of anyone but me. This was probably for the best. The names were awful, but my choices would have been worse. Rather than literary, I would have been literal. Whenever one of our cows produced a male calf, I was permitted to name that, as it would survive only a few months before we slaughtered it for meat. I came up with, successively, Veal, Biltong, Ragout and Tartare.

We were a truly carnivorous family. One day I started on the washing up and found myself eyeball to eyeball with a pig's head which had been left on the long, low wall opposite the kitchen window. It looked serene and rather amused, even when Achilles tried to fight it. In the absence of other dogs, Achilles would fight anything. Sweeping up was impossible when he was around. You would end up dragging about a dog on a stick, while drool-coated bristles blanketed every surface like needles on a pine-forest floor.

* * *

WHEN WE made sausages – which we did a lot, most frequently when a calf had just been slaughtered – Achilles would position himself by the kitchen counter, staring not up but down. Alone among our dogs, he was smart enough to realise that it's easier to snap up scraps of minced meat from the floor than to catch them in mid-air. He resembled a parody of the His Master's Voice dog, with a sausage machine substituted for the Victrola.

Our preferred sausage mixture was Boerwoers, the South African farmers' sausage, which we ground very lean and seasoned with whole coriander seeds and peppercorns. There is no better breakfast sausage.

The sausage machine was the hand-cranked variety, with a spout onto which one rolled several feet of paper skin. Anything with a crank on it, my father would buy, usually at an auction. He and my stepmother had become addicted to auctions. It may have been a coincidence, but their relationship had become much more stable and calm since the first time they attended an auction together. On that occasion they came back with an enormous oak dining table plus chairs, a gargantuan brown L-shaped sofa, and sundry articles of jetsam for which my father had over-enthusiastically bid.

'You should have seen the things he didn't buy,' said my stepmother, rolling her eyes and carrying in Lot 30, 'a dozen assorted glasses' – a selection which included a Kenya Railways brandy snifter, an eyeglass and a lidless jam jar. 'They had a ladle which was just a piece of driftwood nailed to half a coconut. I had to hold him back on that one.'

So big was that first, unexpected haul that to bring it back they had no choice but to hire the only available delivery service: a 30-year-old Peugeot 403 pick-up operated by a firm called Typhoid Transport. It's not an easy thing for a motor vehicle to look diseased, but Typhoid Transport lived down to its puzzling choice of name. Additionally, both car and driver had a wheezing, consumptive air about them, suggesting that tuberculosis ran clammily at the heels of typhus. The pick-up bed sagged beneath its cargo, describing a U-shape that knocked against the pebbles and divots on our driveway.

'I don't want that couch in my house until it's been fumigated,' said Joan.

'It's now or never,' said my father, as half a dozen of us struggled to direct the outsize object to the window bay in the living room.

'How about never?' said my stepmother, to no avail.

From subsequent auctions my father and Joan brought back a Victorian milk separator and a 1920s American ice-cream maker. The former was a hulking Heath Robinson contraption of black iron, bearing a series of concentric steel funnels that rotated via the inevitable crank handle. It took two men to start the thing turning, but once it picked up speed, it would have required Charles Atlas to stop it. Had you negligently reached across it, the spinning crank could have snapped your arm like a twig. The funnels whirled about at a dizzying rate, creating a metal vortex into which we poured the whole milk, while skimmed milk and cream streamed out of two separate spouts. Previously, Obisa had been happy, as part of his duties, to quietly spoon off the cream from the top of the milk. But Obisa didn't come with a crank handle.

Wooden, barrel-like and painted in green, the ice-cream maker contained a small inner tub for the liquid custard, which was turned and smoothed by, of course, a crank handle. The outer layer had to be packed with ice and rock salt. For reasons only a chemist could explain, ordinary salt would not do. This led to a hitch. There wasn't a grocer in Nairobi who stocked rock salt. There wasn't a grocer in Nairobi who had heard of rock salt. There wasn't a grocer in Nairobi who, when you asked for rock salt, didn't look at you as if you had requested three drachms of jellied ocelot and a caddy of pixie dust.

The ice-cream maker was supplanted by a modern, electric-powered, self-stirring version approximately one-twentieth the size. This also delighted my father, as the only thing he liked better than gizmos with cranks was gimcracks with plugs.

My father always has been a devil for gadgets, what would nowadays be known as an early adopter – a person who permits the rest of us to own cheap and reliable machines by purchasing expensive and capricious prototypes two years ahead of everybody else. He had snapped up his gas pistol when it was new on the market. His wardrobe was a repository of unused shavers, camera accessories and assorted battery-powered dohickeys of uncertain purpose and origin.

When home video took off, he was among the first in the country to obtain a video-cassette recorder. It was a peculiar, unwieldy item – already a curio by the time we took delivery of it – made up of two separate boxes. Hooked together with a number of highly specialised cables, they functioned, intermittently, as a home video player. I'm not sure the player didn't run on valve technology. It also featured a remote-control handset, which operated the main box not by infra red but via yet another cable, acting as a highly effective tripwire between television set and sofa.

Having bought the thing, my father was determined to use it. Every week, he would bring home half a dozen cassettes from a rental shop near his office that stocked bootlegged copies of films from the previous 15 years. As the selection on offer was of a uniformly low grade, both technically and artistically, before long he stopped bothering to pick them out, and merely grabbed the nearest tapes to hand. It became a nightly ritual to sit through one of these after supper. My stepmother would unfailingly drop off to sleep within three minutes, although when the film was the kind with plenty of gunfire, screams and explosions, she could hold out for five.

Thanks to this immersion in junk cinema – not the trashy, sensational type of junk cinema that some find so exciting, but the dull and second-rate variety – I can now name in a matter of seconds almost any substandard motion picture filmed between 1967 and 1986. Channel surfing on television late at night, I have been known to identify in succession five different and justly obscure movies in the time it takes to flick past them: 'That was *She Married Her Schnauzer* . . . that's *Escape to Bootle* . . . . there goes Peter Sellers in *Brothel Commandos of the Third Reich* . . . that's *Bob and Carol and Carol's Psychiatrist* . . . . Whoah, we just missed *Miserable and Promiscuous in New York*.' This information takes up space in my brain that might otherwise be occupied by something valuable or useful.

We knew that we had overdone the video business when we found ourselves in a state of near-catalepsy one hot Saturday afternoon, with the curtains drawn and motes of dust slowly turning in what little light could drag itself through the heavy air, transfixed before a sepulchral, turgid prison drama set in nineteenth-century Canada and entitled *Mrs Soffel*. It was hard to say which was more stifling and oppressive, the room or the film. Each seemed to act upon the other, until by the end I felt as if it were I and not Mel Gibson who was festering in a gloomy cell awaiting death's liberating kiss.

For a few months after my father purchased it, the video player not only became the fulcrum of our life at home, but also accompanied us on safari. When you disconnected the two sections, the half with the tape in it became a portable recorder – portable in the sense that a Queen Anne credenza with a suitcase handle glued to its face is portable. A metallic cuboid roughly two feet square and eight inches deep, it weighed no more than a slightly chubby nine-year-old. It came with its own customised brown leather carry case and strap, and after a few minutes of toting it slung across your shoulder, you would forget it was there – and, for that matter, that you had a shoulder. The entire *tzimmis* was powered, although not for long, by a battery the heft and mass of a breeze block. So swiftly did this run down that my father made sure always to carry a spare, in a long pocket attached to the case for that specific purpose.

Coupled to this peculiar rig by another of its proprietary cables was a video camera so large that it lacked only an old-fashioned double-reel cartridge on top and a crank handle for the operator, which would have pleased my father even more. This camera my father pointed at everything we saw, until the batteries ran down. Over the weeks and months he filled hour after hour of videotape.

'I thought,' he said one night, as we gathered around the television, 'instead of watching a film, we could have a look at all our safari movies.'

The thought of sitting through *On a Clear Day You Can Air Your Knickers* was not so enticing as to make anyone object. We settled down, with some anticipation, to our home-made viewing. The first portion of the tape contained only crackles and static.

'The tracking needs adjusting,' said my father. He crouched by the player and held down a tiny button on the underside of the control panel. An image briefly leapt into vision, only to be subsumed by a jagged ripple of colour.

'Why's it going up and down?' said my sister.

'I'm working on it,' said my father. 'There. Has it stopped?'

'It's still going up and down,' said my brother.

The screen, with startling clarity, had revealed a pair of copulating warthogs.

'There we go,' said my father.

We sat and watched.

'Didn't you film anything else?' said my stepmother after a minute or two.

'Hang on,' said my father, and pressed the fast-forward button. The warthogs, which up until then had conducted their tryst in a fairly leisurely fashion, began to move with real vigour.

'Why did you film them for so long?' said my sister eventually.

'How can they carry on for so long?' said my stepmother.

A fuzzy line wiped away the warthogs and replaced them with elephants, which were doing nothing more lewd than browsing in a copse. My father slowed the tape back to its regular speed.

'That's nice,' said my stepmother.

'There's always something quite soothing about elephants,' my brother observed.

The fuzzy line abruptly reappeared, erased the elephants, and revealed a different warthog couple, in a new setting, this time rutting furiously without the aid of any technological enhancement.

'Oh, phooey,' said my stepmother.

'If you had to film this,' said my brother, 'couldn't you have picked a better-looking animal?'

My father hit the search button again, and the warthogs became a vertical blur. On and on they went. These were true endurance hogs, marathon fornicators in a never-ending spool of piggy porno. Even at five times its original pace, their sex session carried on and on until we gave up and watched the movie instead.

'I didn't know this one had Barbra Streisand in it,' said Joan.

'Can we have the warthogs back?' said my brother.

* * *

SEX IN our household was treated matter-of-factly. As a topic, it was rarely discussed, but nor was it avoided. It was simply assumed that from a very young age we children knew all about it. And if we hadn't, the films we watched every night would have filled in any gaps. Sex, and more specifically its consequences, formed the basis of our livelihood. When my father left for work in the morning, he would say, 'I'm off to the orifice.' It started as a joke, but soon became another piece of family slang.

Obstetrics was a more commonplace subject. At mealtimes my father often discussed cases from the operating theatre with my stepmother or with colleagues on a social visit.

'She said she'd had a regular discharge over the last few days,' he would recount, between forkfuls. 'When we got her to the OR, she was haemorrhaging quite severely . . . Would you pass the wild rice, please. Thanks. Then I had Mrs Ali's husband come in today. I'd asked her for a urine sample, but it's Ramadan, so they're fasting until sunset. He said to me, "Dr Bennun, I want to know, should we take this sample before bitings, or after bitings?"'

'So what did you tell him?'

'I told him it didn't really matter. But I had a hard time not using the word "bitings".'

Growing up among animals both wild and domestic, sex was never far away. We came back from safari one Sunday to find that Achilles was gone. Obisa told us that our friend Hans Glass had turned up in our absence and driven both Obisa and Achilles to his house.

'Why?' said my stepmother. Obisa looked embarrassed. It turned out that Hans, who prized Achilles's combative spirit, had unilaterally decided to put him to stud. The lucky bitch Achilles was not another Jack Russell, but a pointer – a dog which stood more than twice as high as Achilles. Achilles rose to the task admirably, but only with the help of Obisa, who had to hold him in place.

Hans returned with Achilles later that evening.

'I hear you took my dog away for a dirty weekend,' said my father.

'I'm trying to breed the perfect hunting dog,' said Hans. 'The instincts of a pointer with the fight of your Achilles. Nothing will stand up to that.'

Sadly, the union bore no fruit. Hans went back to raising pure-bred Jack Russells.

'With five or six of them,' he said proudly, 'you can take on a leopard. They have no fear. One of them will get killed, but the others will be too quick. They'll get it in the end.'

Achilles really did have no concept of fear. It was this that put an end to him. Soon after I turned 17, Achilles finally lost a fight so savage that he lost his life. Even Dr Cision, who must have mapped every inch of Achilles's anatomy by rote, couldn't reassemble the parts into working form. My stepmother was inconsolable.

'He was only a dog,' said my father, whose lack of sentimentality about animals I had inherited, and it was true; but I think he was secretly just as upset as she was.

I had already buried enough of my contemporaries to know that I shouldn't grieve for an animal. They had been claimed by car crashes, by snake bites, by heroin addiction. Three years before, Knollpeak Secondary's students had snickered when our headmaster, Mr Hendry, warned us about the dangers of hard drugs. He might as well have been weighing in against soma, or kryptonite, for all that these things were available to us. Since then, Kenya had become a waystation for brown heroin from the Far East, plenty of which was shaken loose in transit. Kids I had seen join the school as short-trousered scallywags were now being carted off to rehab by their distraught parents. At the time, I couldn't think of anything more degrading. A few years on the fringes of the music business and the media would later put me right on that one.

With the unnatural death toll in my own social circle, the passing of Achilles should not have mattered so much to me. But it did. Our homestead had lost something of its character. Achilles had been part of this household for almost as long as I had. The time wasn't far off when I too would be gone. Although not, I hoped, in an assortment of bloody fragments by way of the vet's office.

'He thinks he's a person,' my father had often said about Achilles. I'm sure that wasn't the case. It was we who thought he was a person. If he had been a person, he would have spent his life behind bars. It was a good thing he was only a dog.

chapter nineteen

The Venison Suitcase and Other Camping Tips

WHEN MY family went on its first Kenyan safaris, in the early seventies, we were accustomed to roughing it. As time went on, we developed a taste for luxury. Of course, luxury is relative. In the middle of the *bundu*, far away from the nearest standpipe or power point, there are several luxuries that in more amenable circumstances would qualify as necessities. A wash, for instance. Or a clean set of underwear. On safari my father would often boast that he had been wearing the same underpants for a week, turning them inside out and then back again on an alternating daily basis. He was exaggerating to wind up my stepmother, but not, I'm guessing, by much.

Our initiation into a more gracious mode of camping was brought about by a family friend, Finn Kopje. Finn laid on safaris for very wealthy tourists. Among his regular clients he numbered Robert Redford, Jimmy Stewart and the late US television celebrity Marlin Perkins, whom he had once abandoned in the middle of the Serengeti.

Perkins presented a nature series called *Wild Kingdom* and may be best described as an American David Attenborough without the boyish charm. He was as old as the hills through which he was being driven, accompanied by an female friend of similar antiquity. Perkins asked Finn to stop, and, leaving his door open, walked behind a knoll to relieve himself. Hearing the door slam shut, Finn threw his Land Cruiser back into gear and bounced away down the track. He had been driving at a fair clip for five minutes when a trembling voice from the back seat asked:,

'Whe-e-re's Ma-a-rlin?'

Finn looked around. Wherever Marlin was, he wasn't in the car. Finn wheeled the Toyota around and rattled back up the road, fully expecting to find a circle of feasting lions on the spot where he had last seen his elderly charge. Instead, he found Perkins standing by the knoll as if he were waiting for a bus. Not only was the ancient zoologist quite unrattled, he seemed blithely incognisant of anything out of the ordinary having taken place. Either Marlin was a man of intrepid imperturbability, or he was long since away with the fairies.

Such lapses on Finn's part were rare. His patrons had the best of everything – including, on one occasion, fresh Jersey cream from our cow Ellie, which was hurriedly collected by a flunkey and flown off to camp for a film-star breakfast. Joan was very excited about this, and for weeks afterwards boasted that Ellie's milk was supplied 'by appointment to Robert Redford'.

Finn's camps were manned by a crew of cooks, waiters and general factotums. When, rather than break camp right after a client had departed, he invited us for a two-day visit, it was a revelation to us. He had canvas cubicles in which dangling buckets of hot water discharged themselves through shower heads. He had a dining tent with linen and silverware. And best of all, he had the venison suitcase.

Most of Finn's comforts were far beyond our budget. We could not afford a travelling staff, and we had neither the time to set up the frills they provided, nor the space in which to transport them. But the venison suitcase was brilliantly simple, a low-tech masterstroke, and we improvised our own version immediately.

First, we acquired a cheap, small, metal chest, about eight inches deep, with a snugly fitting lid. It was covered with green paint, which we burned off. The resulting ashen cuboid might have been pulled from the smouldering wreckage of a pillaged pioneer wagon train. It was now ready for use. The procedure was to build a very large fire, and leave it to burn, while a few feet away we dug a moderately sized and shallow hole. We embedded a head's worth of peeled garlic bulbs in a leg of lamb, and threw it in the suitcase, along with potatoes (ordinary and sweet), onions and a few sprigs of rosemary. When the fire had reduced itself to white-hot embers, we shovelled half of these into the hole, lowered in the suitcase, heaped the remainder on top and smoothed out the cinders level to the earth. Ninety minutes later, the meat was pink and perfect. We eased the suitcase from the ground with a *jembi* (hoe) beneath each end. It was suppertime.

Later, we sourced haunches of Grant's gazelle, for which the suitcase made an ideal oven. Everything that came out of the venison suitcase was a delight to the palate, but in truth we were amateurs, dilettantes, our technique rudimentary and our timing crude at best. Finn's chef, Ahmad, was a venison suitcase virtuoso. I once watched him create, using only his tin box and the campfire, an immaculate cheese soufflé – a dish so fragile and finely balanced that most cooks cannot produce it on an ultra-modern gas range.

Ahmad was an authentic genius, and Finn was lucky to find him. The same could not be said for the only cook we ever hired, during a stay at the coast in 1983. He basted our roast chicken with washing-up liquid.

'This is horrible,' I said.

'I'm sick of your moaning,' growled my father. 'You'll shut up, eat it and like it.' He speared a first, truculent forkful from his plate and put it in his mouth. His face transformed to that of a fountain gargoyle emitting soap bubbles in place of water.

* * *

BY THE time I turned 17, our safaris had evolved into expeditions so well planned and equipped that they bore scant resemblance to our earliest outings. We still spent several weeks a year in the bush. With the end of my school career looming, and the unspoken assumption that I would go to college in Britain, I began to savour these trips with a new acuity. Every time we struck camp and set off on the long drive home, I felt as if something was slipping away from me. Once, it turned out to be my shorts. I had worn the same frayed denim cut-offs on every trip since I was 14, refusing to accept I had outgrown them. The waistband wasn't so stubborn.

In addition to the venison suitcase and our reliable little fridge, we had acquired big, drum-shaped torches of sufficient wattage to illuminate a landing strip; an automatic pump which connected to the Land Cruiser's carburettor and filled up our air mattresses; plastic sacks with shower nozzles, which utilised solar energy to heat up water; Chinese kerosene-powered pressure lamps, bright as electric lights, and a magnet for every moth and beetle in a two-mile radius.

Breakfast was cooked on a ploughshare – a dense, concave, black iron disc over two feet across which served as a griddle for trencherman-sized portions of eggs, bacon, sausages and French toast, accompanied by White Cap lager and flies. Frosty beer at 11 a.m., following an early morning game drive, was one of the great safari pleasures.

In the Mara, there was no convenient source of fresh water. Washing water had to be fetched from the river – on the same river bend into which, as we drove back to camp, a sixteen-foot crocodile could often be observed to slip. My sister and I would crouch by the bank, as nervously as any thirsty antelope, and fill up our plastic *debes*. We reasoned that the crocodile, should it attack, would strike at the *debe* first, leaving us time to escape.

We'd been doing this for years when, one night in Nairobi, we watched a wildlife film shot by a family friend for British television. It included a slow-motion shot of a crocodile taking a wildebeest from a river bank much like the one by our Mara camp. We had always thought that a crocodile would glide up unnoticed, seize the feet of its prey and drag it beneath the surface. We stared, aghast, as the giant lizard flung its entire body out of the water, six feet into the air, clamped its razor-studded jaws around the neck of the gnu before the startled beast could so much as flinch, and disappeared with its kill, leaving only froth and a series of wavelets which washed up against the empty riverbank.

'Oh my God,' said Lesley. 'Oh my God. Oh my God. Oh my God. I am never getting water from that river again.'

'Oh, come on,' said my father. 'There was no chance it would have got both of you.'

I said nothing. I was too shocked. I'm still too shocked. I have come close to death now and then – in cars, in extreme weather, at the mercy of *shifta* bandits from Somalia with automatic rifles – but on all those occasions, I was aware of it at the time. To discover that I had willingly and repeatedly placed myself in a peril greater than any of these was nothing short of gobsmacking. Even my father was swayed, in the end.

'OK,' he said, in the tone of one humouring a toddler. 'Maybe next time we'll drive to the hotel and fill up the *debes* there.'

* * *

WHEN WE camped in the Aberdare range, near Mount Kenya, it was easy to take water from the small, chilly streams that ran along the slopes. The main game park is relatively light on wildlife; the land is too high and cold for big game. Above the treeline, most of it is moor, tufted with fibrous, slippery grass. The attraction is a thrilling series of waterfalls, some of which can only be gawped at across plunging valleys, while others may be marvelled at from above, below or – in the case of a handful of foolhardy tourists each year – both in swift succession. There is one cascade which conceals, at its base, a cave behind the falling stream. It is as enchanted a spot as I have ever known.

There was, for a while, a lion problem hereabouts. Lions are not indigenous to the mountains. They are plains dwellers, and this high up there is nothing of suitable proportions for them to eat – aside from the bongo, an antelope so shy and elusive that even the most expert big cat would have trouble locating one. And these lions were anything but expert. I once saw them trying to hunt a warthog. It was like watching the Keystone Cops attempt to trap a bank robber with a butterfly net.

Rumour had it that a group of European eco-dolts, eager to emulate Joy Adamson, the author of *Born Free*, had raised a pair of orphaned lion cubs with the intention of returning them to the wild, then unleashed them in the Aberdares – the equivalent of marooning a New Guinea tribesman in Lapland. The lions, having never learned to hunt, immediately went in search of the one source of food they knew: people. They invaded tents and terrorised campers, and, when human rations inevitably proved inadequate, began to prey on the humans themselves.

Keeping food sealed and inaccessible was important, as we

discovered in the Aberdare Salient. This forested annexe to the main park, down the slopes towards Nyeri, became our favourite safari spot. It was open to professional tour operators only; so for the duration of our visits, thanks to a fake rubber stamp, that is what we became. In a nation of petty bureaucratic fiefdoms, the rubber stamp was seal and signet. It was also easy to obtain your own at one of many Nairobi street stalls:

'I'd like one which says, "Department of National Parks",' my father would tell the stallholder, 'one which says "Ministry of Finance: Approved", and two from the Ministry of Works.'

The Salient was cut off from surrounding farmland by a deep trench and a wire fence. On one side, elephants browsed the trees, while a few feet away, cattle grazed the pasture. It was a game-spotters' utopia, packed with such hard-to-find sights as leopard, rhino, bushpig, giant forest hog, the skunk-like zorilla, colobus monkeys with long, silken, black and white fur, and an oddity known as the crested rat.

This largish nocturnal rodent, measuring almost two feet from nose to tail, is maned lengthways with high ridges of soft, bristling fur, lending it the appearance of an ambulatory doormat from an East German punk rockers' squat. A specimen which lived in our favourite campsite ate twice its own weight in supplies from our tent one night. A fully grown crested rat tips the scales at around seven pounds. We dined on tinned spaghetti for the rest of that trip.

After that, we bought a pair of big tin boxes in which to seal up our foodstuffs. This didn't deter the crested rat. On our next trip to the Salient, it came back in the small hours and – in what could have been interpreted as an act of symbolic literary defiance – chewed its way through my stepmother's treasured copy of *The Joy of Cooking*.

'Why did you bring it on safari?' I asked her.

'It has a recipe for pancake batter,' she said.

'Is that hard to remember?' I said hopefully. Joan's pancakes were excellent.

The crested rat got its comeuppance when, on our next visit, we inadvertently pitched our tent over the opening of its burrow. The luckless rat, surfacing for a midnight forage, found itself trapped beneath the groundsheet. We woke up to a scuffling sound. I aimed my torch in its direction and lit up a swiftly moving bulge tracing an erratic route beneath our temporary floor. My sister shrieked and, grabbing a flip-flop, began to pursue the bewildered lump around the tent, flailing at it in time to her cries. 'Aaah! Aaah! Aaah! Aaah!' screamed my sister. '*Schwak! Schwak! Schwak! Schwak!*' slapped the flip-flop. The more desperately the harried rat scuttled below the tarpaulin, the more ferociously Lesley whacked it: 'Aaah! (*Schwak!*) Aaah! (*Schwak!*) Aaah! (*Schwak!*)' After at least 90 seconds of this, the poor, persecuted beast reached the edge of the groundsheet and wriggled off into the merciful darkness. This, my sister later claimed, was her idea all along.

'I was trying to guide it,' insisted Lesley.

'You were trying to exterminate it,' I said.

Compared to other intruders, the rat was a minor inconvenience. I woke up one morning with the feeling that the day was well under way. Through the tent's fibre-netted window, I saw nothing but gloom. As I was puzzling this over, the gloom began to move, revealing itself to be of a greyish tinge, wrinkled and possessing a tail. We had a campsite full of elephants. There was nothing to do but wait, in utter silence, until we no longer had a campsite full of elephants, a situation which arrived at around tea-time.

At the other end of the scale, and no more welcome than the elephants, were the *siafu*. Drawn to the merest traces of food, these migratory colonies of army ants will devour anything too slow or unwary to move, such as me, in my sleep. They had a habit of swarming into the tent, fanning out around one's dormant body, and all biting at once. Having suffered the occasional electrocution, I can report that this is similar, but worse. The occupants of the tent would then flee into the night, yowling, rolling around and plucking ants from neck, armpits, groin and between the toes. The ants favoured the more tender spots, as would anybody. Again, there was no option but to sit out the invasion.

Once in a while, our house in Nairobi would be infested. We would move out for a day or two and return when the ants were done picking clean the entire homestead.

* * *

THERE IS a certain valley in the Aberdare Salient – small but steep, lavishly green, bisected by a quick-running stream – which we called Leopard Drift, because, as you might guess, we had once seen a leopard there. Often, as we drove through it, my father would remark that he would like his ashes to be scattered there.

The fifth or sixth time he did this, my stepmother, without looking up from her knitting, asked, 'When, dear?'

'I'd rather you waited until after I'm dead,' said my father.

I understood very well why he felt so strongly about Leopard Drift. It was a place of immaculate tranquillity. There could be no finer spot to be spread by the breeze until nothing of you remained.

This, after a fashion, accounts for the fact that since I left Africa, I have not once been camping. In Europe, where you are never more than half a mile from some form of fixed lodging, living in a tent is a pointless act of masochism. The three-day canvas slums that spring up at music festivals, for instance, are so far removed in sense and spirit from Kenya's loneliest and loveliest regions that I have never felt more homesick than when walking through them. To long for a home which was never really mine may be the cheapest and most spurious kind of nostalgia. But it's the only kind I've got, and it won't let go of me that easily.

chapter twenty

The Great Rift

MORE NONSENSE has been written about Africa than almost any subject under the sun, and not all of it by me. As an inspiration for solipsistic, cod-mystical blathering on the part of visitors, only the Indian subcontinent edges it out. This, of course, bothers the Africans no more than it does the Indians. As long as tourists come, and bring their wallets, their motives are of no moment to the locals. Whether they seek their roots, or ancient wisdom, or a primal communion with nature, or two weeks of sunshine with a tad of game-spotting thrown in, travellers still need restaurants and hotels. Even Africa's nick-nacks are adaptable; they sit just as well beside crystals, birthstones and Hopi dream catchers as they do on a mantelpiece full of sombrero-capped Spanish donkeys.

As a political symbol Africa itself is no less versatile. It fits any agenda. Horrified by the legacy of colonialism? Enraged by Western cultural and economic imperialism? Bitterly opposed to globalisation? Point to Africa and cry foul. Conversely, if you wish to trumpet the virtues of liberal democracy and the benefits of truly free trade protected by the rule of law, you need only cite Africa as a tragic example of what happens in their absence.

What none of these debates and analyses and lectures and raptures acknowledge is the vast ordinariness of Africa. To those who live there, Africa is simply the place where they live – a fact so redundantly obvious that it often goes not only without saying, but without thinking.

When people ask me where I'm from, I tell them, 'Brighton'. It's less complicated that way. If they press me, and I mention Kenya, they say, 'That's unusual', or 'That's exotic'. The only reply I can think of is, 'Not where I come from.'

When I was a child, the most exotic place in the world to me was London. London was concrete flyovers. Terraced avenues and conker trees. Brown Ford Cortinas with too many digits on their numberplates. Golders Green had a McDonald's in it. What could be more beguiling than that?

By my final year at school I was clawing at every scrap of imported culture I could find. To the British, Live Aid meant feeding the desperate and dying of a distant continent. To me – just down the road from the famine, geopolitically speaking – it meant crackly concert videos which ran for hours; much more satisfying than the occasional 30-minute edition of *Top of the Pops*. Even crouched six inches from the television set, I couldn't see the big picture.

Most A-level students are required to choose between colleges. I had to choose between countries. If I wanted to stay in Kenya, the bureaucratic intricacies were daunting. This alone was no basis for leaving, but a decision had to be made.

My father tried to reason with me. 'Look,' he said, 'it makes very little difference to me if you go to college. In the long run it's just a few thousand pounds. But it could make a huge difference to you.'

There was also the question of what work I might do if I stayed. If you were white, you could be a safari operator. I did consider this prospect. I had got my family lost in every major game park in the country. While they weren't best pleased about it, they were a good deal more patient than paying customers might have been. To run safaris, you didn't have to be the brightest bulb on the Christmas tree, but the job did demand patience, authority and unflappability. I could offer panic, stupefaction and a proven magnetism for chaos. This was not the occupation for me.

But what was? I was interested in music, literature, the arts. The majority of job opportunities in Kenya, had they been advertised, would have appeared under the heading 'Wanted: Subsistence Farmer'. It could be argued that as fields of professional expertise go, music, literature and the arts would benefit from all aspirants undergoing an obligatory stint in subsistence farming. Never a trailblazer, I opted for the more traditional and less arduous route of applying to university.

* * *

MY PARENTS had hoped that I might follow my brother to Cambridge. I doubted whether I could make the grade, but in the event, the question proved irrelevant: my chances were effectively scotched by the administrative assistant at Knollpeak. Entrusted with ensuring that my entrance papers matched my A-level subjects, she dealt with the matter in the way she knew best: by ignoring it completely. I found myself sitting down to an examination in French, a subject I had last studied two years previously. If only I had been required to translate the paper into demotic balderdash, I would have aced it. Unfortunately, they wanted the answers in English.

The admissions board at my first-choice college wrote back to say that I had not been accepted, but it would circulate my exam papers to other colleges at the university. It was tactful enough not to add, 'So they can all share the joke.'

Thanks to exam results based on courses I had actually taken, the University of Sussex did accept me. That was the future taken care of, so far as I could see. I was 17 years old. I had the use of a car. I had ten months' of free time until the academic year began. I was living the teenage dream. I could do anything I wanted. From an ocean of possibilities, I selected hanging around at my old school. I was a sorry case. But my tennis game had never been better.

My freedom was not entirely wasted. The little diesel VW Golf, in which I had hit a tree on our driveway, was still in service. It was cheap to run, and reliable. I could take it wherever there was a tarred road. I started driving into the Rift Valley on my own. Adolescent solitude is generally associated with retreat to a dark bedroom hung with posters and pin-ups signifying a longed-for and unattainable world. I had one of the planet's greatest spectacles in which to lose myself. It's hard to overstate my happiness at such moments – following the hairpin bends down the escarpment, marvelling at the enormity and ever-changing drama of the sky. Where workaday skies seem to turn about nature and art – poor art at that – by mimicking the flat functionality of the pedestrian watercolour, the sky above the Rift was colossal, curved and unfathomably deep, an upended bowl of alpha and omega. At night, with not a light inside the horizon to dim them, its constellations were dazzling in their number and density.

Maybe a more profound individual would have found in the Rift Valley and its sky reasons to dwell upon humanity's place in the cosmos, or turned his mind to thoughts of eternity. I just thought it looked ravishing. Far from perceiving myself as small, although I was less than a pinprick on this tapestry, I felt as if I were the biggest thing alive. This was my backyard – mine to do as I pleased. And if that meant driving through it with the Beatles at full blast on the tape deck, that's what I was going to do. *Sgt Pepper's Lonely Hearts Club Band* alternated with *Abbey Road*, unendingly. I was barred from playing them at home.

'I thought you liked the Beatles,' I protested to my father.

'I did,' he said, 'until about a month ago.'

I was once, and only once, stupid enough to drive home under the influence of a Kariabangi special. I was aware of my condition, but thought I had it covered. I never let my speed rise above ten miles per hour.

'Remember to check your rear-view mirror,' I told myself, as the outskirts of Karen crept by. I checked my rear-view mirror. It was empty. 'Hm,' I thought. 'I'm really good at this checking the rear-view mirror thing.' After two minutes had passed, I became aware that I was still staring at the rear-view mirror, and it might now be time to look out of the windscreen. I looked out of the windscreen. I had meandered halfway across where the central marker would have been if the money to repaint it hadn't been funnelled out of the country somewhere between the Ministry of Works and the local council. A medium-sized Mercedes-Benz truck was bearing down on me. The driver's face bore an expression of unhurried curiosity as to what might happen next. I swung back into my lane and the truck rumbled past me. It was loaded with hay bales.

* * *

AND THEN, UNACCOUNTABLY, I was at the airport.

There are times in one's life when a lever is pulled and one backdrop is abruptly replaced with another. My freewheeling year at ease was gone, and I was hugging my family at the Kenya Airways check-in desk.

We had always stuck to the same, simple principle for farewells: say goodbye and go. Alone in the departure lounge, hours ahead of my flight, it was at last impossible for me to deny that I was leaving. I had known it for months. If I was to be honest, I had known it for years. But in all that time, I had never once believed it.

I found a payphone and dialled a number.

'Karen two-three-oh-six,' said my father.

'It's me,' I said. 'The plane's delayed.'

'How much?' said my father. 'Should we come and get you?'

I wanted desperately to say yes.

'Just a couple of hours. I thought I'd say hello.'

'How do you feel?'

'I feel strange. I feel as if I'm already there.'

'No you don't,' said my father. 'You feel as if you're still here with us.'

'You're right,' I lied. My mind had already made the switch, as it always did so quickly with every change I faced.

On the night flight, I couldn't sleep. And even if I had been able to, the cabin crew would have guaranteed I didn't. The stewardess handled her drinks cart like an assault vehicle. As I fretted and speculated, she thundered up to my row and wrestled the trolley to a clangorous halt.

'*What?*' she snarled. I took her to mean, What would I like to drink?

'Orange juice, please,' I said, in as placatory a tone as I could muster.

She slammed a carton of tinted acid onto my tray and bundled her trolley up the aisle to the next passenger.

'*What?*' I heard her ask again.

I opened the university's prospectus and made the latest of many attempts to read it. I still had no idea what to expect, and this chunky document was of small assistance. Perhaps I should have struggled through it before I had sent in my application, or accepted the offer. I gave up once again, opened the airline magazine to an article about tropical orchids, and pretended to read that instead.

I did perceive that going to college would mean a chance to reinvent myself. I reckoned that I would soon be thousands of miles away from anyone who could expose me as an edgy, ineffectual oddball. Naturally, I was wrong. Everywhere I went, the person most likely to give me away would be right there, awaiting his moment.

When I arrived in October 1986, the University of Sussex was a hotbed of strident radicalism, moral posturing, and hot beds. I had no luck with all three, thanks in large part to my colonial-style accent, which invariably saw me mistaken for an Afrikaaner.

ME: 'Hello.'

FELLOW STUDENT: 'Get away from me, you murdering fascist Nazi!'

To the inescapable bewilderment of any 18-year-old who starts at college was added the confusion of a country utterly foreign to an African-bred boy. Everything at the university was named after Nelson Mandela, but that didn't help. The student union couldn't set up a birdbath without paying tribute to the then imprisoned ANC leader. When I went to Mandela House and ordered a drink at the Mandela bar, the staff reacted as if I was the one behind his incarceration.

ME: 'Half of snakebite and black, please.'

BARTENDER: 'I'm not serving you, you murdering fascist Nazi.'

Once I had squandered most of my remittance on black denim, I looked normal enough, by the dubious lights of late eighties college students. But beneath the ill-clad surface I remained a forlorn outlander – eager to be assimilated, but confounded at every turn. I voraciously absorbed every iota of pop culture I could find, and acquired a new accent which even today – having taken detours through most of the English regions – wobbles uncertainly between estuary and Received Pronunciation. By these means I eventually managed to pass as, if not exactly local, then at least as somebody who wasn't necessarily a murdering fascist Nazi.

At night, I stared at the ceiling of my tiny room in the Essex House hall of residence. Twice a week some or other waggish halfwit would obscure the first two letters on the sign by the front entrance with marker pen or paint, in the evident belief that this was an altogether novel jape. It was all the same to me – both Essex and sex were *terra incognita* as far as I was concerned.

Faced for the first time with the reality of meals dictated by my budget, which was modest, and my culinary competence, which was zero, I mopingly slopped tins of Heinz ravioli into my one saucepan and, like any student, daydreamed about the good times back at home.

My mind, when it wandered, always wandered down the same road – the one leading into the Rift Valley. The switchback descent along the escarpment, dynamited through sheets of volcanic rock and threaded past impossibly balanced stacks of giant boulders, then the long, straight and flat stretch south towards Magadi.

A few miles short of the soda lake, if you turned down a track surfaced with loose pebbles, you would soon reach the Stone Age archaeological heritage site of Olorgesaile. The standard of curatorship at Olorgesaile was nearly as primitive as its contents. I had been here as a child on school trips, and feigned interest in flint tools indistinguishable from the rocks among which they had been found. In the months before I went to England, my brother had taken up residence there, in one of the basic *bandas* laid on for overnight visitors. He was studying the breeding habits of yet another small brown bird, the social weaver, for his doctorate.

It wasn't an easy life out in the Rift, but my brother seemed to like it. Every so often, the whole family would load up a car with food, drink and folding chairs, and head out to spend an evening with Leon and his assistant (cataloguing the behaviour of the social weaver was a labour-intensive business). The first two men to hold that post were companions as agreeable as any researcher in the wild could hope for. The third, Esau, turned out to be a rather more reserved and brooding character. He was a man of few words, and even fewer enthusiasms. When we laid out a spread of fresh chops, prime ribs and steaks, with cold beer and cola to wash it down, Esau tucked in more heartily than anyone; but never did he offer a word of thanks or even a gesture of appreciation. You didn't win Esau over just like that.

On my eighteenth birthday, the whole family drove down to Olorgesaile to celebrate. Knowing that it might be the last birthday I spent in Kenya, my mother and my stepmother both joined in – the first time since my parents' divorce that the two had been present at the same family gathering.

We staged the blow-out to end all blow-outs. Rather than bring down our customary coolbox of chops, we arranged for my brother to buy a goat locally. We slaughtered, butchered and cooked it on the spot. We had marinated chicken and *piri-piri* prawns to join it on the barbecue. There was Russian salad, coleslaw and garlic bread on the side. Crates of satin-smooth Tusker Premium were unloaded into tubs of ice, along with freshly squeezed orange juice and every variety of soft drink sold in Nairobi. For dessert, Joan conjured up fresh brownies, still moist and warm from the oven, and two kinds of home-made Jersey ice cream, one flavoured with vanilla pod and the other full of fresh strawberries. It took us hours to work our way through this banquet. At last we sat panting in our camp chairs by the firelight, spoiled and sated.

'Well,' said my father, turning to his nearest neighbour, 'how did you find that, Esau?'

Esau thought about it. He raised an eyebrow – for Esau's features, a seismic shift. You could tell he was impressed.

'It was not the worst,' he magnanimously conceded.

* * *

THREE DAYS ahead of my departure for university, I drove down to Olorgesaile on my own. Leon, surprised to see me, took the afternoon off from tracking the social weavers' nesting patterns. We walked, under a hard blue noonday sky, to the nearest settlement, a couple of miles across the main road. As we entered the tin shack that served as general store and tavern, my brother greeted a woman sitting on a plastic chair by a low wooden table. Her white, starched-cotton dress held a small silver pin in the shape of a cross over the breast pocket.

'Hi, Kaziah,' he said. 'This is my brother, David.'

Kaziah, a nurse, ran the hamlet's only medical facility. She wasn't having a very busy day. She bought us a round of White Cap export.

Then she bought us another, despite my protestations. And another.

'You mustn't pay,' said Kaziah. 'You're a guest here for the first time.'

Kaziah told us the story of a public health campaign funded by an aid agency in the Maasai territories of southern Kenya.

'They are good people,' she said, 'but they do not always understand. They wanted to warn everyone about malaria. So many people die from malaria.'

Malaria, until the near-apocalypse of Aids blighted the continent, could claim the grisly distinction of being Africa's biggest killer. In addition to its physical horrors, the disease saps its victims' will to live. Nairobi was malaria free, but on our travels my family had always been careful with our anti-malarials; except for my father, who mistakenly believed he had built up an immunity. There is no such thing. He found out how wrong he was when he became infected on a trip to the coast. The malady attacks in cycles; for a few days, existence is unbearable. Then comes blissful but temporary relief, to be replaced once more by misery. Once the fatal danger is past, the symptoms may return at any time. Curiously, my father's malaria left him debilitated during the week, but always abated by Saturday, enabling him to take part in his regular softball games against the Japanese embassy and the US marines.

'Many of the Maasai,' said Kaziah, 'do not know that malaria comes from the mosquito. Just as the tsetse fly spreads the sleeping sickness. They do not know. That is why the people from the agency made pictures. They put them on the walls of every *duka* and every bar. It was a picture of a mosquito. They had made the picture very large, like this –' here Kaziah spread her hands about four feet apart '– so everyone would see it. And underneath they wrote, "This is your enemy."

'They came here to put one up. I told them, "There is no malaria here. No water." I said, "If you want to save people from malaria, you should give them pills, not pictures." They did not listen.

'After a few months, they went back to all the places they had put the pictures. To find out what had happened. And do you know what had happened?'

'No,' I said, taking a pull on my fourth stumpy bottle of warm White Cap. 'I don't.' By now it was just one of many things that I didn't know, such as which way was up.

'Nothing had happened,' said Kaziah. 'Everybody was still getting sick. The agency people said, "Why have you not killed the mosquitoes?" And the Maasai told them, "We feel very sorry for you *wazungu*. Where you come from, the mosquitoes are so big. Here we don't have this problem. Ours are only small."

In Kaziah's company, the afternoon melted away. I hope that there were no medical emergencies that night; Kaziah was in no state to tend the ill. She would probably have prescribed another round of White Cap. My brother and I lurched and stumbled across the rocky terrain back to his *banda*, where I flung myself upon the spare bed as it spun past me.

The next morning, Leon was up with the larks and out with the weaver birds. I didn't speak to him again until weeks afterwards. He was visiting Nairobi when I called from England to say hello to my family.

'Kaziah is asking after you,' he told me. 'She wants to know when you're coming back to buy her some beers.'

* * *

I HAVE NEVER been back to the Rift Valley. I haven't been to Kenya in 13 years. And now Kaziah's generosity is just one more item on an interminable list of debts: a lifetime's worth of unmerited and unreciprocated kindnesses.

I don't think I could go back now. I've become a European. In Kenya, that was the term applied to anyone with white skin: European. What it meant was Not African. To be a European in Africa was to presume entitlement. To believe yourself deserving of special consideration. I may have received it, but I never deserved it. I was nothing more than an itinerant. A vagabond with privileges, but a vagabond all the same. In the end, my race was not the problem. It was my detachment, my self-imposed remoteness, that made me a stranger there, and so often makes me feel like a stranger here.

When you are raised as a nomad of sorts, accustomed to moving between houses, between towns, between countries, you let things go too easily. You fail to grasp them when you fail to grasp their value. The truth is, I didn't grow up in Africa. I merely got older there, and taller. The growing up has been done since I left, since I came to understand what – through my own complacency and thoughtlessness – I have allowed myself to lose.

Kenya was good to me. The people I knew in Kenya were good to me. I drifted away from the country and from those people. I negligently permitted friends to retreat into the distance, until I looked around and could no longer see them. I lost touch with an abundance of joys and oddities, which proved impossible to duplicate between the South Downs and the pebble beach of Brighton.

Blind luck brought me unscathed through Africa, and blind luck deposited me in the room where I'm now typing out the last words in the last chapter of another life. You can't expect luck to stay blind for ever. But if luck can keep its eyes averted a little while longer, I'll think of it as yet another unearned favour.